D0367765

Media and the Path to Peace

This is the first book to examine in detail the roles that the news media can play in an ongoing peace process. Gadi Wolfsfeld explains how the press's role in such processes varies over time and political circumstance. He examines three major cases: the Oslo peace process between Israel and the Palestinians; the peace process between Israel and Jordan; and the process surrounding the Good Friday agreement in Northern Ireland. Wolfsfeld's central argument is that there is a fundamental contradiction between news values and the nature of a peace process. This often leads the media to play a destructive role in attempts to make peace, but variations in the political and media environment affect significantly exactly how the media behave. Wolfsfeld shows how the media played a mainly destructive role in the Oslo peace process, but were more constructive during the Israel–Jordan process and in Northern Ireland.

GADI WOLFSFELD is an Associate Professor of Political Science and Communication at the Hebrew University of Jerusalem. He is the author of *Media and Political Conflict: News from the Middle East* (1997).

Politics and relations among individuals in societies across the world are being performed by new technologies for targeting individuals and sophisticated methods for shaping personalized messages. The new technologies challenge boundaries of many kinds – between news, information, entertainment, and advertising; between media, with the arrival of the World Wide Web; and even between nations. *Communication, Society and Politics* probes the political and social impacts of these new communication systems in national, comparative, and global perspectives.

Media and the Path to Peace

Gadi Wolfsfeld

Department of Political Science
Department of Communication and Journalism
The Hebrew University of Jerusalem

CAMBRIDGE
UNIVERSITY PRESS

CAMBRIDGE UNIVERSITY PRESS
Cambridge, New York, Melbourne, Madrid, Cape Town, Singapore,
São Paulo, Delhi, Dubai, Tokyo, Mexico City

Cambridge University Press
The Edinburgh Building, Cambridge CB2 8RU, UK

Published in the United States of America by Cambridge University Press, New York

www.cambridge.org
Information on this title: www.cambridge.org/9780521538626

First published 2004

A catalogue record for this publication is available from the British Library

Library of Congress Cataloguing in Publication data
Wolfsfeld, Gadi.
Media and the path to peace / Gadi Wolfsfeld.
p. cm. – (Communication, society, and politics)
Includes bibliographical references and index.
ISBN 0-521-83136-9 – ISBN 0-521-53862-9 (pb.)
1. Mass media and peace. I. Title. II. Series.
P96.P33W65 2003
070.4′4930366 – dc21 2003053221

ISBN 978-0-521-83136-9 Hardback
ISBN 978-0-521-53862-6 Paperback

This book is dedicated to the victims of violent conflict and their families.

Contents

Acknowledgements

This book is the result of a number of years of research and I have received a good deal of support along the way. First I want to thank a number of foundations and institutes who provided financial support for carrying out the research. The first group of sponsors are all affiliated with my home institution, the Hebrew University of Jerusalem: The Levi Eshkol Institute for Social, Economic, and Political Research in Israel, the Harry S. Truman Institute for the Advancement of Peace (who provided a grant from the Turner Fund for Peace), and the Smart Family Foundation Communication Institute. I also received a generous grant from The Tami Steinmetz Center for Peace Research at Tel Aviv University.

I owe a special debt of gratitude to the United States Institute of Peace, who granted me a yearlong fellowship to work on this project. The institute also provided the funds for me to carry out the research in Northern Ireland. I am especially grateful to Joe Klaits and John Crist, who provided a seemingly endless supply of support and assistance during my year in Washington. My research assistant during that year was Guy Ben-Porat; his intelligence and insight were major assets.

I also want to thank all of those who have read previous versions of this manuscript. I hope they will all identify the significant contribution they have made to the final product: Lance Bennett, Robert Entman, Liz Fawcett, Bill Gamson, Tamir Sheafer, Steven Livingston, Greg McLaughlin, Farida Viz, and Gabi Weimann.

Finally I want to thank my family – Lauren, Noa, and Dana – for their love, their support, their values, and their courage.

Introduction

The news media can play a central role in the promotion of peace. They can emphasize the benefits that peace can bring, they can raise the legitimacy of groups or leaders working for peace, and they can help transform images of the enemy. The media, however, can also serve as destructive agents in the process. They can emphasize the risks and dangers associated with compromise, raise the legitimacy of those opposed to concessions, and reinforce negative stereotypes of the enemy. This work will attempt to explain how, why, and when the media take on each of these roles.

This work can be seen as an expansion of previous efforts of mine to explain the role of the news media in political conflicts (Wolfsfeld, 1997a). The theoretical approach developed in that work was referred to as the political contest model. One of the central themes of that theory was that the best way to understand the role of the media in politics is to view the competition over the news media as part of a larger and more significant contest among political antagonists for political control. Thus, when political leaders are able to exert control over the political environment – say in the level of support they mobilize – they find it much easier to promote their policies to the news media. A lack of political control, on the other hand, leads to a more independent press that is reluctant to accept official dictates.

This basic approach remains intact within this study. The research examines the ongoing competition over the news media among antagonists with different attitudes towards a given peace process. This assumes that there is a genuine process in place and that government leaders are attempting to promote it to the public. In addition to the government there are two other major actors that compete over the news media: those opposed to the peace process and the other side in the conflict (the "enemy"). Understanding the rules of competition between these various antagonists brings us closer to understanding the actual role the media will play in any peace process.

Despite the clear link between the two studies, there are also some important differences. The shift in focus from conflict to peace leads one down a somewhat different theoretical path. Many of these differences are rooted in the problematic relationship between news and peace. Simply put, it is a hell of a lot easier to promote conflict to the media than peace. While conflict can be considered the *sine qua non* of news, peace and news make for awkward bedfellows. A successful peace process requires patience, and the news media demand immediacy. Peace is most likely to develop within a calm environment and the media have an obsessive interest in threats and violence. Peace building is a complex process and the news media deal with simple events. Progress towards peace requires at least a minimal understanding of the needs of the other side, but the news media reinforce ethnocentrism and hostility towards adversaries. The reasons and ramifications of these difficulties are detailed throughout this study. For now, it will suffice to say that what might seem like a small change in the research question has led to a relatively large change in the rules of the game.

This work is also seen as an expansion of the previous book in that it attempts to flesh out a number of concepts that were missing from that previous study. Two ideas are especially worthy of note. While the first study emphasized the importance of the political environment, this work also examines the effects of varying *media* environments on the role of the media. The norms and routines that journalists adopt for covering politics vary and this also has an important influence on the role the news media will play in a given political process. Journalists working in a more sensationalist media environment, for example, will construct very different stories about conflict and peace than those operating in a more reserved milieu.

A second area of innovation has to do with the ways in which the news media and the political environment interact with one another. It will be argued that the best way to understand this relationship is to think of it in terms of a cycle in which changes in the political environment lead to changes in media performance that lead to further changes in the political environment. This dynamic will be referred to as the politics-media-politics cycle. I also attempt to develop some ideas about this interaction by examining "political waves." Political waves take place when critical events (e.g. the Rabin assassination) lead to a dramatic increase in the amount of public attention focused on a particular issue or event. The news media play an important role in such waves, and examining this dynamic also provides some helpful insights concerning the role of the news media in political processes.

The initial spark for this research project can be traced to the inauguration of the Oslo peace process between Israel and the Palestinians in the fall of 1993.[1] It continued through the many years of negotiations and partial agreements, the assassination of Yitzhak Rabin, and a number of changes in government in Israel. These many variations in the Israeli political environment provided important insights into just how the role of the news media varies over time and circumstance. The fact that Oslo also enabled Israel and Jordan to negotiate and sign a peace agreement allowed for an additional avenue of research. As detailed later, the political environment surrounding this process was very different than the one associated with Oslo. The inauguration of peace between the two countries also created a unique opportunity to collaborate with a Jordanian counterpart and to collect comparative data from that country.

More comparative data was collected when I was able to travel to Northern Ireland in the spring of 1999. The Good Friday agreement had been signed about a year before, but the two sides were still having serious problems moving forward. The case of Northern Ireland provided a critical piece of the puzzle for it not only constituted a dissimilar political environment, but also a very different media environment.

The final part of the research deals with what many saw as the end of the Oslo peace process: the failure of the Camp David summit between Ehud Barak and Yasser Arafat and the outbreak of the Second Intifada in the fall of 2000. The return to violent conflict between Israel and the Palestinians afforded a graphic demonstration of the significant differences between promoting war to the news media and promoting peace.

The overall research strategy combined inductive and deductive components. Based on what I know about communication and conflict I began to ask questions about the role of the media in the various peace processes. Two major methods were used to collect data (for details see the methodological appendix). The first consisted of in-depth interviews with a wide variety of individuals who were responsible for promoting

---

[1] The actual research began in the summer of 1994. There is a certain amount of temporal overlap between the previous study and this one. This explains why one of the case studies presented in the previous book investigated the attempts of the anti-Oslo political movements to mobilize the news media against the government.

messages and events to the news media and the journalists who covered the different peace processes. Those interviewed include political and military leaders, their advisors and spokespeople, and reporters and editors from both the print and electronic media. Such interviews provide a wealth of information and insights about the norms, routines, perceptions, and strategies that explain how these various actors interact with one another. In addition, interviews with functionaries who are involved in each peace process provided first-hand knowledge about the impact the resulting coverage had on the process itself.

The second method consists of content analysis of news stories about peace. These stories are seen as the final cultural product that result from the ongoing interactions between sources and journalists. While many of these content analyses are quantitative, I also attempt to carry out a more qualitative and critical reading of these materials in order to better understand the underlying story lines. The stories journalists tell about peace vary tremendously and examining the reasons for such differences provides important pieces of the puzzle.

The theoretical principles that emerged from this research are all rooted in the comparisons between the different peace processes that were studied. Nevertheless, despite the fact that all of the studies adopted the same research strategy, there are methodological differences that prevent a full and ideal comparison. These variations have to do with both logistics (e.g. the relative difficulty in obtaining certain news materials) and the fact that some of the newer ideas emerged at a later stage in the research. At the same time, there are also certain advantages to this circumstance. It allows us to look at the role of the news media in peace from multiple angles, each of which provides somewhat different insights and perspectives.

There is another flaw in this research that is best dealt with at the outset. Although an important part of the study focuses on the role of the media in the Oslo peace process, there is virtually nothing written about the Palestinian press. The reasons for this omission are both theoretical and practical. The theoretical rationale is that the ideas that are presented here refer to situations in which the press enjoys a certain amount of freedom to make decisions. When the news media almost always reflect the official line, one needs to adopt an entirely different set of principles to explain the role the press will play in the political process. The practical problem is that I do not consider myself sufficiently knowledgeable about the Palestinian press to analyze it. One can only hope that Palestinian scholars will carry out research on this important topic.

I should also say something at the outset about my political views. Researchers writing about peace face some of the same dilemmas as journalists. It is almost impossible to take a neutral stand towards the issue. The very fact that the relevant fields are entitled "peace studies" and "conflict resolution" tells us that the implicit goal of such work is to promote peace and prevent violent conflict. This type of bias can threaten the integrity of the research. When the news media make it more difficult to promote peace, for example, this will be considered a "problem" that needs to be solved. Yet those opposed to a particular peace process would argue that such media are demonstrating their independence and protecting national interests.

Although there is no solution to this problem, it is helpful to state one's biases in order to allow readers to look for any faults that are rooted in such prejudices. My own bias is that I supported the peace processes discussed in this work. I believe that the Rabin government took an important step forward at Oslo and like most Israelis I hoped it would succeed. I also supported the peace accords that were signed between Jordan and Israel. Although I have no personal involvement in the Northern Ireland conflict, my position is the same. I believe the Good Friday agreement was a major achievement and that it offers a real possibility for bringing peace to the area.

I also believe that journalists have an ethical obligation to encourage reconciliation between hostile populations. This does not mean that they should blindly accept every peace proposal that calls for compromise. Nor should they serve as propaganda organs for a pro-peace government. Policies intended to bring peace should be scrutinized as carefully as any other government initiative. Everyone wants peace and prosperity; the important question is how to achieve it. The goals of journalism working in conflict-ridden areas should be to provide as much information as possible about the roots of the problem and to encourage a rational public debate concerning the various options for ending it. At the very least, journalists should do no harm. They should refrain from practices that raise the level of hate, distrust, and violence between communities. These issues will be discussed more fully in the conclusion of this work.

ORGANIZATION OF THE ARGUMENT

The book is divided into seven chapters and a conclusion. The first chapter presents the major theoretical arguments of the study. After introducing some initial principles for thinking about the issues, six central arguments are developed about the role of the news media in peace processes. These propositions attempt to deal with both the fundamental contradiction between news and peace and how different political and media environments can either ameliorate or worsen the situation.

The next three chapters all examine the role of the media in the Oslo peace process between the Israelis and the Palestinians. Thus, the second chapter looks at Oslo from the perspective of the Rabin and Peres governments, who were attempting to promote the process to the Israeli media and the public. The third examines the opposite vantage point by looking at the ongoing interactions between those opposed to Oslo and the Israeli news media. This discussion is important because it helps explain some of the problematic influences the news media can have on political debate about a peace process. The fourth chapter looks at the attempts of Palestinian leadership and opposition to convey their own messages to the Israeli public about Oslo. Among other topics, this chapter deals with the types of influences a changing political environment can have on media images of enemies.

The fifth chapter deals with the role of the media in the peace process between Israel and Jordan. As noted earlier, one of the reasons why this case is so instructive is that while the Oslo agreements were extremely controversial, the accords with Jordan received almost unanimous support within Israel. This section is also important for it also includes empirical evidence about the Jordanian press, which does enjoy a limited amount of autonomy. The news data collected for that particular study extends over a considerable length of time and this also provides a more dynamic understanding of the issue. While the findings from this part of the study do suggest some rays of light, most of these results reinforce the same dismal picture concerning media and peace.

The next chapter deals with the case of Northern Ireland. Those who know something about that conflict may be surprised to learn that this is the one place in which the news media appear to play a more supportive role in a peace process. This has certainly not always been the case. However, the relatively high level of elite consensus surrounding the Good Friday agreement as well as the professional norms journalists have adopted for covering that conflict all contribute to making this case to be the exception that demonstrates the rule.

Chapter 7 deals with the role of the news media in the final stages of the Oslo peace process and the outbreak of the Second Intifada. Despite the high hopes that were raised when Ehud Barak was elected Prime Minister he was unable to come to any agreement with Yasser Arafat. This chapter provides a tragically appropriate finale to the entire story. For as the situation in the Middle East turned from bad to worse, so did the role of the news media. When one compares the ease with which leaders can promote a violent conflict to the press to the tremendous difficulties they faced in sponsoring a peace process, it serves as a striking demonstration of some of the major themes that are developed throughout this work.

The concluding chapter summarizes the major findings and discusses some of the major implications for researchers and policy makers. Although this study is not intended as a political diatribe, I do believe that researchers working in the area also have certain ethical obligations. Assuming that striving for peace is a valuable objective, then it is also worthwhile to think about how scholars can make at least a modest contribution towards that goal.

CHAPTER 1

Building theory

M uch has been written about the role of the news media in conflict and war, but very little about their role in peace. Searching through the hundreds of studies on peace building and conflict resolution, it is difficult to find even a passing reference to the press. There is not a single major study that has looked at the role of the news media in an ongoing peace process.[1]

This lack of interest in the topic is even more glaring when one considers the tremendous amount written on media and conflict. There are countless articles and books about the role of the media in protests, terrorism, and war in popular and scholarly publications. Why is there such a gap? Considering possible answers to this question provides some initial insights into the general topic of media and peace. Examining some of the reasons why researchers prefer dealing with conflict also tells us something about similar choices made by the news media.

---

[1] There are a number of studies that deal with such topics as the role of the media in foreign policy, diplomacy and conflict resolution (R. Cohen, 1987; Y. Cohen, 1986; Davison, 1974; Entman, 2003; Fromm *et al.*, 1992; Gilboa, 1998; Gowing, 1996; Henderson, 1973; Naveh, 2001; O'Heffernan, 1991, 1993; Robinson, 2002; Serfaty, 1991; Strobel, 1997; Weimann, 1994), several that relate to the problems peace movements face in attempting to mobilize the news media (Gitlin, 1980; Glasgow University Media Group, 1985; Hackett, 1991; Ryan, 1991; Small, 1987), a few articles that deal with the role of the news media in disarmament and international cooperation (Bruck, 1988, 1989; Dorman, Manoff, and Weeks, 1988; Gamson and Stuart, 1992), and several that have to do with images of the enemy (Ayres, 1997; Becker, 1996; Eckhardt, 1991; Ottosen, 1995). There is also some work on the topic of "peace journalism," which talks about the need to change journalists' norms and routines for covering peace and conflict (Adam and Thamotheram, 1996; Bruck and Roach, 1993; Galtung, 1998; Himmelfarb, 1998; Lynch, 1998; Manoff, 1996, 1997, 1998; Roach, 1993; Shinar, 2000).

The first reason that comes to mind is that the link between media and conflict is simply more obvious. Conflict and violence are the mainstays of the news industry, whereas stories about peace are few and far between. It is also clear that the media play a significant role in protests and terrorism because the need for publicity is a central component of these strategies. The role of the press in wartime is similarly conspicuous. The massive amount of public discussion concerning the role of the news media in the recent wars in Afghanistan and Iraq provide the most recent examples of this phenomenon. There is an enormous amount of publicity associated with wars and such coverage is replete with striking, dramatic images. In addition, when democratic nations go to war the role the media should play often becomes a subject for public debate. The role of the news media in a peace process, on the other hand is usually more hidden and subtle.

Another reason for researchers' preference for studying conflict may be that pundits and scholars simply find conflict more exciting than peace. The drama of terrorism and war is difficult to resist, and it is small wonder that so many people get swept up in the emotion. The numerous studies dealing with the role of the media in the 1991 Gulf War provides an excellent example of this tendency.[2] The high level of public and media interest in such topics provides an added incentive to write about this topic.

Some might also argue that dealing with the part the media play in conflicts is also less complicated than studying their role in a peace process. Protests, acts of terror, and even wars are often short-lived and the major events associated with these conflicts frequently take place in the open. A peace process on the other hand can go on for years and some of the most important developments take place behind closed doors. While this would be a perfectly suitable topic for historians, social scientists prefer more straightforward and overt case studies.

Yet another reason for the gap might be the fact that most communication scholars are located in the United States. The US has certainly experienced a good deal of political violence and war, but it has not been engaged in a major peace process since the end of Vietnam. The closest example would be the détente between the US and the Soviet Union that led to the end of the Cold War, but here too the role of the press was mostly ignored. The President and the State Department have served as both

---

[2] See for example Bennett and Paletz, 1994; Gannett Foundation, 1991; Kellner, 1991; Mowlana, Gerbner, and Schiller, 1992.

mediators and facilitators for peace processes in other parts of the world, including the Middle East, Bosnia, and Northern Ireland. But given the parochial nature of most American research, it is hardly surprising the US scholars are more concerned with their own problems.

It is often said that it is much more difficult to build peace than to initiate conflict. The same can be said perhaps about communication research concerning peace and war. It is to be hoped that this book will provide some ideas for redressing the imbalance.

INITIAL PRINCIPLES

This study will attempt to examine the role of the news media in situations in which a democratic government is actively attempting to promote a peace process. The authorities in such situations hope to exploit the media as part of a more general struggle to mobilize elites and the public in support of their policies. In such cases one normally finds some type of opposition to that peace process that is attempting to promote its own views to the news media. It is an ongoing competition in which both sides attempt to use information and events to support their positions on the peace process.

The need to focus on democratic countries comes from the fact that the role the media play in a political process is related to how they construct news stories. When governments have complete control over the media, news is simply another form of propaganda. When dictators decide to change policies the press becomes a passive – albeit important – tool for executing those policies. The more intriguing questions concern the impact of a relatively autonomous media on a peace process. For it is in these cases that the media are most likely to have an independent influence on the process. Therefore, while many of the points being made here can be applied more generally, the role the news media play in non-democratic entities will for the most part be left out.[3]

The major goal of the theory is to explain when the news media are most likely to play either a constructive or destructive role in a particular peace process. We shall look at this issue from the perspective of

---

[3] There are two exceptions to this approach, one major the other minor. The major exception can be found in chapter 5, where we deal with the role of the Jordanian press in the peace process. The second and more minor exception takes place in chapter 7, where I make a number of allusions to the role of the Palestinian press in covering the outbreak of the Second Intifada.

the governments attempting to promote the process. A particular peace process may be misguided or even dangerous but such questions are beyond the scope of this study. The major question being asked here is when the news media are more likely to either facilitate or frustrate government efforts to move forward.

The theoretical model will be developed in three stages. The first section will be devoted to detailing four major types of influence the news media can have on a peace process. This discussion provides a helpful introduction to the topic by clarifying why it is important to study this topic. The second section attempts to look at what can best be thought of as the "static model." It establishes some fundamental principles about why the news media generally play a negative role in peace process. The third and final section goes one step further by explaining ways in which the role of the media can vary. This dynamic model attempts to explain when the news media are likely to play a more constructive role and when they can be expected to be the most damaging of all.

FOUR MAJOR TYPES OF INFLUENCE

The news media can have four major types of impact on any peace process. First, they can play a major role in *defining the political atmosphere* in which the process takes place. Second, the media can have an important influence on the *nature of the debate* about a peace process. Third, they can have an impact on antagonists' *strategy and behavior*. Fourth, they can *raise and lower the public standing and legitimacy of antagonists* involved in the process and their positions. Let us consider the underlying logic of each of these effects.

Perhaps the most obvious influence concerns the media's impact on the political atmosphere surrounding the process. Many would argue that a peace process is most likely to succeed when it is carried out within an environment that is conducive to compromise and reconciliation. In many ways decisions about whether to go forward on such a path can be considered analogous to making a financial investment. While most people realize that any investment entails a certain amount of risk, the financial climate can have a critical influence on perceptions about the extent of the risk involved. People are much less likely to invest in the stock market when everyone is talking about a recession. A general mood of economic optimism, on the other hand, inevitably leads to increased investment. The same can be said about investing in peace: people are more likely to support a peace process when the general mood appears to be upbeat and optimistic.

News reports provide citizens with important clues about the political climate surrounding a peace process. Is the process moving forward or back? Does the overall level of hostility and violence appear to be rising or declining? Is the "other side" keeping its side of the agreements? Are those opposed to the process succeeding in their efforts to stop it? How much of the public supports what the government is trying to do? Is this process really going to work? The answers to such questions – which are often provided by ongoing news coverage – help determine whether the political atmosphere is conducive to making peace.

The ways in which the news media report on the peace process are, of course, directly related to external events. If negotiations have been halted and violence has broken out, the media cannot be expected to provide upbeat news stories. A peace process however, is usually long and complex, and the direction it takes is often open to interpretation. Journalistic norms and routines, which dictate the selection of sources and the construction of story lines, can have a significant effect on which interpretation appears to make the most sense.

The press also has a major impact on a peace process by influencing the nature of public debate. The news media have become the central arena for political debate in western countries and those who hope to promote their ideas to the public have few alternative channels. It is the news media that determine who gets to speak and what is considered an appropriate form of argument. Just as legal debates held in a courtroom have a prescribed language and demeanor, so do arguments carried out on television, radio, and in newspapers. It is a procrustean bed in which ideologies and positions are often reduced to slogans and sound bites.

The fact that so many leaders, activists, and citizens monitor such public debates increases their significance. A democratic decision about whether or not to proceed with a particular peace process should be based on people being exposed to a wide and representative set of voices. The news media should serve as a forum in which proponents and opponents are encouraged to express their views in an open and reasoned fashion. While such an ideal is rarely achieved in any political system, it is important to identify those structures and processes that limit the range of discourse.

A third form of influence has to do with antagonists' strategies and behavior. In this study, the term "antagonists" refers to all individuals, groups, or institutions that are attempting to have an influence on a particular peace process. This includes actors involved in any internal debate over peace as well as those from "the other side." Because most antagonists attribute so much importance to the news media, they often find themselves adapting their plans and actions in accordance with media needs. The greatest impact will be felt among weaker challengers who must adapt themselves to media demands in order to achieve standing (Gamson and Wolfsfeld, 1993). The surest way for such groups to get into the news is to become more extreme (Gitlin 1980; Wolfsfeld, 1997a). While this strategy also has inherent risks, the alternative is to be left on the sidelines; groups who chose to ignore the media may be excluded from the debate.

The media can also influence the strategies and behavior of those in power. When violence breaks out, for example, leaders come under tremendous pressure to "do something" and the press is an important agent for creating this sense of urgency. Such events are often accompanied by massive amounts of media attention and a dramatic increase in public anxiety. These political waves (Wolfsfeld, 2000) are often short-lived, but can lead to policy shifts. On the international level this dynamic is referred to as the "CNN effect" but media pressure can also have an impact on domestic policy.[4]

The effects of the news media on negotiations should also be considered within the "strategy and behavior" category. One of the working assumptions of such talks is that giving too much access to the news media reduces the chances for success.[5] Secrecy is considered an essential element in any negotiating process. When the negotiations become too open leaders and negotiators must constantly defend themselves against charges of "giving in" to the enemy. Leaks about concessions provide valuable ammunition to opposition forces in their attempts to discredit the government. Concessions, especially costly ones, are seen as failures. Both sides find themselves spending more time engaging in public posturing than in bridging the gaps that divide them.

---

[4] The simpler notions about the CNN effect are most likely misguided (Livingston, 1997; Livingston and Eachus, 1995). These studies show that the effects of the international news agenda on decision makers tend to vary over time and circumstance, a conclusion that is quite in keeping with the theoretical approch taken in this model.

[5] The situation is, however, more complicated than this. As discussed later in this work, the causal relationship between media presence and negotiating success runs in both directions. It is true that the presence of the news media is likely to inhibit progress. However, it is also true that antagonists are more likely to *turn* to the media when there is a crisis in the talks.

The news media can also play an important role in modifying public perceptions about various antagonists. The fourth type of influence concerns the ability of the news media to raise and lower the public standing and legitimacy of various antagonists. There are many political actors who want to have an influence on a given peace process, but few are considered important enough to warrant media attention. There is a direct and often circular relationship between media status and public status. This ongoing competition over media access is what motivates antagonists to develop media strategies. Even if they have to batter down the door, it is still better than being left outside in the cold. The first step to political influence is to be considered a player.

It is important, however to make a distinction between achieving public standing and attaining public legitimacy. This is especially important concerning images of the enemy that are based on long histories of conflict and hate. In times of war, the press is an important agent of vilification, a tool that enables leaders to mobilize public support for their policies. American press coverage of Saddam Hussein during the (first) Gulf War was an excellent example of this phenomenon (Dorman and Livingston, 1994; Manheim, 1994a, 1994b; Wolfsfeld, 1997a). Leaders pursuing a peace process may have opposite goals. They must lower the level of suspicion and hate in order to convince the public that there is a viable partner on the other side. By modifying images of the enemy, the press can play just as important a role in mobilizing the public for peace as it does for war. In a relatively successful peace process such changes will come about naturally as the events themselves become more hopeful. Coverage of negotiations and breakthroughs will gradually replace previous scenes of violence. The press may also adopt changes in norms and routines that can soften images of the enemy. Assigning a reporter to spend time living on the "other side" would be a good example of such changes. Such reporters develop new sources and perspectives that provide a less ethnocentric form of coverage.

The press can also raise and lower the legitimacy of political actors involved in the internal debate over peace. The success of any political position depends, at least in part, on public attitudes towards the sponsors themselves. Media portrayals of proponents and opponents to a peace process are important factors in the overall struggle for political support. Does the government appear competent or incompetent? Does the opposition appear reasonable or extremist? Here too one needs to consider both what is actually happening in the political arena as well as the manner in which the press constructs frames of that reality.

Leaders are often given too much credit for success and too much blame for failures. Perhaps one of the most vivid examples is the way in which George Bush Sr. was framed as a hero after the victory in the Gulf War and as an incompetent when the American economy took a downturn.

The remainder of the discussion is devoted to detailing the independent variables that determine how, when, and why the news media have these types of influences on a peace process.

THE STATIC MODEL

Journalists tell stories. How they construct stories about a peace process can have an important impact on the process itself. Citizens depend on these stories to learn about what is happening. Is the process moving forward or backward? Does the overall level of hostility and violence appear to be rising or declining? Is the "other side" keeping its side of the agreements? How much of the public supports what the government is trying to do? Is it really going to work? Although members of the audience also apply their own interpretations to such stories, news represents a major reference point for public discourse.

All other things being equal, journalists prefer to tell stories about conflict. News is first and foremost about conflict and disorder. Protests, violence, crime, wars, and disasters provide the most natural material for news reports. Journalists become famous and win awards for covering such stories. Many reporters dream of becoming war correspondents for this is considered the height of professional accomplishment. The very idea of a "peace correspondent," on the other hand, sounds strange, even contradictory (Galtung, 1998; Manoff, 1998). When peace appears to be taking hold in a particular area, it is time for journalists to leave. Understanding that peace and news make strange bedfellows is an important starting point for all that follows.

The first major argument of this work can be stated as follows: *due to a fundamental contradiction between the nature of a peace process and news values, the media often play a destructive role in attempts at making peace.* This incongruence is rooted in the professional norms and routines that dictate how journalists construct news about peace. As illustrated in table 1.1, there are four major values that are the most problematic in the production of such news: immediacy, drama, simplicity, and ethnocentrism. Each of these values dictates what is and is not considered

Table 1.1 *News of peace: the editorial process*

	News	Not news
IMMEDIACY	Events Specific Actions	Processes Long-term Policies
DRAMA	Violence Crisis Conflict Extremism Dangers Internal Discord Major Breakthroughs	Calm Lack of Crisis Cooperation Moderation Opportunities Internal Consensus Incremental Progress
SIMPLICITY	Opinions Images Major Personalities Two-sided Conflicts	Ideology Texts Institutions Multi-sided Conflicts
ETHNOCENTRISM	Our Beliefs Our Suffering Their Brutality Our Myths/Symbols	Their Beliefs Their Suffering Our Brutality Their Myths/Symbols

news.[6] Editors use these norms as evaluative criteria to decide what to cover and how much space and time to devote to a particular topic. The best story lines are novel, dramatic, simple to follow, and deal almost exclusively with "us."

These criteria influence how items are selected for the news, the tone of coverage and how political actors adapt themselves to get into the news. It influences the selection process because journalists are trained to look for certain types of stories and editors ensure that only items that meet at least some of these criteria will be allowed to appear. Journalists also follow these guidelines when they construct the stories. Political actors look at the same criteria in their attempts to promote their messages to the media. When all of these processes are combined, it significantly increases the impact of these criteria on the final news product.[7]

---

[6] These criteria also have negative influences in other policy areas.

[7] These are clearly not the only criteria that determine whether or not a story is considered newsworthy. The political status of the actors, for example, is another important

Although all western news media employ these criteria, there are also some important differences in the amount of emphasis each news organ places on them. It is helpful therefore to view them more as variables running along a theoretical continuum. Thus, in a more sensationalist media environment one will find greater emphasis on all four of these problematic criteria. As a consequence, it will be argued, such media are especially likely to play a destructive role in a peace process. This point will be developed more fully below.

The first order of business, however, is to explain how each of these values contributes to the difficult relationship between news and peace.

IMMEDIACY

The first problem is the news media's focus on the immediate. The press covers events, not processes. This presents the public with an extremely narrow and simplistic view of what is happening and makes it difficult for leaders to promote long-term policies. A peace process is usually marked by drawn-out, difficult negotiations spotted with occasional breakthroughs. Adopting a short-term perspective often leads to a sense of impatience and frustration. The media's emphasis on the here and now makes it difficult for governments to maintain public support for the process over a long period of time. Leaders will have little to provide journalists on a daily or even a weekly basis. While experienced policy makers realize that negotiations take time, journalists are not in the business of waiting.

Ironically, this problem is often exacerbated by the fact that such negotiations are considered a major news story. Reporters are often assigned to provide frequent coverage of such talks, which leads to unrealistic assumptions about what "should" be happening. Even if there is some progress, negotiators will normally attempt to keep it secret, in order not to prevent any possible backlash. Continual reports about a lack of progress are more than likely to produce a sense of failure among the general public.

Many events that do take place during these periods are negative, and the press has no trouble gaining access to these developments. In fact, the degree to which negotiators seek out journalists is a good indicator of how the process is proceeding. Breakdowns in talks are often marked

criterion. In this work we place an emphasis on those criteria that are the most likely to influence the role of the media in a peace process.

by each side going public with their accusations, in an attempt to use the media as a means of mobilizing domestic and international forces against the other side. Negative events can also include protests and violence by those opposed to the peace process and this can also make for a more hostile political environment.

The analogy of a financial investment again comes to mind. Consider a situation in which citizens purchase shares in a peace stock. Although they are understandably concerned about the risks to their security, they are hopeful that the stock will eventually pay off. The problem is that they are almost never provided information about the overall trend of the stock. Instead they are given daily highlights, especially when there is a dramatic crash in the market. Over the years, the stock may actually be going up in value, but many investors will be scared into selling. Given the lack of long-term perspective, it is difficult to blame citizens for being pessimistic.

THE SEARCH FOR DRAMA

Journalists' obsessive search for drama also contributes to the problematic relationship between media and peace. This need for excitement can have a devastating impact on the course of a peace process. Every act of violence, every crisis, and every sign of conflict is considered news. Areas of calm and cooperation, on the other hand, will be ignored because they are not considered interesting. Extremism is exciting while moderation is dull. Reports of imminent dangers are considered breaking news, but opportunities made possible by peace are not. Stories about internal discord are a mainstay of news, but points of internal agreement are taken for granted and are not worth mentioning. As can be seen in table 1.1, the one exception to this general pattern concerns major breakthroughs in negotiations, which are dramatic enough to be considered newsworthy. Incremental progress, on the other hand, is much less likely to be considered newsworthy.

As suggested earlier, the emphasis on drama not only affects *what* will be covered but also *how* it will be covered. Reporters have a professional interest in making all confrontations appear dramatic and extreme. Drama is the quintessential element of any "good" news story. There are of course important differences among the news media concerning just how much dramatic license is acceptable. The more serious news organs will make a conscious attempt to present materials in a less emotional format. In many western countries however, the line between entertainment and news has become increasingly blurry (Delli Carpini and Williams, 2001).

This emphasis on strife and discord has a number of negative consequences for peace building. First, presenting conflict between the two sides in dramatic terms serves to inflame the political atmosphere. Such presentations, especially when they are amplified and reinforced by different media, have the potential of becoming self-fulfilling prophesies. Headlines that focus on threats, accusations, and confrontations generate anger on both sides and demands for retaliation quickly follow. Minor glitches become major problems, disagreements are turned into crises. Enemies become more frightening, opponents more vicious. The inevitable result is that the news media are more likely to escalate a conflict than to pacify it.

This dynamic not only intensifies the level of conflict between enemies, it also raises the level of rancor in the *internal debate* over a peace process. The emphasis on drama and conflict leads journalists to seek out the most extreme voices and actions for the purpose of exciting audiences. This routine can inflame the internal debate over a peace process in two major ways. First, political actors feel pressured to escalate their tactics in order to successfully compete for access to the media. Second, by highlighting the most angry and violent forces within a particular society, the media make it almost impossible to carry out a reasoned public debate over the issue. Both governments and those from the opposition feel compelled to respond to the threats, accusations, and insults that make for such dramatic headlines.

This emphasis on drama can also have more long-term influences because the emphasis on violent conflict leads to the conclusion that we all live in a very frightening world: a world full of dangers and brutality where no one is ever completely safe (Weimann, 2000). Research in the area known as "cultivation theory" tells us that the more people are exposed to news, the more they see the world as violent (Weimann, 2000; Griffin, 1996; McQuail and Windahl, 1993). Notions of peace and reconciliation appear naïve against this backdrop. Concessions to the enemy look at best foolhardy and at worst like acts of treachery.

This editorial process also leads to a pessimistic view of how a peace process is unfolding. Although news always deals with deviant events it is difficult for the average citizen to avoid the conclusion that these incidents provide information about what is "really going on." Knowing that thousands of planes land safely every day offers little reassurance to those viewing pictures of a plane crash. Few can avoid thinking about those images when taking their next flight.

The demand for drama can also have a direct impact on the behavior of political actors, especially of those in the opposition. As noted, many activists come to the conclusion that they must pay the "dues of disorder" in order to be heard. A peaceful demonstration will obtain less coverage than a disorderly one and a disorderly protest will receive considerably less publicity than an act of terrorism. This does not mean that every movement will turn to violence; the vast majority of groups are ideologically opposed to such tactics. What it does mean, however, is that challengers feel pressured to become more extremist in order to be heard.

Equally importantly, it means that radical voices will often get preference over temperate ones. Every single step in the news-making process is designed to eliminate moderation in order to make the story more interesting. Reporters search for "action" and when they find it their editors are more likely to place these stories in a prominent position. The rules of competition among journalists assure that whoever brings the most stirring story wins. This need to create exciting news stories provides the worst possible atmosphere for reasoned dialogue and debate.

This dynamic is not, of course, limited to public debates over a peace process. Nevertheless, the potential for damage in this area may be especially great. Citizens' feelings about peace and conflict are likely to be particularly intense and thus even the smallest of political sparks has the potential of turning into a major fire. In addition, a calm political environment is an essential element in the promotion of peace. It will be difficult for leaders to convince the public about the benefits of peace when so much attention is focused on extremism and violence.

In sum, the media's search for drama is the primary reason why conflict is considered more newsworthy than peace. It is an uneven playing field in which violence is always given the upper hand.

SIMPLICITY

The next criterion concerns the media's emphasis on simplicity. Simple story lines, especially when they are accompanied by good visuals, are the key to reaching a mass audience. The lack of space and time, especially in television news, means that journalists must construct stories that are short and uncomplicated. The news media are more likely to cover personalities than institutions, to prefer good visuals over complex texts, and to deal with specific opinions rather than general ideologies.

Journalists' unwillingness to deal with ideologies is especially problematic for it severely limits citizens' ability to fully understand debates over a peace process. Ideology is an important aspect of any major political conflict and to ignore these beliefs lowers the level of public discourse. Instead of focusing on the complex political and historical underpinnings of an event, the standard professional routine is to ask leaders and citizens to relate to what has just happened. Political arguments that go beyond the specific incidents are normally left on the editor's floor.

Here, too, this tendency is especially problematic in media coverage of issues having to do with peace and war. Both the internal and external conflicts over the process are almost always rooted in deep ideological divisions. Political leaders and activists find themselves frustrated by their inability to express these views in the media. Robbed of its ideological context, media coverage of a peace process turns the issue into a meaningless struggle for political advantage. The conflict over peace is always newsworthy, but the deeper roots of the debate often get lost. The high stakes involved in the final decision compound the effects of this norm.

The need for simplicity also lowers the level of public discourse in other ways. News reports and talk shows generally confine the range of discussion about political issues to those viewpoints represented by the major political forces within the society. Bennett's (1990) "Index Theory" centers on this issue (see also Mermin, 1999; Robinson, 2002). He argues: "Mass media professionals, from the boardroom to the beat, tend to 'index' the range of voices and viewpoints in both news and editorials according to the range of views expressed in mainstream government debate about a given topic" (p. 106). When editors design debates to be held in either the electronic or print media, they often invite two spokespeople to represent "the two camp." This practice makes it extremely difficult for citizens to even consider political ideas that are located outside this space. The media thus becomes a major agent in defining the borders between acceptable and unacceptable opinions. As further discussed below, such a dynamic can be especially dangerous when there is a broad consensus within a society concerning political "realities."

As with all such routines, the emphasis on simplicity becomes even more significant because political actors adjust themselves to these demands. Leaders and activists learn to package their messages in ways that are easily integrated into news formats. Many also hire public relations professionals whose training and experience allow them to speak in sound bites (Hallin, 1994; Manheim, 1998; Patterson, 1993) and to design events that can provide good visuals.

Some would argue that this entire line of argument smacks of elitism. Journalists, after all, are giving the people what they want. What good is sophisticated news coverage if the mass public refuses to read or listen to it? It is surely better to water down the coverage in order to increase the number of people who consume it. There is a lot to be said for this criticism and it can also be applied to the other news criteria that have been discussed.

Nevertheless, the goal of research in this area is to point to some of the serious social and political costs associated with this approach to news. Pointing to these dangers could encourage journalists to consider creative ways of providing greater substance to their audience without losing money. It is also important to support the more serious news media to ensure that the public has more options. Finally, it is critical to debunk the notion that the news media provide an accurate representation of political reality. The more knowledge and awareness citizens have of these problems, the more they can become critical consumers of news.

ETHNOCENTRISM

The final reason why the media often make peace more difficult is that they foster an *ethnocentric* view of the world. Every news medium operates from a certain political and cultural base that defines its language, beliefs, values, attitudes, and prejudices (Bar-Tal and Teichman, in press; Liebes and Curran, 1998; Liebes, 1997; Shudson, 1996; Wolfsfeld, 1997a). Many of these beliefs are simply taken for granted; there is no need to actually state them. The news media play a critical role in the reproduction of shared myths, symbols, and traditions that mostly increase loyalty to the state (Edelman, 1988). News stories are almost always about "us": about what is happening or could happen to us. When there is news about "others," it centers on how they affect us.

This is especially true about enemies. News editors assume, probably correctly, that the mass public has very little interest in learning about the life and society of enemies. Enemies are only of interest as threats, and thus such news stories focus almost exclusively on the level of danger posed by the other side. As with the other rules of selection, this routine has a decidedly detrimental effect on the prospects for peace. Willingness to compromise is unlikely to take root when the public is constantly exposed to threatening, one-dimensional images of the enemy. Even journalists who support a peace process will avoid writing stories that offend "local sensitivities." Self-censorship can be an extremely effective means of filtering out unpopular viewpoints.

This ethnocentrism becomes especially blatant in times of crisis. When a peace process breaks down, the news media of both sides emphasize their own righteousness and the other's evilness. Such breakdowns are often accompanied by violence and the news media are easily mobilized for the vilification of the enemy. News stories provide graphic descriptions of the other side's brutality and our people's suffering. The tragic stories of the dead and the wounded leave collective scars that remain for many years to come. Claims about our own acts of aggression and the other's suffering are either ignored, underplayed, or discounted. We are always the victims, they are always the aggressors.

Given this, one must always remember that some of the most important effects of the media on the prospects for peace take place long before the negotiations begin. No peace process ever starts from zero. Each public has been exposed to years of tragic images and stories about evil enemies who have killed one's people. It is difficult to exaggerate the overall impact of this constant flow of ethnocentric information on public perceptions of the enemy. The news media are extremely powerful and omnipresent mechanisms for intensifying and solidifying hate between peoples.

THE PRINCIPLE OF UNINTENDED CONSEQUENCES

Some readers may perceive a discrepancy between these arguments and what they know about journalists. Most journalists, they would argue, have a deep moral objection to violence. The underlying message of most news stories has to do with the tragedy of war. When peace breaks out, it is considered good news and reported as such. Compromise between antagonists is considered reasonable behavior and obstinacy is condemned. Many journalists also have a liberal and cosmopolitan view of the world and thus are often among the first to support efforts towards peace and reconciliation. Those who use violence are treated as deviants, especially if they resort to terrorism. How can there be a fundamental contradiction between news and peace when the desire for peace is such an important value in conflict coverage?

The best way to answer this question is through analogy. Think if you will, of a set of parents with two children. One child is extremely well behaved and successful. The other is a problem child: difficult to discipline and always getting into fights at school. The parents get nothing but joy from the first and mostly aggravation from the second. Although they may be reluctant to admit it, they have much more trouble loving the difficult child than their angel. It turns out, however, that they end up devoting much more time, energy, and attention to the difficult child. In doing so, some might argue, they may in fact be reinforcing the exact behavior they are attempting to prevent. This would certainly be the case if a need for attention were one of the reasons for the disruptive behavior. The better-behaved child might justifiably feel neglected. The parents certainly had no intention of rewarding bad behavior, but may inadvertently be doing just that.

The same can be said about the way the news media deal with peace and conflict. While the media place a high value on peace, they act as if they prefer conflict. They devote almost all of their attention to confrontation and violence and mostly ignore areas of cooperation and reconciliation. In some instances – such as terrorist acts – they may indeed end up encouraging the very violence they abhor. This is because the competition over the news agenda is an important element in any political struggle; it is often better to receive negative coverage than no coverage at all. Due to this dynamic, peace-loving journalists can become inadvertent mechanisms for the promotion of war. These are the unintended consequences that are rooted in the standard norms and routines for the construction of news.

To sum up, the news criteria discussed above explain why the news media will usually play a negative role in most peace processes. This impact can be found with regard to all four of the potential influences that were discussed earlier. The emphasis on drama means that the political atmosphere surrounding the peace process is likely to be negative, pessimistic, and heated. This obsessive search for drama can also have an inflammatory influence on the actors' political strategies and on the nature of the political debate. The media's search for simple messages and their focus on immediate events severely lower the level of public debate and deliberation concerning the process. Finally, the completely ethnocentric orientation of the news media serves to reinforce suspicion and hatred towards the enemy and severely inhibit attempts to modify such attitudes. When taken as a whole the combined impact of all of these phenomena is likely to be extremely powerful and pervasive.

CHANGES OVER TIME AND CIRCUMSTANCE:
THE DYNAMIC MODEL

Despite all that was said till now, the role of the news media does vary. There are situations in which the press can play a more constructive role in a peace process. The challenge for researchers is to identify those factors that influence such variations. There are two sets of variables that are especially likely to have such an influence: those associated with the *political environment* surrounding the peace process and those that have to do with the *media environment* in which the journalists operate. The political and professional context for news stories about peace has a major impact on how they are written. As noted, all media work from a particular cultural and professional base that helps define the construction of news (Gamson, 1992; Gamson *et al.*, 1992; Ryan, 1991).

The political environment refers to the aggregate of private and public beliefs, discourse, and behaviors concerning political matters within a particular setting and time. It is a "macro" concept referring to the political "situation."[8] What is the political mood concerning the possibility for peace? What issues are people talking about? What are various leaders doing and how are people reacting to these activities? How are the news media covering political issues at that particular time and place? What is the distribution of opinion on a particular issue? What are the most common interpretive frames being employed to explain and evaluate what is happening in the political realm?

The impact of the political environment on the role of the news media was a topic developed in my previous book (Wolfsfeld, 1997a). It was argued that the authorities' ability to take control over the political environment was a key factor in explaining their ability to promote their messages to the news media. In other words, political control leads to media control. A major reason for this relationship is that the construction of news is a mostly reactive process. Editors and reporters respond to stimuli that are provided by a multitude of sources and events and then attempt to provide their audience with a report about the state of their world. It is a process of social construction not only because of how these inputs are turned into news, but also because of what political sources

---

[8] A similar approach is taken by Japanese researcher Ito (1990, 2002) who talks about "*kuuki,*" which can be translated as climate of opinion.

are saying and doing. Most changes in the tone and content of news coverage reflect shifts in the political process.[9]

Probably the most influential aspect of the political environment has to do with the level of elite consensus in support of a peace process. This brings us to the second major thesis of this work: *the greater the level of elite consensus in support of a peace process, the more likely the news media will play a positive role in that process*. When leaders are able to generate a high level of political support in favor of peace, the press has little problem coming along for the ride. When elites are divided, on the other hand, the internal conflict itself becomes a major part of the story (Entman, 2004). When a peace process is considered controversial, journalists will also be much more conscious of the need to cover it in as balanced a fashion as possible.

Hallin (1986) makes a similar point in his work about the behavior of the American news media in the Vietnam War. Contrary to popular belief, US news coverage of the early stages of the conflict was extremely supportive. This was in keeping with the almost universal agreement about the need to stop the spread of communism in South-east Asia. As the level of elite consensus declined, news reports and editorials began to focus on more negative aspects of the war. The media may also have accelerated the decline in public support once the negative story took hold. Thus, these changes in the political environment had a direct influence on the news media moving from a supportive role to a more independent and critical role.

The influence of elite consensus on the role of the media can also be seen in the example of the Gulf War. The US Senate was split almost completely down the middle when it was asked to give Bush a green light for attacking Saddam Hussein. Once the war began, however, American journalists found it difficult to find members of the opposition who were willing to speak publicly against Bush's policy (Wolfsfeld, 1997a). The changing level of consensus (or at least expressed consensus) had an important influence on the media. While early news coverage and editorials focused on the fierce debate in the United States, the coverage of the war itself can only be described as enthusiastic (Bennett and Paletz,

---

[9] This approach downplays the significance of public relations. While it is true that governments can devote tremendous resources in their attempts to "manage the news," their ability to manage the political situation is far more important. This premise provides a better explanation for the varying ability of leaders to promote their positions to the news media. While a leader's skills and resources in public relations remains mostly constant, the political situation always changes.

1994). The normally cynical journalists found themselves swept up in a wave of patriotism and it was difficult to find elite sources that were willing to publicly criticize the American intervention.

The most important indicator for the news media in these situations is the positions taken by the major political parties. Journalists depend on party leaders as their dominant sources for assessing the state of the political environment. The major opposition parties define which issues are contentious and worthy of public debate. The level of political consensus among the general public can also have an impact on media coverage, but this type of influence is less direct and less significant. The indirect influence comes from the fact that political leaders consider the climate of opinion when forming their own positions (Entman, 2004).[10] However, in keeping with Bennett's (1990) notion of indexing, the range of debate expressed in the news media is mostly shaped by the range of debate among the mainstream political elite.

This process can also be understood by examining the way the news media construct frames about political issues. The news media routinely employ interpretive frames as a device for providing meaning to events.[11] Media frames are perhaps best thought of as organizing themes that journalists use to place events into a package that is *culturally resonant* and *professionally valuable*.[12] Gamson and Modigliani (1987) take a similar approach, claiming that a frame is: "the central organizing idea or story-line that provides meaning" (p. 143). The construction of such story lines to deal with an event can be understood as a process in which journalists attempt to find a narrative fit between incoming information and existing media frames concerning a particular topic (Wolfsfeld, 1997a).[13] The frames that are available for use by journalists vary over time, culture, and political circumstance. The frames that are available in most western

---

[10] Entman (2003) has developed a "Cascade Model" that attempts to deal with the complex set of influences between the political leaders, the news media, and the public. One particular argument is worth noting here. Entman argues that even in those cases when the news media do express independent opinions on policy issues, oppositional forces may be reluctant to promote such ideas if they sense that the climate of opinion will run against them. This mechanism tends to inhibit the emergence of counter-frames.

[11] The notion of media frames has become a central area of research in the field of political communication, and thus this is only one of many possible definitions. For a review of this literature in this area see Reese and Gandy, 2001, and Scheufele, 1999.

[12] A similar approach can be found in Gamson *et al.*, 1992.

[13] Similarly Entman and Herbst (2001) see the process of framing as "selecting, highlighting, and sorting into a coherent narrative some facts or observations and deleting many others" (p. 203).

countries for covering women's issues, for example, have gone through important changes in recent years. The notion of "women's rights" has become more resonant within these societies and news coverage serves to reinforce this change in social values.

When there is a widespread elite consensus about a political issue, one frame tends to dominate media discourse and few questions are raised about its validity. If the level of opposition grows, alternative frames emerge and this competition is reflected in changing media coverage.[14] The public debate in the United States over Vietnam is again instructive. The Cold War frame dominated public discourse during the early years of that conflict and, as noted, this had a major impact on news stories (Hallin, 1986). Given the high degree of consensus, sponsors of Anti-War frames were either ignored or treated as deviants. In later years the growing disenchantment with the war among important elites increased the prominence of competing frames. The Vietnam issue entered what Hallin (1986) labeled "the sphere of legitimate controversy." Journalists who covered such issues felt obligated to present a more balanced form of coverage in which government critics were given a significant amount of time and space to present their views.

This helps explain why it is so important to evaluate the level of elite consensus concerning a peace process. The lower the level of controversy among elites concerning the process itself, the more likely Pro-Peace frames will dominate media discourse. Peace frames will be used to organize information about both successes and setbacks: successes will lead to more optimistic coverage and setbacks will be seen as "problems" that must be solved. Here, too, those who oppose peace will be treated as troublemakers, especially if they resort to violence. The news media in such cases become active agents in the promotion of the peace process, constantly amplifying the existing consensus.

When, on the other hand, there is a serious competition among frames about the peace process, the news media will legitimately give expression to both perspectives. In such cases a good deal of the news coverage will focus on the internal debate over the process and journalists will actively search for sources from both camps. Another means for the news media

---

[14] Simon and Xenos (2000) make a similar distinction in their article on "Media framing and effective public discourse." They differentiate between situations that are "univalent" (one dominant frame), "bivalent" (two dominant frames competing), and "multivalent" (many competing significant frames). See also Mermin (1999), who makes a similar point in his study of the role of the news media in American foreign policy.

to achieve balance when consensus is low is to alternate between frames in accordance with changing events. The news media can employ a Pro-Peace frame when the process is moving forward, for example, and more nationalistic frames during times of crisis.

It is important to consider a possible objection to the stated relationship between consensus and media coverage. Some might argue that it is difficult to make a clear distinction between the independent variable (level of elite consensus in support of peace) and the dependent variable (use of Pro-Peace media frames). The news media, such critics would suggest, may simply make an independent decision to support the peace process. They would then marginalize the opposition and the level of consensus would appear to be much greater than it actually is. The media could also take the opposite stand and highlight the internal dispute over the process and this would give the appearance that there is less consensus than actually exists. This criticism suggests that the argument is circular.

There is a difference however between a circular argument and a circular relationship. I would argue that the social and political forces within a given society are far more powerful and enduring than any editorial decisions about how to cover a particular peace process. The major political parties and movements within a given society develop over an extended period of time and do not simply appear and disappear in response to news media coverage. The political positions such organizations take with regard to a given peace process can be studied independently by looking at their institutional histories. Ideological changes among such institutions are normally slow and incremental.

In addition, editors do not simply invent interpretive frames; they absorb them from the society in which they operate. As noted, the construction of news is a reactive process and journalists attempt to create stories that are politically acceptable to their readers. Editors working in western democracies use major political parties and movements as central sources of information. Journalists report on such organizations, they do not invent them. The news media can be important agents in *accelerating* political changes within a given society, but to suggest that they *initiate* such changes contradicts most of what we know about how journalists operate.

It is important, then, to make an empirical distinction between measures that are intended to gauge the state of the political environment and those that tell us something about the nature of media coverage. Examining the level of elite consensus involves looking at the positions taken by the major parties: the smaller the official opposition, the greater the consensus. The amount of support among the general public (which may also have some influence on news coverage) can usually be measured using survey data. The measurement of media coverage can be ascertained by content analyses of actual news stories and editorials. Distinguishing between political and media variables reduces the chance that researchers are merely measuring different aspects of the same construct.

NUMBER AND INTENSITY OF CRISES

A second variable associated with the political environment has to do with the number and intensity of crises affecting the peace process. Every peace process is marked by a certain number of breakdowns and setbacks. The third major argument is that: *the greater the number and severity of crises associated with a peace process, the more likely the news media are to play a negative role in the process.* In other words, when things get bad, the news media often make them worse. The media's need for drama and their lack of a long-term perspective lead them to exaggerate the intensity and significance of such crises. Political leaders are pounded with huge headlines and angry questioning. By heating up the political atmosphere, this type of coverage can become a self-fulfilling prophecy. Political leaders may feel compelled to overact to this sense of crisis and the cycle begins again. The role of the news media in a relatively calm peace process will be very different. The tone of the reporting will be generally low-key and many stories will be relegated to a less prominent position in the line-up. Contrary to what has been alleged by their more ardent critics, the press rarely invents stories. If the peace process is not producing anything interesting, journalists will look somewhere else for drama. The more stable and trouble-free a peace process, the less likely that the news media will play a destructive role.

Here too the level of political consensus can play an important role. Leaders are in a much better position to ride out a crisis when they can afford to lose a few percentage points in their performance ratings. They will be in a very different position if such a crisis means losing their majority. As discussed, the amount of consensus will also have an effect on how the media view a crisis, on the meaning they give the events. When, for example, opponents to a peace process carry out acts of violence, journalists can either see it as a sign that peace is impossible or that peace is even more urgent.

The news media, then, often play the role of catalysts in such conflicts. A useful metaphor (which I have admittedly used in the past) is to think of the effects of wind on a fire. A fire can spread even when there is no wind. However, the same fire becomes more dangerous when there is a strong wind blowing. The overall impact of the wind will depend on its strength and the nature of the physical environment. The same can be said about the influence of the news media on conflicts and crises. The impact of the media will depend on the intensity of the coverage and as well as the nature of the political environment in which they are operating.

There is an important lesson from all this for political leaders: nothing succeeds like success. Leaders who can mobilize a broad consensus for their policies and successfully manage to keep the peace process on a steady course with a minimum of setbacks have little to fear from the media. Taking control over the political environment is the key to achieving success in the press (Wolfsfeld, 1997a). The news media, however, are fair-weather friends. When those same leaders slip and fall, when consensus breaks down, the media amplify those failures into disasters. The more problematic the peace process, the more destructive is the role of the news media.

THE POLITICS-MEDIA-POLITICS CYCLE

The fourth argument is somewhat more complex, for it deals with the ways in which the news media and the political environment influence one another. It is formulated as follows: *the influence of the news media on a peace process is best seen in terms of a cycle in which changes in the political environment lead to changes in media performance that often lead to further changes in the political environment.* It is not a chicken and an egg problem; politics almost always comes first. A useful rule to follow in these matters is to start by looking at a particular political context, attempt to understand how political actors and journalists interact within the situation, and then examine how the resulting news stories influence the process itself. As noted in the introduction, I shall refer to this principle as the politics-media-politics (PMP) cycle.[15]

This notion was implied in the earlier discussion about the impact of elite consensus and political crisis on the media. The degree of elite consensus, it was argued, has a direct impact on journalists' norms, routines, and coverage. The greater the level of consensus surrounding

---

[15] Although I believe that this proposition can be applied more generally, the discussion will focus specifically on the role the news media play in peace processes.

peace, the more likely the journalists will adopt a pro-peace approach to their work. They will be enthusiastic about the process and grant relatively little access to those opposed to the peace process. Should the environment begin to change, however, the news media can also become important *catalysts* for accelerating such changes. An increasing number of violent crises coupled with a rising number of elites expressing opposition to the government would inevitably lead to a change in both media routines and coverage. Such media changes would increase the political standing of oppositional groups and make it easier for them to mobilize others to the cause. It is a question of momentum, and the news media are critical agents for intensifying and amplifying political momentum.

The importance of this cycle becomes especially conspicuous in the midst of political waves. The term political wave was mentioned earlier but this would be an appropriate juncture to go into more detail. Political waves are *sudden and significant changes in the political environment that are characterized by a substantial increase in the amount of public attention centered on a political issue or event.* Such waves are often marked by major *triggering events* such as a terrorist attack, a war, or an election.[16] The focus on the political environment distinguishes this approach from related issues concerning "news cycles" or "feeding frenzies" (Sabato, 2000). Once again, the argument is that politics comes first.

Nevertheless, the news media do play an extremely important role in such waves. First, they increase the *political impact* of such waves by *amplifying* them. This amplification comes from the fact that so many different news media are providing so much space and time to the story. Journalists love big stories and once a wave has begun no one wants to be left behind (Lawrence and Bennett, 2000). The topic dominates the news on television, radio, talk shows, and phone-in programs. These are the stories people talk about and there is a predictable spike in news consumption. The story is everywhere and political actors are expected to respond to it; it is the type of story that is almost impossible to ignore.

The news media also provide a *temporal structure* for such waves by making an editorial decision about when these stories are "over." Such

---

[16] The term "triggering event" comes from Cobb and Elder, 1983. A number of researchers have used different terms to describe similar processes. Kingdon (1995) as well as Baumgartner and Jones (1993) use the term "focusing events," while a number of German scholars (Brosius and Eps, 1995; Kepplinger and Habermeir, 1995) have used the term "key events."

decisions are clearly influenced by both the size of the wave and what happens in the field. When the major event is followed by a series of related episodes media attention will continue. A new, unrelated event can also create a fresh wave that replaces the old. Often, however, it is the editors who decide when the story is no longer newsworthy. Interestingly, the news media seem to have an almost unspoken agreement about when it is time to move on to other topics. This is an important editorial decision because once the wave is over, political actors adjust their political strategy accordingly. Government leaders may decide, for example, to suspend a peace process in the wake of a serious act of violence. They will resume their efforts only after the political climate has cooled. For opponents to a peace process the end of a crisis wave will mean that they must find alternative strategies for promoting their frames. Here, too, the news media not only signal the fact that the climate has changed, they also play a part in producing that shift.

The media also provide *narrative structure* for political waves. Journalists construct a limited number of story lines that provide guidelines for the collection of information and the production of news stories. The news media become massive search engines frantically looking for information and events that are consistent with a particular frame. German scholars have provided useful evidence on this point in their studies of "key events" (Brosius and Eps, 1995; Kepplinger and Habermeir, 1995). They found that major events having to do with traffic fatalities, AIDS, and attacks on aliens and asylum seekers in Germany changed the criteria for the news selection. After key events, journalists apparently go out looking for related stories and thus give the false impression that there has been a rise in the occurrences of such incidents.

These narrative structures can become especially important when political waves run in a particular *direction*. The notion of direction refers to the extent to which a wave provides political advantages to one set of antagonists and political disadvantages to another.[17] The wave associated with the Columbine "massacre" in April of 1999 provides an excellent demonstration of the political impact of such narratives. Two high school students opened fire, killing twelve classmates, one teacher, and themselves. In many news stories the National Rifle Association stood as the accused in that incident and was forced to devote a considerable amount

---

[17] Lawrence (2000) makes a similar point by arguing that particular news events provide journalists with "story cues" that "push emerging problem definitions in particular directions" (p. 179).

of time and resources to damage control. The entertainment industry also came under serious attack and a number of policy changes were suggested. The massive amount of publicity associated with that event provided an important opportunity for gun control advocates to rally support for new legislation.[18]

News stories about Columbine devoted a considerable amount of time and space in an attempt to find a solution to the problem of youth violence. Yet, the 1998–99 school year was actually one of the safest school years in a decade. In fact statistical data suggested that schools were the safest place for children (Bowles, 1999). The real policy question, one could argue, was not what the authorities were doing wrong, but rather what they were doing right. Nevertheless, given the obvious direction of the wave, it was almost impossible to find stories that talked about schools being safe.

The news media will play a similar role in construction of political waves associated with a peace process. A major breakthrough in negotiations, especially when accompanied by massive amounts of international support, provides important political and media advantages to the government. Officials find it much easier in this type of atmosphere to promote optimistic frames to the media and the public. Peace frames seem to make sense within this context: it all appears to be working out. Those opposed to peace are put on the defensive and find themselves swimming against a powerful tide. When disaster strikes, on the other hand, it places a pro-peace government on the defensive. Such disasters can include a complete breakdown in talks, aggressive statements or actions from the other side, leaks about major concessions by the government, or a terrorist attack. Within this context it is the opposition frames that make sense because the events provide graphic demonstrations of the risks and dangers associated with the process. Peace appears impossible as more traditional fears and hates return to the fore.

Not all political waves provide such a clear direction. Some are more ambiguous and do not provide advantages to either side.[19] A major summit between the two leaders engaged in a peace process can lead to a

[18] The question of whether such brief opportunities can be exploited for long-term changes in policy is a separate issue. One can assume, however, that the greater the number and intensity of waves that run in the same direction, the more likely they will have a long-term impact on the political process.

[19] Entman (2004) argues that ambiguous political events have become much more prevalent in the United States since the end of the Cold War. He argues that this has provided the news media with more power to shape the argument over government policies.

good deal of public and media attention. This still leaves ample room for spokespeople from the government and the opposition to provide their own "spin" on such an event. The authorities will argue that such a meeting demonstrates that the process is moving forward while opponents will focus on government concessions. The results of such a summit can also be open to different interpretations.

The PMP cycle does not only take place in the midst of waves; it also helps explain the role of the news media in more long-term political processes. It is helpful in this regard to think about two types of changes in media coverage that are likely to characterize such a dynamic. The first has to do with the changes in the *news slots* that are used to cover a conflict and the other with variations in the construction of *media frames* about peace. While the first change is more structural in nature, the second is best thought of as a change in the way journalists interpret ongoing events linked to a peace process.

News slots can be defined as topic areas that are routinely covered by journalists. The initiation of an ongoing peace process inevitably leads to the creation of news slots that were unavailable in the past. An important example has to do with the opening of negotiations between the two sides. Until such talks begin, the vast majority of news stories deal with the threat posed by the enemy and the ongoing confrontation. Once negotiations have begun editors must retool in order to cover a different type of news story. Journalists with knowledge and experience in diplomacy, for example, will become more important than those who have spent their careers covering the military beat. This change in news slots will also necessitate a change in setting – say from the battlefield to a location more conducive for such negotiations. There will also be an important adjustment with regard to the prominence of various sources. Thus, political leaders who are linked to the peace process will enjoy a higher level of media status while the proportion of exposure allocated to military sources is likely to decline. Perhaps even more important is the effect a change in news slots can have on media images of the enemy. The general public will be exposed to an entirely new set of personalities from the other side, many of which will be speaking positively about the possibility of peace (Weimann, 1994).

These changes in coverage have the potential of making a positive contribution to the promotion of peace. The very fact that the term "peace process" is being constantly discussed implies that peace is possible. The inevitable changes in setting, stories, emotional tone, and language may very well serve to reduce tensions between the antagonists. Even bad news about a peace process is less likely to do more serious damage than negative news that centers on violent confrontation. Thus, despite all that was said about the fundamental contradiction between media and peace, the possibility of changing news slots may provide an important exception to this general rule.

News slots should not be confused with media frames. While there are some interesting overlaps between the two constructs, news slots have to do with administrative decisions about the assignment of reporters, the search for certain types of sources, and the amount of news space devoted to certain topics. Media frames, on the other hand, have to do with interpretive themes that govern the collection of information and the construction of news stories. Thus, one would want to make a distinction between an increasingly important diplomatic news slot – meaning that there is more time, space, and resources allocated to covering that topic – and a Peace frame that (among other things) portrays those who oppose a peace process as extremists.

This brings us to the question of how the PMP cycle can also explain changes in the way the news media frame public issues. It was argued earlier that the news media construct frames that are culturally resonant and professionally useful. Public notions about what is considered culturally acceptable tend to change over time and here too the news media can reinforce or even accelerate such changes. Gamson and Modigliani (1989) made a similar point in their study of media frames of nuclear energy. In the early years nuclear energy in the US was seen as simply a form of "progress" and thus reporters tended to downplay any reports of problems or accidents. Thus, a very serious accident that took place at the Fermi nuclear reactor in Michigan was barely noted in the news. As anti-nuclear groups became more successful at convincing people about the risks and dangers of nuclear power, the press became more open to employing a "Danger" frame in their news reports. It is not that one frame replaced the other, it was that different frames were now competing with one another.

This case provides a good illustration of how one could employ the PMP cycle to explain the role of the news media in long-term changes. Political mobilization increased the number of anti-nuclear opponents among elites, which was then reflected in the construction of media frames. Increasing use of such frames by the press, especially after the disasters at Three Mile Island and Chernobyl, gave important new advantages to anti-nuclear activists. Changes in the political environment (alternative ideological frames among elites) led to media changes (competing media frames) that led to further changes in the political environment (growing awareness about possible dangers of nuclear power) and in the political process (reduced support for nuclear power).

This argument suggests that the level of elite consensus may be the most important variable of all in determining the role the news media will play in a peace process. It was argued that when journalists construct media frames they attempt to find a narrative fit between existing frames and incoming information. It was also claimed that when there is a high level of consensus, one frame tends to dominate media discourse. Thus, the first question is whether one is dealing with a situation in which the Peace frame is dominant or one in which there is a genuine competition between frames. When the Peace frame dominates, the nature of the incoming information will be less important. Even a crisis will be viewed with the pro-peace context. In a more competitive situation, however, journalists will have at least two alternative frames they can bring down from the shelf: one that provides advantages to the peace camp and one that helps the opposition. In these cases, the construction of media frames will be more event driven. Such situations will be characterized by a more open contest between the two camps. Nevertheless, given what was detailed earlier about what is and is not considered news, the playing field will usually remain tilted against those promoting peace.

DON'T THE MEDIA SOMETIMES INITIATE SUCH CYCLES?

There are a number of scholars who would object to the dominance being attributed to the political environment in this formulation. Dearing and Rogers (1996) for example believe that political outcomes are rooted in the interaction between three sets of agenda: the media agenda, the political agenda, and the public agenda. The assumption is that it would be a mistake to attribute more weight to one component than another – at least when it comes to the topic of agenda setting.[20] One also finds elements of this approach in the work of Lawrence (2000), who makes a helpful distinction between "institutionally-driven news" and "event-driven news." Institutionally-driven news, she argues mostly focus on routine events in which officials are the "key providers of news narratives and frames" (p. 174). Event-driven news focuses on unexpected and accidental events; in these cases the news media become a dominant force in defining the nature and intensity of the problem. A central

---

[20] This approach can also be found in an earlier work by Cobb and Elder (1983).

example in Lawrence's work focuses on the role of the news media in defining and amplifying the beating of Rodney King by the Los Angeles police department.

The major question being asked is how often do the news media take the lead in such stories. There are of course many stories that are initiated by challengers, but this merely reinforces the claim that politics comes first.[21] In addition, as Entman (2003) points out in his work, even when the news media do initiate independent positions, unless they are "picked up" by a serious political force such ideas are unlikely to spread. There are cases in which unplanned news can have an impact on public discourse; the Columbine incident provides a useful example of such a phenomenon. The news media may also publish a scoop that can have a major impact on a political process. A diligent reporter can ruin peace negotiations by publishing details of the talks.

I would argue, however, that such cases are very much the exception, especially when it comes to major political issues such as those associated with peace and war. In addition, even when unexpected or media-initiated events do occur, they take place within a wider political context. The example of the nuclear accident at the Fermi nuclear power station was used earlier to illustrate this point. As further detailed below, the news media do play an important role is controlling the flow and direction of political tides; but they rarely initiate them.[22]

THE INFLUENCE OF THE MEDIA ENVIRONMENT

The nature of the media environment also has an important influence on the role of the news media in a peace process. As noted, journalists construct news stories that are culturally resonant and professionally worthy. The nature of the political environment determines what is culturally resonant while the media environment establishes what is considered professionally worthy. The news media play a significant role in this process by deciding how to translate political events into news. The media environment can be defined as the aggregate of professional beliefs, values, and routines that journalists employ in the construction

---

[21] Lawrence, for example, includes terrorist attacks as an example of event-driven news but such acts are neither unplanned or even (at least in recent times) unexpected.

[22] Critics might argue that the very notion of a cycle makes it impossible to determine where such processes begin and end. I would respond by suggesting that the intensity of the "influence current" varies over time and circumstance. If the political process is not providing any new stimulants the story will quickly die.

of news stories. These definitions vary over time and culture and this is one of the reasons why the role of the news media in political processes also varies.

Political leaders in democratic countries, have relatively little control over the media environment. This is an important distinction from what has been said till now concerning the political environment. To put it differently, the media environment is much more stable than the political environment. Journalists' professional practices are slow to change, and this helps explain why political leaders often feel frustrated in their relations with the press. There are some important exceptions to this rule. Thus, the news media are much more willing to accept government restrictions during wartime in the interests of national security. One also finds that there are also "partial democracies" where governments exert both formal and informal power over the news media. Jordan is a good example of such a country, as will be further discussed in chapter 5. For the most part, however, leaders in democratic countries have no alternative but to take the media environment as a given and to adapt their strategies accordingly.

This study will stress two important dimensions of the media environment: *the degree to which sensationalism has a major foothold among journalists* and the *extent to which antagonists in a conflict share the same news media*. These two factors push in opposite directions. A greater level of sensationalism will increase the likelihood of the media playing a destructive role in a peace process, while an increase in the amount of shared media will increase the chances that the press will make a positive contribution to a process.

THE DANGERS OF SENSATIONALISM

There has been growing concern in the field of political communication about the influence of sensationalism on public discourse. The phenomenon has also been referred to as "infotainment" (Blumler and Kavanagh, 1999; Brants, 1998; Brants and Neijens, 1997; Graber, 1994) or "tabloidization" (Newton, 1999; Owen, 2000; Sparks, 1992; Swanson, in press). Despite the differences in emphasis, most of these works center on the same point: the greater the influence of commercialism on news content, the less likely that the media can serve as serious and responsible forums for public debate. An important aspect of the present research is to demonstrate how sensationalism can become an especially dangerous problem when the news media deal with peace and war.

The fifth argument reads as follows: *the more sensationalist the media environment the more likely the news media are to play a destructive role in a peace process.* The notion of sensationalism refers to the extent to which journalists feel obliged to use a melodramatic style of presentation in the construction of news stories. Sensationalist norms place a high value on emotionalism rather than reason, on entertainment rather than information. Sensationalist media place a special emphasis on the four problematic news criteria that were highlighted in the earlier discussion: immediacy, drama, simplicity, and ethnocentrism. It is helpful to think of these criteria as a set of continua on which one can rate various media organs and systems. All news media, I argued in the first section of this chapter, employ these four criteria in the production of news. Nevertheless, the degree of emphasis varies and this can have a significant impact on the role the news media will play in a peace process: the higher the level of sensationalism, the more damaging the role.

Emotional news coverage is designed to stir passions and nothing could be more damaging for those engaged in conflict resolution. When sensationalism is considered a central news value it influences every stage of the news production process. Journalists search for the most dramatic and emotional stories while photographers, camera operators, and editors attempt to capture and publish the most shocking images. Drama becomes the primary criterion for decisions about story prominence. Those responsible for layout and graphics also contribute to this process by using formats and headlines that magnify conflicts.

The other end of this continuum can perhaps be labeled responsible journalism. The norms in this type of media environment emphasize the need for reporters to maintain emotional distance when covering political events. More responsible news media place a premium on informing at the expense of entertaining and aspire to provide more serious analyses of the political world. Such news media also make an effort to provide a broader view of the political world that includes a commitment to including foreign news. This brand of journalism is more sophisticated, less emotional, and less ethnocentric. There is still a contradiction between news routines and the nature of a peace process, but here it is less severe.

There are no absolutes in this area: every modern media system is characterized by at least some sensationalist media and most also include some responsible news organs. When carrying out comparative work, researchers need to look at the relative importance of sensationalist values within the overall media environment. The approach taken in the present work centers on the *norms and values* that dominate the media environment. While looking at news formats (e.g. the size of headlines) can also provide important information about the level of sensationalism, it is critical to focus on how such norms regulate the interactions between leaders and journalists. Journalists working in a relatively sensationalist environment feel more pressured to supply their editors with melodrama and they pass these expectations on to their sources. Political leaders and activists operating in this type of environment are forced to be more dramatic in order successfully compete for space. This often leads to a good degree of tension in the relationship between journalists and their sources, as leaders become frustrated over the media's unwillingness to deal with substance. Sensationalist news values can also have an important impact on journalists working for the mainstream media as well.

Interviews with journalists and political actors can provide important insights about the extent to which such values have an impact on the interactions between them. The higher the demand for drama, the more political leaders will feel pressured to provide it. The major advantage of focusing on sensationalist values is that it allows us to look directly at how such professional guidelines influence the behavior of both journalists and political leaders. As noted, the testimonies of leaders involved in a peace process are especially critical, because they are in the best position to tell us about the impact such pressures has on the course of the process.

Sensationalist news media have a vested interested in conflict. The best-known historical example of this phenomenon is the flagrant attempts by publisher William Randolf Hearst to stir American anger against Spain at the end of the nineteenth century. The oft-repeated story claims that a bored illustrator asked to come home from Cuba because "there will be no war." Hearst alleged reply was: "You furnish the pictures and I'll furnish the war." While some have questioned the veracity of the story, there is no dispute about the fact that Hearst and others were able to significantly increase circulation by sensationalizing the Spanish–American conflict.

There is an even more poignant demonstration of this phenomenon that is less well known. Ito (1990) reported on a number of research projects carried out in Japan concerning media coverage of the Russo–Japanese war in 1904. This research shows that those newspapers that carried "chauvinistic and sensationalist" articles and editorials during that conflict greatly expanded their circulation, while those that did not lost many of their readers. One of the newspapers that opposed the war had its premises set on fire by angry mobs and eventually went bankrupt. All this may explain the comments attributed to the newspaper journalist Kuroiwa Ruiko later in that century: "Newspapers should be anti-government during peace time, and chauvinistic during war time" (Ito, 1990, p. 431).

The world constructed by sensationalist journalism is an especially frightening place: filled with threats and violence. The cynical saying associated with sensationalist journalism is: "if it bleeds it leads." Enemies appear powerful and unwilling to compromise and citizens need to be constantly on their guard. It is also a world in which the internal debate over peace is likely to be especially intensive. Reasoned debate becomes impossible. Sensationalist news media turn every public debate into a shouting match. While there is always a certain contradiction between media and peace, the discrepancy becomes particularly glaring when entertainment becomes the central goal of journalism.

SHARED MEDIA

The notion of a shared media refers to the extent to which antagonists engaged in a peace process receive their news from the same news organs. Here, too, the level of shared media should be seen as a continuum rather than a dichotomy. While there is often at least some political or ethnic overlap within the audience, the extent of this intersection will vary among conflicts.

The sixth and final argument is as follows: *the greater the extent of shared media, the more likely it is that the news media will play a constructive role in a peace process.* There are cultural, commercial, and political reasons for this dynamic. As noted, journalists always write stories within a particular cultural framework. Presumptions about collective identity are an especially important element in the construction of news and this can provide a basis for dialogue. In an environment dominated by shared media the underlying theme concerns what can be done to resolve conflict within "our" community. When, on the other hand, there are little or no shared media the perspective is inherently ethnocentric. Routine coverage of a peace process focuses on the threat that "they" pose to "us." The news media in each culture reinforce existing myths and stereotypes about the other.

There are also commercial motivations that point in the same direction. Broadcasters and newspaper publishers working in an environment with shared media will be extremely reluctant to offend major segments of the audience. However difficult, they must find a tone and language that speaks to the largest possible population. Editors will also hear from

42

their audience if they appear to move too far in a particular direction. The most sensible editorial position in these situations is to find a middle ground that appeals to a broad range of consumers. This is probably the only example in which commercial interests actually *increase* the probability that the media will play a constructive role in a peace process.

The existence of a shared news media will also have an important influence on how political leaders and groups shape their messages. Leaders employ a less extremist form of rhetoric when they find themselves talking to multiple audiences. This process may even have an influence on the ideologies of the warring groups as more moderate messages become familiar and acceptable. Those who only have to communicate with their own people, on the other hand, will emphasize sectarian loyalties in order to maintain their power base.

One is more likely to find a shared media in domestic conflicts than in international disputes. This is another example of how the role of the media is influenced by the political context in which they operate. When a conflict breaks out between different groups within the same country journalists will be more likely to construct news stories that will bridge the cultural gap between the two sides. This does not suggest that such stories will be completely "objective"; they will still be more likely to reflect majority views. They are unlikely, however, to be as ethnocentric and stories written by two sides engaged in an international conflict, in which citizens from each country receive all of the information from their own media. The news media operating in these situations will reflect and reinforce all of the cultural animosities towards the other side.

IN SUM

The model that is being put forth in this book sees the news media as important actors in a peace process. They are not the most important players because they are far more likely to react to events than to initiate them. Yet they do play a significant role because they are important catalysts that can have a serious influence on the chances for success. Supporters and opponents from all sides of the conflict invest a significant amount of resources in an attempt to promote their positions to a variety of publics and leaders. In addition, many depend on the media as their major source of information about the peace process and how the media relate to the process can have a significant influence on public perceptions and attitudes.

All other things being equal, the news media are more likely to hinder than to help. This is because there is a fundamental contradiction between the nature of a peace process and what is considered news. The editorial process systematically highlights information and events that raise doubts about peace and excludes information that could raise confidence. Given this tendency, the news media are more likely to sour the political atmosphere than to improve it, more likely to encourage violence than to discourage it, more likely to lower and intensify the level of internal debate than to raise it, and more likely to lower the legitimacy of a pro-peace government than to enhance it.

The challenge for researchers is to explain how this process varies over time and in different circumstances. The key to understanding such variations is to look at the nature of the political and media environments in which the media are operating. Some environments are more likely to produce positive news about peace because they fundamentally alter journalists' working assumptions. The nature of the political environment is important because journalists reflect and reinforce the existing climate of opinion. The nature of the media environment is significant because it helps define the norms and routines for producing news about peace.

The influence of four specific variables will be dealt with in this work, two that have to do with the political environment and two with the media environment. The most important political factors are the degree of elite consensus in support of the policies and the number and intensity of crises associated with the process. The greater the degree of elite consensus and the lesser the degree of crisis, the more likely it is that the news media will play a constructive role in a peace process. The two variables having to do with the media environment are the level of sensationalism and the extent to which antagonists share a common media. Sensationalism leads to the media playing a more destructive role and having a large number of shared media has the opposite effect.

The next step is to illustrate the utility of these principles by applying them to different peace processes.

CHAPTER 2

The initial stages of Oslo

Israeli journalists recall the last days of August 1993 with both embarrassment and excitement. The media had been following the ongoing peace talks in Washington, which seemed to be going nowhere. Suddenly, Israeli and Palestinian leaders announced that they had achieved a breakthrough in secret talks taking place "somewhere in Scandinavia." The agreement called for Israel to pull back from Gaza and from the city of Jericho in the West Bank and for the PLO to take administrative control of these areas. Within a few days the media learned that the agreement was even bigger. Israel intended to formally recognize the PLO as the legitimate representative of the Palestinian people, and the PLO would formally recognize the Jewish state. In addition, the Declaration of Principles (DOP) would set out a series of steps for moving the peace process forward.

The initial weeks after the breakthrough were euphoric, and the Israeli media were enthusiastic partners in the celebration. This period came to be known as the "peace festival" and the newspapers, television, and radio were full of rosy predictions about the new dawn (Wolfsfeld, 1997b). The Peace frame dominated media discourse during this initial wave of enthusiasm. There were stories about Israel becoming the "Switzerland of the Middle East" and that peace with Syria was just around the corner.

The problem was that peace had not arrived; it was not even close. The Declaration of Principles signed by Israel and the Palestinians merely established a framework for negotiations. While the signing of the Olso accords was an important breakthrough, the road to peace would prove long, difficult, bloody, and (at the time this is being written) unsuccessful. The leaders themselves were well aware of these difficulties but assumedly felt they should ride the wave of optimism for as long as it would last.

It did not last very long at all. The initial stages of the Oslo peace process provide a good starting point for demonstrating the problematic role the news media can play in a peace process. The major reasons for this have to do with the nature of the political and media environments surrounding the process. The Rabin government was never able to mobilize a broad consensus in favor of the Oslo accords and the long negotiations were marked by some of the worst acts of terrorism Israel had ever seen. These problems were exacerbated by an extremely sensationalist Israeli press dedicated to turning every event into melodrama. The role of the news media during these stages was to make a problematic peace process much worse.

Despite the initial enthusiasm, the political environment was not conducive for the promotion of peace. Prime Minister Rabin had been elected by an extremely slim margin in the 1992 elections and had a great deal of difficulty maintaining his majority in the Knesset during the long months of negotiations. The initial agreement with the PLO passed the Knesset by a vote of 61 to 50 in September of 1993. The "Oslo B" agreement that was signed two years later was barely approved at all. By that time Rabin headed a minority government and the agreement was passed by a mere two votes. Public opinion about Oslo was also split. An ongoing poll carried out by the Tami Steinmetz Center for Peace Research (1996) revealed that the amount of support among the Jewish population rarely reached 40 percent; about 35 percent were opposed and the remaining quarter was undecided.[1] Rabin was never able to mobilize a massive amount of support for Oslo in either the Knesset or among the public.

The Israeli polity had long been split over the question of what to do about the occupied territories. Many in Israel still regarded the PLO as a terrorist organization responsible for hundreds of deaths and the opposition was both extensive and fierce. Immediately after the initial accords were announced, the political right wing organized two of the largest demonstrations ever held in Jerusalem, with numbers reaching over 100,000 participants in each. Countless protest movements were organized against the agreement (see Wolfsfeld, 1997a). It was clear from the beginning that the struggle over Oslo would be bitter.

---

[1] Unfortunately, at this stage in the surveys, the Arab citizens of Israel were not included in these polls. They represent about 12 percent of the voting public and the vast majority supported the Oslo accords. Thus, the overall level of public support is somewhat higher than this.

The period under consideration in this chapter runs from that first announcement in August of 1993 to a few weeks after the Rabin assassination that occurred in November of 1995. The majority of this period was marked by complex negotiations that led to two important agreements between the Israelis and the Palestinians. The first Declaration of Principles was signed in September of 1993 and the second ("Oslo B") in September of 1995.

The major ideological frames being promoted by the two camps were firmly rooted in the long-standing debate in Israel between left and right. The Rabin government promoted the Peace frame, which emphasized the need for compromise with the Palestinians in order to end the conflict. Foreign Minister Shimon Peres was perhaps the most eloquent spokesperson for this perspective when he described the "New Middle East," which would be marked by a political and economic boon to the entire area. The initial enthusiasm of the press during the "peace festival" reflected the cultural resonance of that frame.

The frame being promoted by the right-wing opposition is best labeled the "Security First" frame. The term security has an almost reverential status in Israel, as one would expect from a country that has lost so many lives to war and terrorism (Barzilai, 1996; Horowitz and Lissak, 1990; Kimmerling, 1993; Peri, 1983). The minister in charge of the armed forces is called the "Security Minister." The Israeli news media constantly tries to assess the security situation, or have ongoing discussions about security problems. The area in Southern Lebanon that Israel occupied for many years was called the "security zone."

The opposition – led by Likud Party leader Benyamin Netanyahu – argued that any concessions to the Palestinians would pose a serious threat to Israel's security and lead to even more bloodshed. The security card has always been the right's strongest form of attack on the left, because any concessions to the Arabs are considered dangerous risks. The opposition's major hope of defeating the Labor government was to have the debate over Oslo framed as a conflict over security rather than a conflict over peace. One of Netanyahu's advisors talked about the resonance of the security message:

> The security aspect means something to people. What worries them is security, that 80% of the population lives near the coastal plain [which the Likud Party claimed would be under direct threat if the

territories were given back] or just that it is a real problem that everyone is worried about. (O14, August 18, 1995)[2]

Thus the competition between the Israeli left and right was never a question of those in favor and opposed to peace, it was between those who stressed the importance of achieving peace and those who emphasized the need for security.[3] The cultural resonance of these frames is rooted in the fact that every Israeli would like to achieve both of these goals. The centrality of these frames to Israeli politics can be demonstrated by the fact that candidates running for Prime Minister inevitably include "Peace and Security" as among their major campaign slogans.

Indeed, Yitzhak Rabin's rich military background made him an ideal candidate for the left. Only "Mr. Security" would be in a position to convince Israelis that the country could afford to make concessions in the interest of peace. The same argument was made several years later when former Chief of Staff Ehud Barak was chosen as the Labor candidate for Prime Minister. The problem with other Labor candidates, such as Shimon Peres, was that they were considered extreme doves who could simply not be elected.

It was clear from the beginning, then, that there would be a genuine competition between frames over the Oslo peace process and the news media served as the central arena for this contest. The discussion moves on to consider the problems the Rabin government had in promoting the Peace frame to the Israeli media. The first part will look at the overall relationship between the government and the Israeli media while the second will look more specifically at how this relationship was altered during some critical political waves.

PROMOTING PEACE TO THE MEDIA

It is important to begin the analysis by considering the *advantages* enjoyed by the Rabin government. Governments always enjoy a natural

[2] Each of the interviews quoted in this book is signified using a letter notation that associated it with a particular research project. The following is a list of those notations: O= Oslo research project, J = Jordanian project, NI = Northern Ireland project, CD = Camp David project.

[3] This is of course an overly simplistic description of the ideological frames that are being promoted by the various political movements and parties in Israel. However, these two "meta-frames" are useful in two ways. First, they are helpful because they are general enough to be applied to so many different groups and ideologies. Second, while other, more specific frames enjoy shorter "shelf-life," these two frames endure within Israel over an extremely long period of time.

advantage over challengers when it comes to promoting frames to the news media. The most important benefits can be labeled "production assets" (Wolfsfeld, 1997a). Production assets refer to those properties that facilitate the creation of newsworthy information and events. There are two major types of production assets: political standing and resources.

The Prime Minister and the other senior ministers have an extremely high level of political status and almost anything they do or say is considered newsworthy. They also enjoy a high level of organization and resources that are devoted specifically to dealing with the news media. The Rabin government, for example, had four major offices responsible for promoting the government's stand on the peace process: the Prime Minister's office, the Foreign Ministry, the Defense Ministry, and the Government Press Office. Each of these offices employs full-time, experienced staff who are responsible for ongoing relations with the press.

The Rabin government also enjoyed another important advantage: the hope for peace resonates extremely well within the Israeli news media. There was almost universal agreement among all of those interviewed for this research about journalists' support for the Oslo peace process. Even the reporters themselves – who might have been expected to plead "objectivity" – had little problem admitting where their sympathies lay. While some denied that such beliefs had a significant influence on coverage, almost all expressed their personal support for the process. The statement made by one of the best-known political reporters exemplifies this sentiment:

> It's true that Israeli reporters are mostly peaceniks. If I had to judge from the people I know, I'd have to say that is true. If I had to evaluate it or make a guess, I'd say that they don't vote for the right wing and that they support these accords. They went with it and really wanted the dialogue with the PLO I don't think that their personal ideology was part of their coverage but they certainly didn't oppose the accords because that would be against their position. (O5; May 14, 1995)

Another political reporter talked more specifically about the cultural resonance of the peace:

> There's one thing that's true about the coverage of the peace process, it's not objective. The peace process is not some anonymous process that you leave it up to the reader to decide whether it's optimistic or pessimistic. In principle, when the media relate to the peace

process they are primarily relating to the word peace and therefore the attitude [*hityachasut*] is optimistic. I mean that the attitude is optimistic, or even celebratory, let's call it that. Just like it is completely clear that if there is a terrorist attack like yesterday the attitude is negative. When the media come to cover the ceremony, the handshake at the White House, or the historic handshake at Oslo they relate to the word peace and if there are complaints about that [the biased coverage] then maybe they're justified. (O8; July 26, 1995)

On the surface these types of statements serve to support those in Israel who claim that the Israeli news media are biased in favor of the left. However, it is critical to make a distinction between political and professional considerations. As discussed in the previous chapter, journalists as individuals may very well love peace, but as professionals they pay much more attention to conflict. I shall return to this point below.

Thus, despite the advantages enjoyed by the Rabin and Peres governments they both faced serious obstacles in promoting the Oslo peace process to the Israeli press. The most important problems were rooted in their inability to mobilize a clear political consensus in support of Oslo. This point becomes especially clear when the analysis moves on to consider the very different role the media played in the Jordanian peace process. Nevertheless, not all the problems related to selling Oslo had to do with the problematic political environment; there were other difficulties that can be attributed to the values and routines that dictate the construction of news. It is here that one begins to understand the underlying contradiction between news and peace.

POLITICS AS A SERIES OF EVENTS

The first major problem with the Israeli press coverage of the Oslo peace process was its emphasis on short-term events rather than long-term processes. As discussed, the news media define politics as a series of daily events and then attempt to use those events as a means of determining the fate of the peace process. A peace process, however, is mostly marked by long, difficult negotiations with occasional breakthroughs. Governments have very little to offer journalists during these long lulls. A political reporter who followed the entire process talked about this problem and complained about the lack of drama.

It's actually hard to write about the peace process in a sensational manner. Unless you're talking about a breakthrough. On a daily basis you're talking about some very gray things and they're not going to be sensational. I write about personal subjects, or even pseudo-gossip, I write about the trivia. There is very little sensational stuff I can write about. (O6; May 11, 1995)

Another reason journalists have difficulties reporting on a long-term political process is their emphasis on the here and now. The news media were constantly attempting to learn whether the Oslo peace process was a "success" or a "failure," whether it was "over" or "moving forward." That same journalist claimed that this short-term thinking was part of a general phenomenon where reporters and editors increasingly attempt to write short, simple news stories.

I think some of my colleagues – and this comes from the nature of the media, not because of their personalities – are far too definitive. That is why every time there is a terrorist attack, the peace process is over. And these are very respected people. It is caused, among other things, by the tendency within the media for short headlines that leads to short conclusions. (O6; May 11, 1995)

Those who expect quick results from such negotiations are inevitably disappointed. The need to provide daily reports about the negotiations only serves to exacerbate this problem: the constant repetition about a lack of progress provides increasing evidence of deadlock. Policy makers take a more long-range view of such talks and understand that setbacks are an inevitable part of the process. The frustrations expressed by a television reporter almost two years after the first Oslo agreement illustrate this problem.

The negotiations with the Palestinians and the Syrians go very, very slowly. Every phase is a story that goes on for long months and they are dealing with the smallest details of the smallest details and it goes on for days and days. It is not like every day they decide to withdraw from the Golan Heights. Look how little has happened since the Cairo agreement that dealt with "Gaza and Jericho First" till now. You could put all that into a few statements and that's it. (O8; July 27, 1995)

A peace process is not only long, it is also complicated. Negotiations were going on at a variety of locations and dealt with an enormous number of technical issues. The attempt to transfer authority to the Palestinian population involved long and difficult talks about such issues as taxes, customs, trade agreements, energy, water, industry, legal arrangements, and security. None of these negotiations readily lend themselves to sound bites.

Governments also face another difficulty in competing for public attention during such periods. Negotiations must be kept secret in order to succeed. The importance of taking control over the flow of information is especially important within this context. One of the reasons why the initial talks in Oslo were so successful was that no one knew about them. The leaders had no need for posturing, no need to prove they were "winning." It was much more difficult to keep the subsequent negotiations secret and every leak made it more difficult to make progress (Wolfsfeld, 1997c). One of the Prime Minister's advisors put it this way:

> Any deal is better if you don't have to do it under the spotlight. Because the spotlight means "deadlines." Spotlights mean questions that you are not always eager to answer. Spotlights mean that the two sides will be much tougher about things than they would without those spotlights. It's much easier to do it secretly and quietly. (O4; March 19, 1995)

The need to maintain secrecy makes it difficult for spokespeople to provide reporters with any real information. The political reporters, who had been so important during the first days of Oslo, no longer had much to report. When one stops feeding journalists, they find somewhere else to eat.

One of the most fundamental difficulties in promoting a peace processes is that it is extremely difficult to find newsworthy events that "prove" the peace process is working. It is much easier to find events that "prove" that the process has failed. This period was marked by a number of significant changes in Israeli–Palestinian relations, but none of these provided continuing news. The Israelis and Palestinians, for example, carried out hundreds of joint military patrols designed to deal with any tensions that might emerge. These patrols were considered news when they began but then considered routine. The patrols were only covered again when something went wrong, especially if a conflict broke out between the soldiers from the two sides.[4]

---

[4] These patrols were suspended at the outbreak of the Second Intifada (September, 2000) when one of the Palestinian policemen opened fire and killed his Israeli counterpart.

One of the more important examples of "hidden achievements" had to do with the cooperation between the two intelligence communities. It was the first time in history in which Israelis and Palestinians worked together to defeat terrorism. Neither side was anxious to have this cooperation publicized in the media. The Palestinian leadership was concerned about publicizing the cooperation with Israel against their own people, and the Israelis did not want to emphasize their dependence on the Palestinian Authority. Although it took some time, there is good reason to believe that this cooperation led to a dramatic drop in terrorism during the Netanayhu and Barak governments that followed this period. Here, too, however, only the failures were considered newsworthy.

This is clearly part of a much larger issue concerning the inherent negativity of news. Shoemaker (1996, and in Shoemaker and Eicholz 2000) argues that humans are "innately" interested in deviant events and this can be explained by looking at both biological and cultural evolution. People's first priority is to ensure their own safety and this is why so much news deals with threats. Journalists make a convincing argument that people have little interest in "good news."

Here, however, the important question has to do with the *consequences* of these routines, not their causes. Journalists are indeed expected to report on the planes that crashed, not on the hundreds of thousands that reach their destinations. But if news about planes is mostly about crashes and news about peace is mostly about failure, citizens are likely to think about the deviations, rather than the norm. The issue can be referred to as the problem of "representative deviance." If most of the information about an issue or place focuses on deviance, people will be more likely to assume that such exceptions are typical. In the case of news about peace such a process is more likely to lead to fear than hope.

THE PROBLEMS OF SENSATIONALISM

There is another, equally important reason, why the Israeli media proved to be a poor vehicle for peace. As discussed, the need for drama is a central element in the creation of any news story. Nevertheless, it is the emphasis on drama that allows us to distinguish between serious reporting and yellow journalism. A troubling trend in the Israeli press in recent years has been the increasing need to turn politics into melodrama (Peri, 2004). The Rabin government had difficulties maintaining the high level of drama they had provided in the first days of Oslo. The major actors who could provide the drama were those carrying out extreme acts of violence, especially the Palestinian opposition movements Hamas and Islamic Jihad. It is ironic that these terrorist attacks become the major vehicle for the Israeli right wing to promote the Security First frame to the news media and the general public.

The Israeli media environment was not always dominated by sensationalism (Peri, 2004). In the past ideological papers owned by political parties had a wide circulation. Virtually all of these newspapers went out of business as commercial newspapers came to dominate the marketplace. Today, the two most popular newspapers – *Yediot Ahronot* and *Ma'ariv* – both employ a tabloid format that includes large colorful headlines, the extensive use of visuals, and an extremely dramatic and emotional form of coverage. The intense competition between the two newspapers has led to an increasingly high level of sensationalist reporting. Despite this, both newspapers also employ serious writers that allow them to bridge the gap between different types of readers.[5]

There is also a third important newspaper – *Ha'aretz* – that targets a more elite audience. It is the most serious newspaper in Israel and is considered essential reading by the social, political, and economic elites in Israel. The fact that *Ha'aretz* uses a more sophisticated format is one of the reasons why it has by far the smallest circulation of the three papers.

The electronic media in Israel have also become increasingly sensationalist, especially during the 1990s. For many years there was only one television station in Israel, a public broadcasting system modeled on the BBC. Channel 2, a commercially oriented station, began regular broadcasting in 1993, using a more dramatic format. It quickly became the more popular station for news, and the first channel was forced to make changes in order to compete. Another development in this area is that there has been a virtual explosion in the number of radio stations in Israel and here, too, the use of drama is seen as the critical means of increasing ratings. The growing sensationalism of the Israeli news media is a frequent topic for debate. The term "ratings culture" is often used in Israel to describe these problematic changes.

---

[5] Caspi and Limor (1999) disagree, arguing: "although both dailies adopt many of the features of the popular press, one could hardly label them 'sensationalist.' Even if the their editors are at times guilty of banner headlines that border on the hysterical (after a terror attack, for example) they are very careful not to adopt the more common features of yellow journalism such as nude photos or low level language" (p. 81). I would argue that it is important to see the level of sensationalism as a variable that can be placed along a continuum. Israeli newspapers are not the worst of the lot, but they are certainly not the best, especially (as Caspi and Limor suggest themselves) when it comes to the coverage of political violence.

The relative importance of sensationalism in a given media environment can best be ascertained by talking with journalists and their sources. These expert informants are in the best position to tell us about the rules of the game and how such norms and routines influence the interactions between political actors and the media. Israeli journalists are aware of the influence of sensationalism and it is a familiar topic of discussion. While most editors and reporters would probably prefer to engage in a more serious form of reporting, they have resigned themselves to the existing market and its dictates. The prevailing assumption is that dramatic coverage is the only way to compete for audiences. The comments of one journalist on this topic are typical of what was said by many others.

> The media goes too far about every subject under the sun. They went too far about the Oslo process. They went too far about the peace with Jordan. They go too far when it comes to terrorist attacks and they go too far when it comes to scandals. That's the "tabloidization" process that all of the media are going through. It's not related to the peace process. It has to do with the media. (O7; May 11, 1995)

The Israeli authorities were continually frustrated by the sensationalist coverage given to terrorism. They did admit, however, that terrorism represented a significant threat to the peace process and no one questioned that it was a legitimate news story. It was the proportion and tone of the coverage to which they objected. Prime Minister Rabin (1996) himself expressed this frustration in an interview he gave in the *Harvard Journal of Press and Politics*. He complained about the fact that newspaper headlines about isolated stabbings in Jerusalem were larger and more dramatic than the headlines reporting on the beginning of the Six-Day War in 1967. Every act of terror, the government argued, was not war; the state was not about to be destroyed.

The coverage of these incidents was indeed hysterical. The Israeli news media have adopted special modes of operation for dealing with terrorism waves.[6] The electronic media halts all regular programming and initiates round-the-clock coverage that deals exclusively with the tragedy. The national radio stations all have special tapes prepared for such disasters that play somber Israeli music; the usually large proportion of

---

[6] This routine was used more sparingly with the dramatic increase of terrorism that marked the beginning of the Second Intifada. It was reserved for those events which were characterized by a large number of deaths within a single incident.

foreign music is considered inappropriate for such occasions. The ongoing television coverage includes repeated broadcasts of the shocking scenes from the attack, including heartbreaking interviews with the injured, eyewitnesses, and the victims' family and friends. There are also ongoing talk shows in which political leaders are asked to explain the meaning of the event, twenty-four-hour call-in shows, and special programs for children to help them deal with their grief. The newspapers follow a similar format. The two more popular papers – *Ma'ariv* and *Yediot* – are filled with tragic images in full color. The terrorist attack is the only story and it fills every page. A more detailed description of such coverage will be provided in the analysis of the wave associated with the terrorist attack at Beit Lid.

The media's need for drama proved to be a two-edged sword. The media was extremely enthusiastic about the various breakthroughs and the signing ceremonies. That same inclination, however, came back to haunt the government in the coverage of terrorism. Israelis found themselves riding an emotional roller coaster as they went from the grandeur and splendor of the peace ceremonies to the sickening sights of carnage from blown-up buses. In hindsight, one might argue that the government's decision to promote these interim accords with such enthusiasm may have made the fall from grace even more severe.

It is important to emphasize that there is nothing inherent about a terrorist attack that demands such hysterical coverage. The leaders and the journalists who were interviewed all agreed that this approach was a radical departure from media coverage in years past. One of Rabin's closest advisors, a former journalist himself, talked about the change in coverage.

> There's no comparison between the coverage today and what it was like in the past. Twenty-four soldiers died in an ammunition truck after a mission in Egypt . . . There was an ordinary headline in *Yediot Ahronot.* Nothing like what you have today. There were two pictures, a list of the dead that was it. Two days after that there was nothing. Today with all of the pictures, the headlines, and the color, it a completely different world . . . I once wrote about a bomb that went off at the central bus station in Tel Aviv. It was a one-page story. One and a half pages in *Yediot Ahronot* and that was the end of the story. People were killed. Today a bomb in the central bus station in Tel Aviv would be like the end of the world. (O4; March 19, 1995)

The sensationalist coverage of terrorism during this period suggests that audience considerations were more important than political ones in the construction of such stories. This illustrates an important point that was raised earlier. When journalists have to choose between political considerations (supporting the peace process) and professional considerations (increasing audience size), the latter generally win out. The demands of the market proved more powerful than any need to bolster the Oslo process. The first goal of any journalist is to produce the most interesting story possible and few would give up a good story for political reasons. One of the more cynical journalists put it this way:

> I have a theory about whom I work for. I don't work for the public. You can forget about all this stuff about "watch dog" and "the public's right to know." I work for my boss. Why? Because he's the one who can promote me. If I can bring some type of scoop that manages to embarrass the Prime Minister or the Foreign Minister then that places me in a certain position. The second group that interests me is my colleagues. I want to bring a good story, one that tears their insides out. A good story that I have and they don't. My greatest nightmare is to wake up one morning and read in one of the morning newspapers that Israel and Saudi Arabia have agreed to have diplomatic relations and I don't have the story. That's my greatest nightmare. (O11; November 15, 1994)

As implied above, the argument that is being made here runs against the conventional wisdom in Israel. It is assumed that because most Israeli journalists support the peace process, media coverage is biased in the same way. There are three major factors working against this logic. The most important has to do with the professional definitions of news that were discussed in the last chapter. A second (related) factor has to do with journalists' professional reputation and advancement. The journalists most likely to gain a good reputation are those who produce the most interesting stories. Journalists who give up such stories, or demonstrate blatant political bias in their coverage, are unlikely to receive accolades from either their peers or employers. Finally, the need for security resonates just as well with journalists as it does with the rest of the public, especially when it comes to acts of terrorism.

Thus, any government attempting to promote a peace process to the news media must deal with the fact that threats will always be more newsworthy than opportunities. However, the more sensationalist the media environment, the greater the obstacles leaders will face.

AN ANALYSIS OF NEWSPAPER STORIES

A content analysis of newspaper articles that appeared during the first year of Oslo demonstrates some of the difficulties associated with the promotion of peace. The analysis was based on fifty days of news articles that appeared between August 27, 1993 and May 5, 1994. This period starts with the initial news of the breakthrough in Oslo and ends with the signing of an agreement in Cairo which came to be known as "Oslo A" or "Oslo 1." The fifty days were selected at random and the analysis looked at all news articles about the peace process that appeared in the first three pages of two newspapers: *Yediot Ahronot* and *Ha'aretz*. A total of 577 articles were included in the analysis. Editorials and personal columns were excluded.

The news stories were divided into a total of seventeen subject categories based on headlines.[7] The categories were then classified into those considered "positive" news about the peace process, "negative" news, and "mixed news." The positive news categories included stories about progress in the peace process, progress in the negotiations, peace ceremonies (including preparations and the aftermath), economic benefits related to agreement, non-economic benefits related to agreement, international support for agreement, new relations with Gulf states or other Muslim countries, and general optimistic statements in favor of peace process. The negative news categories were: dangers associated with agreement, terrorism (including aftermath), standstill or difficulties in negotiations, parliamentary opposition to agreement, and extra-parliamentary opposition to agreement. The following categories were considered mixed news: mixed reports on the negotiations, reports about the negotiations with Syria, reports about the negotiations with Jordan, reports on the discussions in the Knesset, and (for reasons explained below) the Hebron massacre carried out by Baruch Goldstein.

The 250-day period was broken down into five equal periods. The proportion of positive, negative, and mixed news stories that characterized each of these periods is presented in figure 2.1. These figures should be seen more as an approximation than as an exact count. But the trends do give some sense of the tone of coverage during these periods.

---

[7] Two separate coders were trained and given a sample of seventy-five articles to test the reliability of the coding sheet. There was an 87 percent rate of agreement between the two coders. For more details see the methodological index.

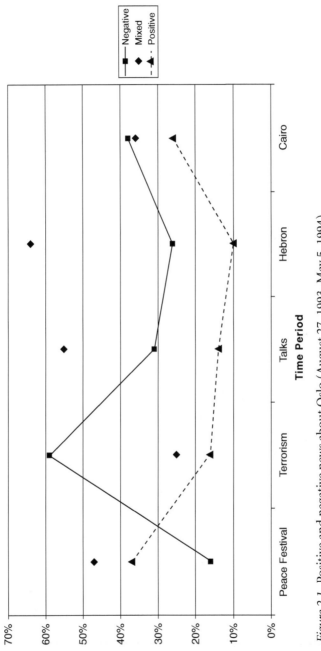

Figure 2.1 Positive and negative news about Oslo (August 27, 1993–May 5, 1994)

The names given to each period help signify the major events that dominated coverage. The first period, labeled the peace festival, represents the only period when the amount of positive news stories outnumbered negative ones. Thirty-seven percent of the stories published in the two newspapers dealt with positive aspects of the peace process such as ceremonies, political and economic breakthroughs, and optimistic statements about the peace process. Only 16 percent of the stories provided a pessimistic view. Stories about terrorism, protests, and the risks associated with the process were all included in this coverage, but these events and information paled in comparison to the greater drama associated with the initial breakthrough.[8] As discussed, this was the period when the government exerted its greatest level of control over the political environment. The country was flooded with optimistic statements, analyses, and events all suggesting that Oslo provided a real chance for peace.

The second period was dominated by terrorism and the reversal in coverage was dramatic. Hamas had taken the initiative during this period and become a major player. The Rabin government was on the defensive in their attempts to reconcile the signing of peace agreements with the increase in Palestinian violence. An extremely high 59 percent of all the news stories were negative during this period and only 16 percent were positive.

The gap narrowed somewhat during the third period but negative stories still outnumbered positive ones. The period is labeled "talks" because a good deal of the coverage at this time dealt with the mechanics and issues that were being discussed in the negotiations. This helps explain why there is so much "mixed" news. The government had very little to show for the talks and, as noted, was doing everything they could to keep the substance of the negotiations secret. There was a drop in terrorism during this time but there were still enough incidents to provide a significant amount of negative news. The peace process was, for the most part, in a holding position, and this was the only period that lacked any major defining events.

---

[8] One receives a similar outcome by looking at the amount of space devoted to each story. What this analysis does not show, however, is the relative *impact* of these stories. As discussed below, one powerful story about a terrorist attack is likely to do more damage than five stories about the benefits of peace. Nevertheless, it should be noted that the terrorist activity in this period claimed far fewer victims than terrorism in subsequent periods. This helps explain why there was a smaller number of stories dealing with these incidents.

The major event characterizing the fourth period was the Hebron massacre. As noted it was decided to classify this event as "mixed news" for the peace process. On the one hand the act served as a means of lowering the legitimacy of those opposed to the peace process. Nevertheless, the act was also interpreted as a sign of the difficulties associated with attempts at reconciliation between Israelis and Palestinians. The massacre also caused a new wave of terrorism and the amount of good news about the peace process reached an all-time low: 10 percent. The events and information that the government had supplied during the festival were by now considered old news, and terrorism provided important advantages to those promoting the Security First frame.

The fifth and final period refers to the breakthrough in the negotiations leading to the Cairo agreement. The Rabin government was finally able to take some of the initiative away from its opponents and the amount of positive news rose to 26 percent. There were stories about progress in the talks, the economic benefits from the news agreement, and the preparations for the ceremony marking the government's achievement. Terrorism, however, continued and over a third of the stories during this period dealt with this issue. Even in this hour of success, the Rabin government found itself getting more bad press than good.

This analysis helps demonstrate why the role of the news media in a peace process is affected by *both* the political and media environments. On the political level, Rabin's failure to take control over terrorism continually inhibited his ability to promote the peace agenda. It also hampered his attempts to mobilize a consensus in support of Oslo. At the same time, media values and routines also played a role. The fact that the proportion of positive stories about the process rarely went past 20 percent is significant. Examining this period from an historical perspective, many would see it as one of the most significant breakthroughs in the Arab–Israeli conflict. Israel recognized the PLO as the legitimate representative of the Palestinian people and the Palestinians recognized Israel's right to exist. This period was also marked by the first agreements ever signed between Israelis and Palestinians, and by an unprecedented amount of cooperation between Israeli and Palestinian institutions. It is the nature of news, however, to focus on the immediate and on dramatic events, which gives important advantages to extremists. Baruch Goldstein, Hamas, and Islamic Jihad, were all attempting to derail the peace process and the Israeli news media were important – albeit unintentional – allies in these efforts.

THE ROLE OF THE MEDIA DURING TERRORIST WAVES

The news media, it was argued earlier, play an especially important role during the political waves associated with major events. Given the importance of such incidents, the media do indeed create the first draft of history. It is, however, a very poor draft. Journalists have a very specific set of professional goals and have little interest in placing the events within a wider context.

The Oslo process was marked by a number of major waves. Some brought important advantages to the Rabin and Peres governments while others placed them on the defensive. The peace festival mentioned earlier is a good example of a government-initiated wave that facilitated the initial promotion of the Peace frame. The political waves following major terrorist attacks, on the other hand, provided important opportunities for the opposition to mobilize the media in support of the Security First frame.

The role of the news media in waves can best be understood by using case studies that allow for an in-depth look at the issue. As noted earlier, waves provide a convenient manifestation of the politics-media-politics cycle. Here I will examine the political wave that followed the terrorist attack at Beit Lid junction in January of 1995. The major goal of this analysis is to demonstrate how the news media amplify waves and provide them with both a temporal and narrative structure. The discussion will also attempt to provide some insights concerning the effects such coverage can have on political actors' strategies and behaviors.

The analysis begins by considering the historical period that preceded the attack at Beit Lid. The period between October, 1994 and January, 1995 was marked by a number of major events in Israel. The first was the kidnapping by Hamas of a soldier by the name of Nachshon Waxman on October 11, a story that carried on for several days and produced an enormous amount of news coverage. In the end Waxman and another soldier were killed during a rescue attempt. On October 17, the mood turned euphoric as the Rabin government initialed a peace agreement with Jordan, an event that will be dealt with in chapter 4. Only two days later the mood again turned grim, when a bus was blown up in the center of Tel Aviv, killing twenty-two people.

The terrorist attack at Beit Lid took place on January 23, 1995. This well-known interchange is not far from Tel Aviv and serves as a major transfer point for hundreds of Israeli soldier in transit. Two suicide bombers blew themselves up on that morning, killing twenty people

Table 2.1 *Number of articles about Beit Lid attack*

Newspaper	Jan. 23	Jan. 24	Jan. 25	Jan. 26
Yediot	30	17	13	0
Ma'ariv	29	29	14	0
Ha'aretz	21	19	17	2
Total	80	65	44	2

and wounding sixty-five. A tide of sorrow and anger once again swept through the country, raising serious doubts about the viability of the peace process.

As in the past the Israeli media quickly went into disaster mode. Television and radio suspended their programming and became the central forums for grief and anger. The images and sounds were horrific and the bloody scenes were shown over and over. Among the most devastating aspects of this coverage were the eyewitness accounts of the carnage. Consider for example the testimony of a soldier who was weeping for his fallen comrades as he tried to describe the horrors he had seen:

> I heard the explosion and I was shaken. The things I saw. A person's head between his legs, hands and legs all over. People screaming "help us," "help us." All my friends from my company, they all flew into the air. By the coffee house there are people with no hands . . . people tried to help . . . but everything was turned into pieces. (*Channel 1 Evening News*, January 23, 1995).

There are frightening items to view. While no one can deny the accuracy of such reports, it is reasonable to question whether they cross an ethical line in terms of sensationalist coverage.

The number of articles published in the three major newspapers about Beit Lid is detailed in table 2.1. This table is important for it provides evidence of how the news media both amplified and provided temporal structure to such waves. As can been seen, the event received a massive amount of attention: 191 articles in three newspapers over an extremely short period of time. These numbers do not even include the large number of pictures that often took up an entire page in the two more popular papers (*Yediot Ahronot* and *Ma'ariv*).

What is fascinating is that the wave ends as abruptly as it begins, and it does so at exactly the same moment in all three newspapers. While

Ha'aretz published two articles on the 26th, the story is basically over on the 25th. The event that had been so enormously important to Israel just three days before was no longer mentioned. The sudden drop is not related to the start of any new wave: there was only routine coverage on the 26th. All of these editors came to the same conclusion at the same time: the story was over. The problem of terrorism was apparently no longer worth discussing until it happened again.

This decision about the temporal structure of the story has important implications for the government, the opposition, and the public. The government is no longer under pressure to find an immediate solution to the problem, and the opposition finds it more difficult to exploit this issue as a means of gaining access to the media. Leaders of political movements return to their normal modes of operation; the office phone stops ringing as supporters go back to their usual routines. For the public the end of media coverage provides a powerful signal that the emotional upheaval associated with Beit Lid is over. It is no longer an issue; Beit Lid has now become an historic event.

Amplification not only comes from the amount of space devoted to the attack, it also comes from the exaggerated, emotional tone of the coverage described earlier. The newspapers – which will be the focus here – play a critical role in this emotional catharsis. A summary of the first day's coverage in the three newspapers is presented in table 2.2. The front pages of the two most popular papers are covered with portrait photographs of the dead staring out at the readers. The massive red headline in *Yediot Ahronot* read: "The children that won't return." The *Ma'ariv* headline was "With tears of rage." A short biographical piece was written about every victim and their grieving families.

A remarkable amount of space is devoted to the pictures and reports of the horror and grief. On the first day *Ma'ariv* devotes ten full pages and *Yediot* nine full pages. On the second day (not shown) *Ma'ariv* devoted another ten full pages and *Yediot* gave another nine pages. The stories include appalling accounts by eyewitnesses and the victims' families.

The coverage in the more quality newspaper *Ha'aretz* provides an important contrast; it illustrates that the same event can be covered in a much less sensationalist style. Here, the emphasis is on detached analysis rather than emotional catharsis. Thus, the first day's headline read: "19 Killed by Two Bombs at Parachute [Beit Lid] Junction; Closure Imposed on the Territories."[9] The portraits of the victims are placed on page 3.

---

[9] The number of dead rose after this headline was published.

Perhaps even more important is the fact that there are also *other* news stories on both the front page and throughout the newspaper, including other stories relating to the Arab–Israeli conflict. These differences in tone also continue on the second day. As noted, the popular newspapers devoted a massive amount of attention to the funerals and the national mourning. *Ha'aretz*, on the other hand, printed almost nothing along this line.

Perhaps there is no objective means of deciding which type of coverage is more appropriate. Eyewitnesses to the horror of a terrorist attack would probably react like the two popular newspapers, so this can be considered a more "authentic" form of coverage. What is clear is that the fact that the vast majority of Israelis are exposed to the more sensationalist, emotional coverage – which is then reinforced by the horrific images being shown on television – serves to dramatically increase the social and political impact of the wave. Leaders operating in a political environment that was defined by the *Ha'aretz* tone might be in a better position to think about terrorism from a long-range perspective. As noted, this apparently was the situation before the rise of sensationalist news coverage in Israel.

NARRATIVE STRUCTURE

The news media also provide a narrative structure to political waves by providing an authoritative account of the major actors and events associated with a wave, and by thematically organizing information in ways that serve both their own professional interests and the cultural sensitivities of their audience. The construction of a narrative structure should be seen as a joint effort among journalists, antagonists, and the public.

News coverage of any disaster wave runs along fairly predictable lines. The news media construct stories that correspond with public reactions to the event: sorrow over the loss of human life, anger at those considered responsible, and an intensive search for solutions. There are also more "technical" stories that provide details about how the disaster took place.

The Beit Lid story ran along just these lines. In addition to the technical details of the incident, news stories centered on three major themes: grief over the dead and wounded, anger at the Palestinians, and an almost desperate search for some way to prevent future acts of terror. The Israeli media conducted a massive search for any information that could be related to these three themes. Given time constraints and the enormous amount of space allocated to political waves, journalists have little choice

Table 2.2 *First-day newspaper coverage of Beit Lid attack*

Newspaper	Page	Headline	Visuals*
Yediot Ahronot	1	The Children Who Won't Return	Individual pictures of victims
	2,3	Red Berets Soaked in Blood	Weeping soldier holding bloody shirt[a]
	4,5	The Children Who left for the Army and Won't Return	Portrait pictures of two victims
	6,7	In One Moment the Intersection Turned into a Deadly Field	Sister kissing wounded brother[a]
	8,9	Death on the Way to the Base: Stories from the Booby Trap	Shocked medic[b]; Overhead picture of site[b]
	10	I Saw by the Coffee House People Whose Entire Head was Burned, All those Hands . . .	Crying soldier being held/led by second soldier
Ma'ariv	1	With Tears of Rage Complete Closure of Territories	Individual pictures of victims
	2,3	Death on the Way to the Base	Sapper going through debris[b]; Female soldier crying
	4,5	19 Black Frames [obituary notices]	Medic treating wounded
	6,7	The Curse of Renne Cassain: 2 Dead Yesterday, 6 Within Last Half Year	Shocked soldier being held by second soldier[a]
	8	Booby Trap at Parachute [Beit Lid] Junction: The Dead	Picture of one victim
	9	The Terrorist Ran Towards the Wounded and the Dead and Blew Himself up.	Scenes of wounded and dead bodies at site
	10	"It was a Terrible Massacre"	Medics comforting weeping civilians
Ha'aretz	1	19 Killed by Two Bombs at Parachute [Beit Lid] Junction; Closure Imposed on the Territories; Islamic Jihad Accepts Responsibility; Beilin to Al-Baz: We will Consider Signing the Nuclear Non-Proliferation Treaty	Sappers going through debris

2	The Terrorist Blew himself up Next to the Soldiers that were Treating Their Friends	Diagram of site; religious workers standing next to bodies
3	Those Killed in the Attack: 18 Soldiers, including One Woman Soldier, and a Civilian	Individual pictures of victims
4	Rabin: In the Intermediate Time-Span, the Entrance of Palestinians to the Sovereign Territory of Israel must be Prevented; In the Security Offices there are Discussion about Possible Actions against Terrorism: "The Intelligence Operations will be Increased"; Parachute [Beit Lid] Junction: Among the Most Crowded, and an Old Site for Terrorist Attacks	None
5	"I am Looking for My Friend", said the Pale Girl"; Senior Members of Likud Party Reject [President] Weitzsman's call for Unity Government.	Wounded being unloaded from helicopter at hospital
6	Islamic Jihad Leaflet: "Our Heroes Blew up the Transportation Station of the Zionist Soldiers"; Yasser Arafat Called Rabin to Condemn the Attack, and to Send Condolences to the families; Hamas Supporters suggest Stopping the Violent Actions in Exchange for Israeli withdrawal from West Bank.	Picture of one of the attackers; picture of "The Engineer"

a Visuals taking up full tabloid page
b Visuals taking up half of a tabloid page

but to lower their normal standards of evaluation. Stories that would not normally be considered worthy of publication are included because they can be easily integrated into existing slots.

The stories about the horror and the mourning in the two popular newspapers were structured by using *organizing captions* to thematically connect a number of different stories under the same headings. This is a standard routine for covering waves in Israel and even includes a (literal) frame to indicate which stories fall under the same heading. The first day's organizing captions (January 23) centered on the initial shock: "Death on the way to the base" (*Yediot Ahronot*, pp. 3–11) and "Hell [*Tofet*] at Paratroopers [Beit Lid] Junction" (*Ma'ariv*, pp. 2–10). The second day focused on the theme that the whole country was suffering: "The country is crying" (*Ma'ariv*, pp. 2–11), "A country in mourning" (*Yediot Ahronot*, pp. 1, 3, 5, 7, 9). These captions not only provide a structural link to the stories, but also allow the editor to integrate the many photo images into the overall narrative.

Decisions about narrative structure influence the collection of information. A good example of this process is the decision by *Ha'aretz* not to put a major emphasis on the grief and mourning theme. Because of this decision, no reporters were sent to cover the many funerals taking place on the second day of coverage. These journalists were then assigned to cover the other aspects of the story deemed to be more significant by *Ha'aretz* editors.

The stories about grief and mourning were dealt with earlier. The discussion turns, then, to the stories having to do with the other two themes: anger at the Palestinians, and the search for solutions. The rage against the Palestinians and the accompanying doubts about the peace process was an important theme in all three days of coverage. The anger is directed at all the Palestinians and specifically at Arafat.

Examining these news stories one gets a better understanding of how sources, journalists, and publics cooperate in constructing such items (see also Just *et al.*, 1996). There were a large number of stories denigrating Arafat and the Palestinian leadership. The President of Israel, who is expected to remain above politics, was one of the first to open the attack. President Weitzman made major news by suggesting that "maybe Arafat is not the right partner" and that "the peace talks should be suspended." This was especially surprising given the fact that Weitzman was traditionally one of the strongest supporters of the Oslo peace process. *Yediot Ahronot* (January 23) also contributed to the antagonistic mood, reporting on its front page that Arafat had been "reluctant" to condemn the attack. A story in *Ha'aretz*, based on information supplied by a former advisor to the previous government, talked about an audiotape in which Arafat was purported to have stated that "we are all suicide bombers" (*Ha'aretz*, January 23, p. 5). There was no information of how long he had had the tape but this was clearly an appropriate time to release it and to publish a story about it.

The next day *Ha'aretz* published an article that contained a leaked report from the meeting of the Rabin government: "Security forces at the government meeting: Arafat is not keeping his commitment to operate against extremists" (January 24, p. 5b). Yediot had a similar story, suggesting that a secret report prepared by the military's legal department suggested that the PLO was constantly breaking the agreement (January 24, p. 3). Here, too, no information was given about when the report had been written. Other stories focused on calls by various leaders to end all cultural contacts with the Palestinians and on those Palestinian groups who were "celebrating" the attack on Beit Lid.

All of these items illustrate how a story line is constructed during such waves. Once the initial theme has been established journalists look for any information that can provide empirical support for that theme and they have little trouble finding sources that are eager to supply it. The theme in this case centers on the anger against the Palestinians. This provided opponents of Oslo with an important opportunity for promoting the notion that Israel could never trust the Palestinians. The emphasis on such threats is an integral part of the Security First frame. Indeed, when violence breaks out, the war against Palestinian terrorism becomes the dominant theme in such rhetoric.

The third important theme in the coverage centered on the frantic search for solutions to terrorism. None of the remedies presented withstood the test of time; terrorism continued. But the public wanted answers and given the extremely high level of anxiety, leaders had to come up with "something."

Prime Minister Rabin's speech to the nation on the night of the attack became the center point of these discussions. As noted by his advisor (in an interview with me), the goal of this speech was to "calm" the people. Part of the strategy was to promise revenge: "We will destroy the murderers: no border will stop us," and a dramatic message to the terrorists: "We will come after you and we will win." The other part was a grand plan for "separation" from the territories using some type of fence or electronic border that would provide a means for controlling the inflow of Palestinians. Rabin's separation proposal provided the news media with an important new angle for the terrorism story, a means of filling the enormous news hole that had been created by the attack. Politicians, experts, and citizens could all express their views on the desirability and feasibility of the plan.

The idea of separation often comes up in Israel during such crises.[10] Leaders are understandably reluctant to talk about trust and reconciliation when there is such anger over terrorism.[11] Claiming that the ultimate goal of the Oslo peace process is to "keep the Palestinians out of Israel" is an attempt by the left to place the peace process within a Security frame. Given the high level of distrust of the Palestinians, the metaphor of a divorce resonates much better than one of marriage. This framing strategy is similar to the attempts by the right to talk about the need for a "true" peace. Neither side is willing to give up the cultural resonance of either Peace or Security.

There were also many other solutions that were suggested for dealing with terrorism, all of which proved ephemeral. The government announced that they would close the territories, not release the Palestinian prisoners as had been promised and would expand their attacks on the terrorist infrastructure. The police announced that they would use an additional helicopter to increase patrols on the border. One well-known reporter suggested that the families of suicide bombers should be expelled to another country. A government minister proposed that Israel forbid Palestinian Muslims to come to the mosques in Jerusalem during the holy month of Ramadan, "so they will know there is a price for mayhem." One of the religious parties claimed that the real cause of terrorism was that Rabin did not observe the Sabbath.

One solution to terrorism that did not emerge in any significant manner was the idea that Israel should *accelerate* the peace process. There were certainly voices within the left who supported such an idea, but it made little political sense to bring them up in the midst of the hysteria surrounding Beit Lid. The pro-Oslo forces were already on the defensive and any suggestion of more concessions would provoke an angry

[10] This idea became especially popular again after the breakdown at Camp David and the outbreak of the Second Intifada. Ehud Barak and other members of the One Israel party became enthusiastic supporters of this policy.

[11] This was one of the important differences between the rhetoric of Rabin and Shimon Peres. Rabin, always the military man, was much more likely to talk about security considerations linked to Oslo. It was Peres who was more likely to talk about "The New Middle East," which would be marked by a dramatic rise in Israeli–Palestinian economic relations.

response from a wide spectrum of political forces. This point will become more important when the discussion examines media reaction to a similar act of terrorism in Northern Ireland.

The search for a solution provides a fitting end to the narrative about Beit Lid. The story begins with the shock and grief over the loss of life, continues with the rage towards the perpetrators, and concludes with a number of proposals for retribution. The sad truth is that there are never any short-term solutions to terrorism, especially when suicide bombers are involved. Nevertheless, given the enormous amount of grief and fear associated with such waves, such a pessimistic conclusion is culturally unacceptable. The end of the wave brings a certain relief. Terrorism is no longer on the public agenda and the political process moves on to other topics. The story – at least for a time – is over.

INFLUENCES OF TERRORISM WAVES ON THE POLITICAL ENVIRONMENT

This brings us to consider the second part of the PMP cycle. The cycle is easier to observe during waves because it takes place within a relatively short period of time. The political wave associated with Beit Lid begins with the attack itself. As shown, the news media then amplify the wave and assign it a certain meaning. The political actors find themselves confronting this new reality and must adjust their strategies accordingly. A useful method for understanding this process is to examine the changing interactions between the political actors and the journalists during such a wave.

Acts of terrorism are a major jolt to any political system. Political leaders, activists, and journalists all abandon their normal routines and move into a crisis mode of operation. At the same time, all of these actors have been through previous waves and have established routines for dealing with them.

Every terrorist attack during this period was considered a major failure for the Rabin government. Israelis had been promised an end to violence; terrorism was seen as a clear indication that the Oslo accords were not working. There was no doubt that the political climate had turned against the government, the direction of the wave was very clear. The euphoria in the early days of Oslo was being replaced by the need for damage control. The Peace frame was simply out of place. One of Rabin's advisors talked about these changes in fortune:

In certain areas my message is the main message. In other instances it is the message of the opposition or other forces that influence the final journalistic product. For example, when it comes to terrorism, you have to remember that I don't have a strong explanation for the terrorism issue. I am hurt by terrorism as much as the opposition. I just say that if I stop the process it would be a mistake, because that would only increase terrorism . . . The problem is that when there is a wave of terror my explanation is not strong, and the explanation or the inputs of the opposition to stop the process are just as powerful or even more powerful than mine. (O3; May 17, 1995)

As noted, almost all of the journalists we spoke to supported the Oslo peace process. Yet the relationship with the Rabin government became strained and even hostile in the midst of these political waves. Reporters were caught up within the surge of pessimism and doubt. Liebes (1998) made a similar point in her study of "disaster marathons," in which Israeli television stops its normal broadcasting and focuses exclusively on a major calamity. These become, she says, "degradation ceremonies" in which the Prime Minister and the Chief-of-Staff are grilled about their culpability. Such a change in the attitude of the media, I would argue, has political consequences, for it lowers the legitimacy of those in power. A political reporter who was interviewed in May of 1995 described the relationship between the political mood and support for the peace process.

I think it depends on when you are talking about. If you are talking about September of '93 [start of the Oslo process], then yes [we supported it]. If you are talking about the day when the peace agreement was signed with Jordan, then yes. But those are not representative days. You have to ask about a day like today (after terror attack). The journalists, including those in the middle politically, are influenced by the atmosphere and I think many support it less, much less than they supported it before. When it comes down to it, they reflect the general political mood, they can't detach themselves from it. (O6; May 11, 1995)

It is impossible to isolate the extent to which the news media are creating the mood or amplifying it. As noted however, the sensationalist coverage of terrorism in Israel is a relatively recent development. In the 1970s and early 1980s, terrorism coverage was much less extensive and emotional. In modern times however leaders must accept the fact that they will be forced to make decisions in the midst of public panic. Another Rabin advisor was asked about the public mood during these waves:

> Anxiety, fear, extreme attitudes on all sides. One side says give it all up, and the other side says we should kill all the Arabs. And the emotional excitement [*hitragshut*] that never existed before. (O4; March 19, 1995)

As noted, there were two other incidents of terrorism that took place right before the Beit Lid attack: the Waxman kidnapping and the bus bomb in Tel Aviv. Rabin held extremely difficult press conferences in which he attempted to defend himself. The journalists – so enthusiastic only a few months before – battered him with hostile questions and accusations. They wanted answers and they wanted them immediately. Rabin was no longer confident or in control, his performance was weak and unconvincing. After the third attack in Beit Lid, Rabin asked for television time in order to speak directly to the people and avoid the antagonistic reporters. His chief advisor talked about that decision.

> Those three incidents, Beit Lid, Waxman, and Dizengoff, were three unsuccessful things. All three were unsuccessful. Because carrying out a press conference in the midst of hysteria is worse than if you shut up. The reporters are hysterical, and the Prime Minister gets angry with them and answers them hysterically and the results are terrible . . . We thought that the broadcast from his room here, with the flag, would be more calming. We thought that would work. Maybe we didn't succeed. (O4; March 19, 1995)

The terrorist attacks and the emotional media coverage that followed also had an influence on the political status of the parliamentary opposition. The terrorist attacks provided graphic "proof" that Oslo had failed. As the death toll grew so did their case against Oslo. The debate over Oslo was transformed into a debate over security rather than a debate over peace. When terrorism was everyone's major concern, the need for dealing with security first was self-evident.

Terrorist waves also offered important political opportunities for the right wing movements who were opposed to Oslo. In many ways these groups were much more effective than the political parties in getting the message across. As with any movement, they were forced to wait for the proper event in order to mobilize their members and sympathizers. Within hours of every terrorist attack people were in the streets all over the country. People were angry and it was up to the movements to channel that anger. One of the movement spokespeople put it this way:

> Everything I plan is planned in advance, but even the advanced planning takes into account that things happen from now to now. So if you're going to plan a demonstration in Kings of Israel Square [major site for massive demonstrations], you need a trigger in order to do it. So people say, "OK, when something happens, when they sign an agreement, when they don't sign an agreement, when the security situation gets bad, then we'll put that plan into action." (O18; August 18, 1995)

The changes in the political environment also had an impact on the relationship between the Israeli journalists and the Palestinian leadership. The Palestinians were also placed on the defensive during every terrorist wave. At the very least it appeared that Arafat was incapable of controlling the Islamic opposition, at the worst that he was cooperating with them. The emphasis on dramatic events made it difficult for the Palestinian leadership to compete with Hamas and the Islamic Jihad movement. A PLO leader argued that the emphasis of the Israeli media on terrorism was destroying the peace process.

> I think the Israeli media in general, and Israeli television in particular, is not passing on our message, or to be more exact it is passing on the unusual situation like the bombing at Beit Lid. They are using the articles and the pictures to inflame the situation rather than to calm it. The Israeli press and especially the Israeli television should be reporting in a way that helps the peace process. They attack the Palestinians for the Hamas actions as if all of the Palestinians are carrying out these kinds of acts, and they're trying to destroy the peace process. But if they really want peace then the Israeli television should be telling the Israeli viewer about the other side of the Palestinian people. (O26; January 16, 1995)

The message of antagonists is always constructed within a particular political context. Just as the Israeli leaders had to change their message in light of the wave of terrorism, so did the Palestinian leadership. Such changes in the message are not merely a question of "public relations"; they often represent significant changes in political strategy. While part of the reason for such adjustments certainly has to do with the changes on the ground, leaders are also reacting to the way the news media are amplifying and framing these events.

In many ways the terrorism waves in Israel accomplished exactly what they were supposed to. The terrorism and the massive amounts of publicity they generated increased the political standing of Hamas and lowered the legitimacy of the Arafat government. They served as powerful counter currents to the euphoric waves that accompanied the peace ceremonies. By January 1995, after the three incidents discussed above, public support for the Oslo peace process dropped to an all-time low (Tami Steinmetz Center for Peace Research, 1996). All of the leaders, activists and journalists were forced to adjust themselves to the new reality. The news media cannot be held responsible for either the initiation of the terrorism wave or for how the various actors chose to react to it. They did, however, play an important role in the social construction of that reality.

IN SUM . . .

The Rabin government had a great deal of difficulty promoting the Oslo peace process to the Israeli news media. The media emphasized the negative aspects of the process and tended to ignore the more positive developments associated with Oslo. The coverage of terrorism was especially devastating. The news media were primary agents in spreading fear and panic among the public and in focusing the blame on the Palestinian leadership.

Looking at the political and media environments surrounding Oslo helps explain why this happened. The political environment was characterized by a lack of elite consensus in support of the process and a large number of serious and violent crises. The ongoing controversy provided journalists with two competing frames about Oslo, while the large number of crises provided important opportunities for the opposition to promote its anti-Oslo frames. As discussed, the construction of news stories about a peace process can only be understood by looking at both the interpretive frames that are available and the events that take place in the field.

One can hardly blame the news media for what happened. The Israeli news media were perfectly justified in raising serious doubts about such a peace process, especially given the fact that almost half of the population was opposed. Given the level and intensity of violence, one could hardly conclude that peace was in the air. Indeed, given the fact that most Israeli journalists supported Oslo, one might even view their coverage as admirable.

What makes their behavior seem less admirable was their constant concern for the bottom line. The interviews reveal a media system in which audience share becomes the primary factor in the decision-making process. The sensationalist coverage of terrorism was not motivated by any ethical considerations for balance or accuracy; it was driven by a clear financial interest in making the story as huge as possible. That same interest drives the entire editorial process and leads to a simplistic, short-term, ethnocentric view of the peace process.

The problem is compounded by the nature of the peace process itself. The negotiations with the Palestinians were extremely long and complicated and many of the most important developments had to be kept secret. The Rabin government did enjoy important advantages in their relations with the news media because of their high levels of status, organization, and resources. Nevertheless, apart from the grandiose peace ceremonies, they had very little material that could compete with flow of negative information and events. It is simply much easier to produce evidence that a peace process is failing than to demonstrate that it is succeeding. People naturally pay attention to large noises, but almost always take the quiet for granted.

This, however, is only one part of the picture. In order to understand the role of the Israeli news media one also has to look deeper into two perspectives that were only mentioned in passing. The first is the vantage point of those opposed to Oslo and the second tries to look at the issue from the perspective of the Palestinians. These are the subjects of the next two chapters.

CHAPTER 3

The Israeli media and the debate over Oslo

A good deal of the debate over any issue takes place within the confines of the mass media. This includes not only news and editorials but also talk-shows and the entertainment media. Each of these forums has different guidelines for deciding who can participate and how the antagonists are expected to conduct themselves. These rules are primarily designed to ensure the largest possible audience. The result is that the public is presented with a narrow, emotional, shortsighted debate in which values and ideology take a back seat to entertainment (Underwood, 2001; Delli Carpini and Williams, 2001).

One of the foundations of any democracy is that citizens be must given an opportunity to deliberate over the major issues of the day. The quality of that deliberation clearly depends on the level of information and analysis available (Bennett and Entman, 2001; Vedel, 2003). The limitations on public debate for those living in undemocratic countries are more obvious for the authorities make a concerned effort to take control over the flow of information. The problems facing western democracies are subtler and less severe. Nevertheless, media routines often prohibit any serious discussion of political issues and citizens are forced to make decisions based on an extremely limited set of information and images. As discussed, this is especially true when the media environment is dominated by sensationalist values.

It is helpful to consider what would constitute an "ideal" forum for public debate about a peace process. Such a forum would allow citizens to hear reasoned arguments from a variety of sources that would enable them to develop an informed opinion about the process. Despite what may have been inferred from previous chapters, one would certainly *not* want the news media to become a blind advocate for either side. A large proportion of the Israeli population was opposed to the Oslo process and they had a right to be heard. Equally important, they had a right to be heard without shouting, threatening, or resorting to violence. The quality of public deliberation on such issues depends on the level and tone of public discourse (Mutz and Reeves, 2001).

This chapter will look at some of the influences the news media had on the public debate over Oslo. A good deal of the discussion will look at this issue from the opposition's perspective. This is because the media's rules of access for such groups have a major influence on how the debate unfolds. Such rules, it was argued, have two major types of influence. First, they determine which voices will be heard. Second, they send a clear message to challengers about the entrance fees for getting into the news. This has a significant impact on the political strategies and behaviors of such groups. Leaders must decide whether they are willing to pay the price of admission or be left out in the cold.

The analysis will be divided into two major discussions. The first part will look at the routine competition over the news media. The goal of this section is to elaborate how media rules helped shape the ongoing debate over Oslo. The second section deals with the significant changes that take place in these routines in the midst of political waves. The particular wave that is analyzed here was initiated by a major historical event: the assassination of Prime Minister Yitzhak Rabin.

THE OPPOSITION TO OSLO

The first thing to understand is that challengers are always more dependent on the news media than the government (Wolfsfeld, 1997a). They have almost nothing else. There is very little challengers can initiate because they have so little political power. The opposition spends most of its time and resources reacting to what the government is doing. The news media represents, for the most part, their most important avenue of political influence. One of the opposition spokespeople put it this way:

Look, the media is our *raison d'être* [said in French] that gives us a right to exist. Where else can we express our opinion? What is an opposition? An opposition is something that yells. I'll try to get on any program I can. (O13; August 28, 1995)

This phenomenon is a good example of what can be labeled the "principle of cumulative inequality" (Wolfsfeld, 1997a): those that need the news media the most are the ones that find it the most difficult to mobilize them.

The right-wing opposition in Israel was extremely frustrated about their inability to get their message about Oslo across to the news media. This may seem surprising given the generally pessimistic coverage of the process that was discussed earlier. The opposition, however, scored points by default; very little news came directly from them. In fact, the content analysis described earlier reveals that during those first 250 days after the announcement, the parliamentary opposition was considered the *main* topic in only 2 percent of all news articles about the peace process.

These figures are somewhat misleading. First, opposition *reactions* were included in news stories that dealt with ongoing events.[1] It is also true that these leaders were much better represented in talk-shows on radio and television (which focus on debates). One could also argue that the extra-parliamentary movements, who received more attention in the news, were promoting similar views (Wolfsfeld, 1997a). Finally, opposition views were clearly represented in the editorial pages of the newspapers. Given the major divisions over Oslo, it was only natural that both major frames were allowed to compete in the opinion section.

Nevertheless the fact remains that the elected representatives from opposition parties found it extremely difficult to set the political agenda. The opposition in any country always faces an uphill battle in promoting their positions to the media. The relationship between political power and access to the press can be easily demonstrated by considering the allocation of reporters to the different beats. Most "routine news" comes from government leaders and officials; unofficial sources must constantly "prove" that they are worthy of space.

In Israel, journalists actively compete with each other for information from the Prime Minister, but it is the 120 Knesset members who have to compete to get their stories accepted by the few parliamentary reporters. Power is best understood by looking at who is running after whom. The journalists run after the Prime Minister and Knesset members run after the journalists. One parliamentary reporter compared his own routine with his colleagues who were covering the Prime Minister's office (the "political" reporters):

The political reporters spend more time trying to collect stories. In other words the more telephone calls they make, the better their chance of getting more stories. And with me, I take all of

---

[1] Unfortunately, the content analysis does not deal with this question.

the tremendous amount of papers I have on my desk – the amount of papers every parliamentary reporter receives is tremendous, it must be a kilo of papers – and that's how I get to stories. First, I have to scan these papers, to filter them, and then maybe 1 percent of all those papers are worth a story. (O16; December 12, 1995)

This description provides important evidence about the severity of the selection process. Knesset members hoping to compete must develop strategies that will allow them to stand out from the rather large crowd. This has a direct influence on the quality of the subsequent debate. Journalists justify the relationship between power and access by arguing that their job is to focus on those political forces that are most likely to have a real impact. One of the reporters who covered the Knesset was asked why the media gave such little publicity to the various peace plans that were proposed by the major opposition party, the Likud:

First because the Likud is not in power, so it is not realistic. When the Likud was in power and there was the Madrid conference then the papers were full of the Madrid conference. If for example Sonia Peres [Foreign Minister's Shimon Peres's wife] were to be interviewed by some paper and say, "I keep telling my husband day and night that he should declare that the Golan is Syrian land and we have to return it," that would get the main headline. Though Sonia doesn't have an official government position, she has influence on Shimon. (O16; December 12, 1995)

The only way for weak antagonists such as the opposition to gain access to the media is to provide either drama or novelty. While government officials are allowed access to the news media through the front door, weaker challengers must enter through the back door that is especially reserved for deviants (Wolfsfeld, 1997a). This makes it extremely difficult for members of the opposition to promote their ideological frames to the public. They are forced to choose between obscurity and extremism. A leading member of the opposition described the rules of entry.

What do the journalists see as newsworthy? Violence and riots, that's what they're waiting for. So when you bring them reasonable opinions, it doesn't interest them. They want blood . . . They want something drastic, some type of scoop so that they will get a medal from their editor. (O19; August 21, 1995)

The competition for media attention among challengers is fierce and difficult. One word that kept popping up in these interviews was gimmick (*gimmikim* in Hebrew). Knesset members hoping to get exposure have to find a gimmick that puts them ahead of the competition. This regrettable trend in Israeli politics has become especially pronounced since the inauguration of primaries in many political parties (Peri, 2004). Getting elected in primaries depends on name recognition, and name recognition depends on gaining exposure, even if that exposure carries a hefty price. A spokesperson for an opposition party told me about a conversation he had with a TV news editor.

> I tried to get a story about one of the Knesset members on television. The editor said no, and I asked him why not. He told me something wonderful. He said, "Look, in our crazy country, there are 100 excellent stories a day that are related to thirty wonderful topics, and I can only put in eight." He's right, He's right. There has to be some type of selection. So what is he going to take, something important? No, he'll take something interesting. (O18; August 18, 1995)

The negotiations over access at this level can be quite blunt. Party spokespeople are put in the position of salespeople trying to convince journalists that they have something especially interesting to sell. Some of those interviewed told stories about journalists "coaching" their sources to say things more dramatically. Given the increasingly blurry line between news and entertainment, it is not surprising that some reporters take on the role of directors.

Challengers not only compete with the government for access, they also compete with each other. The rules of this daily competition are simple. More powerful challengers are preferred over weaker ones, and among the weak whoever provides the best show gets in. In the struggle over the Oslo peace process the parliamentary opposition was competing with the large protest movements, who in turn were competing with the smaller, more radical movements. Reason and moderation were definite disadvantages in this contest. Members of Knesset complained about the movements "hijacking" the cause and the larger, more moderate movements made the same complaints against their more extremist allies.

Interviews that were carried out with movement leaders confirmed that the need to attract media attention was a primary motivation in carrying out violence.[2] The press searches for action, the movements provided it. The more radical the rhetoric and actions, the more likely it would be in the news. Movement leaders found that the only way to be quoted was to escalate their tactics. Strikingly, Rabin's assassin, Yigal Amir, talked about this dynamic in his police interrogation following the murder:

> The root of all this extremism is media coverage. All the vandalism in Hebron and those other places of allegedly extremist organizations are all due to the lack of attention. It all stems from the desire to attract media attention. (Quoted in Peri, 2000, p. 11)

The process of radicalization appears to have followed the same lines described by Gitlin (1980) in his classic work on the influence of the American media on movements opposed to the Vietnam War. Gitlin argued that by focusing on the more radical leaders among the Students for a Democratic Society (SDS), the press was providing these leaders with increasing power. This is an important comparison, for it demonstrates that the influence of the media on right-wing movements in Israel is similar to the impact that Gitlin described with regard to left-wing groups in the States. In both cases, the major goal for journalists was to find the most incendiary images and sound bites that could be integrated into the evening news.

Most of those from the right who were interviewed believed that leftist bias explained a good deal of the coverage they received. The leftist press, they claimed, either ignored them altogether or made them seem like a bunch of lunatics. A major spokesperson for the opposition was one of many to make this point.

> It is very convenient for the left to highlight the extremist circles. The minute you emphasize the extremist actions, everything will stick to the Likud in the end. The media has a certain bias and they want to show the right as a bunch of crazies, a bunch of psychos that do some kind of nonsense and then [journalists can] say here's the right. It's very convenient. (O2; August 13, 1995)

While one cannot summarily reject political bias as a cause for this routine, professional bias makes more sense. Journalists look for drama and whoever provides it receives the most coverage. This is especially true

---

[2] I have dealt more extensively with the competition between the various movements in my previous book (Wolfsfeld, 1997a).

in a more sensationalist media environment such as Israel. As noted, the fact that Palestinian terrorists receive so much coverage illustrates that audience considerations are more important than political ones.

The news media not only served to escalate the public debate over Oslo, they also tended to narrow it. In keeping with Bennett's Index Theory (1990), the Israeli news media had little interest in any opinions that went beyond the debate between the two major parties. One group that was especially deprived was the Arab Knesset members. Their position was that the Rabin government should be making more compromises and speeding up the pace of the peace process. The lack of voice given to the Arab minority in the Hebrew news media is a broader problem that has been studied elsewhere (Avraham, Wolfsfeld, and Aburaiyah, 2000; Wolfsfeld, Avraham, and Aburaiya, 2000). The Arab citizens of Israel represent about 20 percent of the total population. Leaving them out of the public debate over Oslo represents a serious problem that can be directly attributed to how the news media do business. One of the Knesset reporters was asked about this problem:

> We deal with news. You have to understand – the press is not a welfare agency for Knesset members who want to be re-elected. It is also not a pipeline. Today there is a pipeline from the Knesset to the public – Channel 33 [which broadcasts live coverage from the Knesset]. A wonderful pipeline, an objective pipeline. If the Arab parties would bring something new . . . The thing is that the Arab parties always claim the same thing: "There should be a Palestinian state whose capital is Jerusalem" – that's about it. The news is interested in the dynamic not the static. (O12; December 12, 1995)

The same reporter went on to tell us that the notion of balance was "nonsense." If you wanted to achieve true balance in the debate over Oslo, he argued, you would have to bring in the Americans and the Palestinians, and then there is no end to it.

If the Israeli media had presented a wider range of views about the peace process it might also have had some indirect influences on public discourse. The Rabin policies, for example, might have appeared more moderate if they had been placed within the context of demands from right and left. Turning to a wider range of sources may have also have shown some of the areas of agreement between the two major political parties. Areas of agreement are an important aspect of such discussions, but are almost never considered news. Although one can also attribute this divisiveness to the political leaders themselves, a more sophisticated media should be able to deal with accord as well as discord.

The major opposition to the peace process had difficulties finding an appropriate vehicle for promoting their ideas to the media. This made it easier for the Rabin government to discredit and marginalize the opposition. Nevertheless, the public was entitled to hear more from all of their representatives; including the more moderate ones. It is also possible that if the media had served as a forum for a more reasoned debate about the Oslo process, it might have defused some of the anger and frustration of the right wing during those critical moments. The right wing was constantly accusing the government and the media of "shutting their mouths" (*stimat piot*).

The opposition political parties not only had a problem with the media's need for drama, they also had a problem providing novelty. Once the press has heard a particular idea or plan, it has little interest in hearing it again. This dynamic leads to another problem for a parliamentary opposition: how to remain both consistent and interesting. A serious political leader is expected to take a stand and, at least for some time, stick to it. This strategy, however, is in direct contradiction with the media's need for novelty. When Netanyahu was still in the opposition, one of his media advisors talked about this no-win situation.

> First they said he was rash. That he always jumps and says things. When he doesn't say anything, they say: "Well, he doesn't have anything to say," and when he does say something they say: "He's always saying the same thing" . . . Maybe he's careful, but he's not supposed to be a comic, he's not supposed to be a clown who gives the crowd something different each time. He's a statesman with a certain political stand. (O6; May 18, 1995)

The rapid pace of Oslo also placed the opposition in a difficult position. Any positions they had taken about what should be done quickly became outdated. Questions about recognizing the PLO, releasing prisoners, the amount of control to be given to the Palestinian authority, and how much land to give to the Palestinians were no longer relevant. The Likud and the other opposition parties were continually trying to catch up with what was happening on the ground.

Not all of the journalistic values and routines worked against the opposition, there were several that worked in their favor. As pointed out by Entman (2004) journalists have an inherent interest in finding political controversy. Many news stories are built around conflict and it takes two sides to create conflict. This is especially true on the many talk-shows on radio and television. The opposition has a much better level of access, for most of these shows are dedicated to public debate.

Several more prominent opposition members said that they had no problem at all picking up the phone and getting on such programs. The increase in the number of radio and television stations in Israel means that editors need more guests and this provides important opportunities for members of the opposition. Here, too, however, the Knesset members who provide the best "show" were the ones most likely to be invited.

It is also important to make a distinction between the political debate taking place in the struggle over the news and what was happening within the editorial section of the newspapers. Looking at only the editorial section of the newspapers one finds a reasoned, responsible debate over Oslo. One also finds more editorials in favor of the Oslo peace process than opposed to it. A content analysis was conducted of Israeli editorials that were written about the peace process in the wake of seven major events that took place between the start of Oslo in September of 1993 and the major terrorist attacks at the end of February 1995.[3] They include both positive events (the Cairo agreement) and negative events (terrorist attacks). A total of 229 editorials were taken from the newspapers *Ha'aretz*, *Ma'ariv* and *Yediot*.

In the three major newspapers one finds at total of 115 editorials in favor of the peace process, 80 opposed and 34 putting forth a more ambivalent opinion. The more liberal paper *Ha'aretz* is much less balanced than the two popular papers and one finds very few pieces that are opposed to the peace process.[4] Reading the editorials in all of the papers one learns quite a bit about the underlying ideologies of the two major camps in Israel. The proponents talk about the reasons for continuing the peace process despite the problems, while opponents point to the dangers they see in continuing with the Oslo process. The debate that takes place within the confines of newspaper editorials tends to be analytical and intelligent.

Nevertheless, most citizens learn about the dispute through the news, not through editorials. A national survey found that while 75 percent of the Israeli population turn to the news on a fairly regularly basis, only

---

[3] For details, see the methodological appendix.
[4] This finding confirms a statement that was made by one of the interviewees who serve on the editorial board of *Ha'aretz*. He reported that there had been an early decision within the board to provide support for the Oslo process in the editorial pages.

25 percent tended to regularly read editorials.[5] Thus, the ways in which the media construct news about the peace process are likely to have a more significant impact on the public climate than what is written in editorials. This point is borne out by the fact that political antagonists spend an enormous amount of resources competing over the news and relatively few efforts in the struggle over the editorial section of the newspaper.

This brings the discussion back to the competition between the two frames for Oslo. Having dealt with the ongoing contest over the news, it is time to look again at how the media deals with political waves.

THE MEDIA AND THE RABIN ASSASSINATION

In September of 1995, the level of vindictive rhetoric and violence against the Rabin government reached new heights (Peri, 2000; Sprinzak, 2000). Knesset members, settlers, rabbis, and protest movement leaders attempted to outdo one another in condemning Rabin and his government. Rabin was being called a traitor and during one rally he was portrayed in an SS uniform. Channel 1 filmed a "secret" ceremony in which masked gunmen threatened to kill the Prime Minister.[6] There were several outbreaks of violence and a number of attempts to attack ministers. The news become increasingly frightening and the amount of invective appeared to be rising every day. The peak of violence was the assassination of Prime Minister Rabin on November 4, 1995.

It would be a mistake to suggest any one cause for this rise in violence. There were important political forces at work and the settlers and their supporters believed that the Oslo accords represented a direct threat to their existence. Nevertheless, there is every reason to believe that the sensationalist news media of Israel played a role in inflaming the atmosphere during this period. The exaggerated, hysterical coverage of terrorism, the pressure on movements to continually escalate in order to stay in the news, and the continual preference for extremist voices over moderate ones all played a part in making the debate surrounding Oslo more volatile.

[5] The survey was conducted by the Dahaf polling company in November of 2000 as part of a separate research project conducted by myself and Ya'akov Shamir.
[6] This was an extremely controversial piece. Many argued that this type of staged event should never have been filmed. The criticism became even more bitter when it was learned (after the Rabin assassination) that the leader of this group was actually a government agent.

The Rabin assassination was an important turning point in the debate over the Oslo peace process. The struggle for political control is not only a contest over ideological frames (Peace versus Security First), it is also a contest over the political legitimacy of frame sponsors. The Israeli news media placed a good deal of blame for the assassination on the right-wing opposition and this considerably lowered their public standing. Due to the radical change in the political environment, the anti-Oslo movements were no longer able to mobilize mass protests against the government. This allowed the Peres government to carry out a number of territorial withdrawals with a minimum of opposition. Rabin also became a powerful martyr for peace and – at least for a time – this made it much easier to promote the Peace frame to the media and the public.

The assassin, Yigal Amir, was a religious radical whose goal was to stop the peace process. Netanyahu and the religious right were accused of partial responsibility for the assassination by inciting followers to violence. The Prime Minister's widow, Leah Rabin, was one of the most vehement accusers, tearfully recounting the daily abuse she and her husband had suffered in the days leading up to his murder. Rabin had been continually portrayed in protests as a traitor who was surrendering the homeland to the enemy.

As in the terrorist attack at Beit Lid, the Rabin assassination was treated as a disaster wave and thus one finds revealing similarities in narrative themes. One finds shock and grief over the murder, anger at those groups held responsible, and a search for solutions. A surprisingly high proportion of news articles dealt with the question of blame. A content analysis was conducted on all of the news articles and editorials dealing with the Rabin assassination that appeared in *Yediot Ahronot* and *Ha'aretz* during the two weeks following the assassination. Of the 941 articles that were analyzed, 65 percent dealt with possible causes for the murder.

The major explanation given for Rabin's assassination was "incitement." The argument was that by constantly painting the Prime Minister as a traitor and continually fanning the fans of hatred, the right wing had provoked his murder (Peri, 2000). The "dangers of incitement" theme is one that has continued to resonate in Israel for years after the assassination.[7] During the Beit Lid wave, it was the Palestinians who bore

---

[7] Evidence of the enduring power of this frame can be found in statements made by Prime Minister Ariel Sharon during a memorial session of the Likud Knesset faction on the anniversary of the assassination. Sharon defended his party by arguing that there had been plenty of incitement by both left *and* right, so it was important for all to bring such actions to a halt.

the brunt of the blame, and those supporting peace were placed on the defensive. This time the political wave ran in the opposite direction and it was the right-wing opposition who stood accused.

The Incitement frame dominated public discourse and here too the news media played a major role in amplifying it and providing it with narrative structure. Interviewees from the right were constantly being asked whether they were "searching their souls" [*heshbon nefesh*] about what they had done. There was also a frantic search for any stories that would illustrate the Incitement frame. Reporters would go out looking for "inciters" who were willing to confess their crimes. In one particularly strange item, a television news broadcast was interrupted to allow a repentant citizen to confess in front of Rabin's grave. He talked about how sorry he was that he had called Rabin a traitor and that he had participated in a number of violent protests. He swore he would never do it again.

The success of the Incitement frame is particularly interesting here because it has little to do with what was known about the assassin. Almost everything we know about Yigal Amir points to an intelligent, analytical individual who killed Rabin for religious and ideological reasons (Sprinzak, 2000). The statements made during his interrogation and at his trial suggest that he was frustrated that the right "wasn't doing enough" to stop Rabin. He said that when the group doesn't do anything the individual has to act. The killer considered himself a leader, as did many of those who knew him. Amir also talked about several other attempts to kill the Prime Minister that extended over a significant period. Finally, Amir has never expressed regret for the killing. One might have expected such remorse if the act were rooted in the passion of the time.

As discussed earlier, the construction of media frames is a process in which journalists attempt to find a narrative fit between new information and existing frames. The more salient the existing frame the more likely it will be chosen. Labor Party leaders had been promoting the Incitement frame for several months before the assassination. They were reacting to the violent protests, the attack on one of the ministers, and another event where Rabin appeared to be in real danger. In fact, the rally where Rabin was killed was in part a rally against incitement. The organizing slogan was: "Yes to Peace, No to Violence." The Incitement theme had also been developed in previous news stories about the more vehement anti-government protests. Thus, when the assassination did take place it was seen as the climax to an existing story.

The most dramatic evidence of this point comes from the special televised news report, on the evening of the assassination. Haim Yavin, the primary anchor for Israeli television, had quickly arrived at the studio to cover the attack on Prime Minister Rabin. Little was known at the time about the identity of the killer or his motives, but an unknown right-wing movement had taken credit for the attack. A few seconds earlier, Israelis were told that Sky television had reported that Rabin was dead.

Yavin was interviewing Opher Pines, one of the organizers of the peace rally where Rabin was shot. Pines was talking about a visit he had with Yona Avrushmi, who, in the 1980s had been convicted of throwing a grenade into a Peace Now rally, killing activist Emil Greensweig:

> Pines: About a month ago I visited Avrushmi; he told me then, he appealed, through me, to the right-wing camp, he told them to stop this process of incitement, and he said that it [Greensweig's death] happened because of things that he heard.
>
> Yavin: I have to stop you. There is now an official announcement from the Icholov hospital in Tel Aviv. Prime Minister Yitzhak Rabin passed away as a result of the assault . . . Well, we have to pull ourselves together a little . . . The assassin, by the way, is Yigal Amir, a third-year law student, twenty-seven years old, studying at Bar Ilan university.
>
> [*After a few seconds the interview continues.*]
>
> Pines: We went through an evening tonight, an evening that was meant to be a tribute to peace, that was cut off by a person who was incited by the right-wing leaders, just as I was told by Avrushmi last month . . . That was what this rally was about: "No to violence." Not only didn't they say no to violence, they killed our Prime Minister.

A few moments later, Yavin presented a film clip of a previous interview in which Rabin explained why he did not try to come to an agreement with Netanyahu to lower the level of violence:

> I know that there is wild incitement, verbal violence . . . I saw the demonstration where they have me dressed as a Gestapo person. When I see a former Likud minister, David Levy, thrown out of the rally by an incited crowd. And then Knesset member Netanyahu comes to me on Thursday or Friday . . . and asks for a meeting for Friday afternoon. Then I see a protest with Likud banners, with shouts of "traitor," "murderer." I said, it would be wrong of me to play into the hypocrisy of the Likud, of the head of the Likud. He stood there and gave a speech under the picture of [Rabin

wearing a] Gestapo uniform. And then he wants to meet with him.
I don't believe him.

Rabin is quite specific in blaming the Likud, and its leader for the
incitement and the violence. Many of the points Rabin raised in this
interview became central issues in subsequent coverage. The file footage
of the SS uniform and the shouts of traitor and murderer were constantly
shown on television as telling evidence that "the writing had been on
the wall." Ironically, it was Prime Minister Rabin himself who became
one of the first major sponsors of the Incitement frame for his own
assassination.

These two excerpts provide a valuable example of how sources and
journalists each contribute to the construction of media frames. The
television news department turned to Pines as a routine source of information. He helped organize the rally where Rabin was killed and could
also serve as an eyewitness. He believed, as did most others who identified
with the government, that right-wing incitement was the major cause of
the assassination. As he was speaking, the television staff was looking for
a previous clip of Rabin talking about incitement; it was the most natural
frame to apply to the current event. Rabin, of course, had used his own
interview to promote the Incitement frame against his opponents.

The change in the political climate following the assassination could be
felt everywhere. Once again, I would argue, it was not only the event itself
that led to this change, but also media interpretations of that event. The
dominant story line emphasized the victimization of the peace camp and
that Netanyahu and the right were partially responsible for the tragedy.
In interviews given later, Netanyahu talked of that time as one of the
most difficult of his career. He, and other leaders from the right, have
since blamed both the Labor Party and the news media for exploiting
Rabin's death to discredit them. The mainstream Israeli news media
were completely united in disseminating the story: it is unlikely that
there was a single interview where Netanyahu was not asked about the
charges against him and the Likud.[8] They were the accused and given the
intensity of the wave the best they could do was to defend themselves.

---

[8] One can certainly come up with alternative explanations for the assassination. One
example would be to see such violence as the natural outcome of religious fundamentalism. This is certainly consistent with everything we know about the assassin. Such
an explanation would have been far less damaging for the secular right. It would have
also led to different policy initiatives. However, there were understandably far more
sponsors for the Incitement frame.

The Peace frame also received a major boost during this period. As noted, Rabin was instantly transformed into a martyr for peace and one of the major "lessons" from the assassination was the need to fulfill his legacy. The "legacy of peace" theme had an especially impressive list of sponsors. Prime Minister Shimon Peres, all of the other ministers in his cabinet, the President of the United States, and almost every major leader in the world spoke about the need to continue Rabin's quest for peace. The funeral itself and the large number of subsequent memorial events provided a massive audience for promoting the Peace frame. The anti-government forces were driven into an embarrassed silence, and it took many weeks for them to even consider a counter-attack.

The change in climate also had a dramatic impact on public opinion. For the first time over 50 percent of the Jewish population said they supported the Oslo process and only 26 percent were opposed (Tami Steinmetz Center for Peace Research, 1996). Election polls taken at the time showed Shimon Peres leading Benyamin Netanyahu by about twenty points. This was another in a long list of ironies about the Oslo peace process: the assassination of Yitzhak Rabin produced the biggest boon for peace since the initial breakthrough with the Palestinians.

The point to remember is that nothing about the peace process itself had changed during this time. The rapid decline in the legitimacy of the right-wing opposition and the equally dramatic rise in support of the Oslo peace process can be attributed to the "lessons" that emerged from the assassination. The victims of violence are always given significant advantages in promoting their own narratives to the news media. Government supporters were quite adamant in blaming the right-wing opposition and in demanding that the peace process continue to move forward. The news media were important agents in amplifying these frames and downplaying competing interpretations. It was a sort of "sympathy vote" that was totally unrelated to the peace process itself.

It would not be long, however, until other major events would lead to yet another shift in the political environment of Israel. In the spring of 1996 suicide bombers blowing up buses killed fifty-eight Israelis. At the time, it was the worst series of terrorist attacks in the history of Israel and fear was rampant. This event led to an increase in the political prominence, the professional utility, and the cultural resonance of the Security First frame. The hysterical coverage returned and with it the anger against the Palestinians. It was now the Peres government that was placed on the defensive, desperately trying to show that peace still made sense.

An important conclusion from these analyses is that the rise and fall of opposition frames has little to do with their own initiatives. Given their lack of political power in a parliamentary system, opposition parties have few assets that facilitate the production of news. Their fate depends, to a large extent, on what others do. Till then they mostly sit and wait for the next political wave, never knowing in which direction it will run.

There were two types of political actors who were able to bring about major changes in the political environment during this period. The Rabin government was able to do so through its political power, especially in the initial breakthrough with the Palestinians. The extremists on both sides were also able to have a major impact by carrying out shocking acts of violence that reverberated throughout the Middle East. The Rabin assassination provided tremendous advantages for the Peace frame while the subsequent terrorist attacks facilitated the promotion of the Security First frame. Given these set of circumstances, the opposition could only react to these changes. They rode the waves running in their direction and attempted to duck those running against them.

The Israeli media played an important role in defining the nature of the debate over these frames. They had an inherent interest in making the conflict over Oslo as dramatic as possible and also the power to increase the volume. This power was rooted in the news media's strict rules of access that not only weeded out moderate voices but also provided important incentives for violence. They also magnified the inherent advantages of political waves by amplifying them and by constructing simplistic story lines complete with heroes and villains.

Which bring us to yet another change in the political environment: The Israeli elections of 1996.

THE ELECTIONS OF 1996[9]

The elections of 1996 provide a fascinating case in which Israeli voters were, to a certain extent, forced to actually choose between the Security First and Peace frames. The Peres campaign focused mostly on the opportunities provided by peace while the Netanyahu message talked about the security threat posed by Oslo. Peres wanted people to think about the new dawn that was breaking and Netanyahu wanted them to focus on the terrorist attacks that had taken place only a few months before.

---

[9] The research that is reported in this section was conducted by Gabi Weimann and myself (Weimann and Wolfsfeld, 2002).

The struggle over the electoral agenda was a critical component of this race.

Shimon Peres had only been in office for a few months when he decided to call for new elections. Many assumed that due to the sympathy aroused by the Rabin assassination, Peres would ride to an easy victory. As discussed, however, the three buses blowing up in February/March of 1996 had a devastating impact on the Peres government, and the race remained close till the end. Most of the polls leading up to the June election still had Peres leading by about 5 percent, and the conventional wisdom held that he would win.

There was another event worth noting. In the beginning of April 1996, two months before the elections, the Israelis launched a military operation against the Muslim organization Hezbollah, based in Southern Lebanon. During that month Israel carried out a massive attack: the "Grapes of Wrath" operation. Peres also held the position of Minister of Defense and this assured him a great deal of media attention (Arian, Weimann, and Wolfsfeld, 1999). Some of his advisors were hoping this would also allow Peres to demonstrate that he too was concerned with security. One of the important ramifications of this operation was that it served to delay the electoral campaign. Netanyahu was in no position to attack the government when Israel was at war. It is fair to say that the "real" campaign only began at the beginning of May, four weeks before the election. This was also the same point in time when the candidates were allowed to begin broadcasting their commercials on television.

The struggle over the electoral agenda is an important aspect of any campaign. Candidates and parties all attempt to take control over the agenda so that they can compete on the issues that are best for them. Clinton's team in 1992, for example, was convinced that the secret to success was to keep the campaign focused on the economy (Arterton, 1993). The now famous slogan written at campaign head-quarters read: "It's the economy, stupid." Bush, on the other hand, would have preferred that the election be about foreign affairs and personal integrity.

The competition over the public agenda often includes a contest over media frames. It was clear from the beginning that the Oslo peace process would be the central issue of debate in the 1996 elections. Each side hoped to promote its preferred frame to the news media in order to gain more support. Examining the relative success of the two sides provides an important opportunity to test some of the ideas that have been put forth within the context of an election campaign. It is important to bear in mind, however, that the competition over media frames during an election campaign is somewhat different to what has been described till now. The most important difference has to do with the amount of access given to the opposition. Election news centers on the contest between the two sides and this increases the newsworthiness of the major challenger. The media are expected to provide balanced coverage that allows both sides an equal opportunity to present themselves and their positions (Arian, Weimann, and Wolfsfeld, 1999).

Definitions of newsworthiness, however, remain the same. The media are still more interested in drama than in substance. One of the most frequent criticisms of election news is that it is much more likely to focus on the "horse race" than on substance (Just *et al.*, 1996; Patterson, 1993). The most popular election stories focus on telling citizens who is in front and behind, which candidate has made the biggest mistakes, and what's "really going on behind the scenes." As in the debate over peace, candidates often find it difficult to talk about ideology or policy.

There is another similarity in the two types of coverage: the preference for negative news. Patterson (1989) has studied this issue and found a dramatic increase in the propensity of the American media to publish negative news about the candidates. Here, too, the rules of access have an important effect on media strategy. Candidates feel compelled to "go negative" in order to ensure they receive the maximum amount of coverage. Manheim (1991) has refers to this phenomenon as the "multiplication effect": negative messages are much more likely to generate news articles and this means that one gets a much better return on one's investment. Cappella and Jamieson (1997) see this as part of a more general "spiral of cynicism" in which "the conflict-driven sound-bite-oriented discourse of politicians" reinforces the "conflict-oriented structure of press coverage" (p. 9). As those authors suggest, each side argues that they are merely adapting to the demands of the other: the politicians provide information and events that will be considered news and the journalists claim, "they are simply reporting what is being offered" (p. 10). As indicated, these same principles can also be applied to the ongoing political competition that takes place between elections.

COMPETING FRAMES OF OSLO

The Peres campaign strategy promoted the Peace frame by talking about all of the benefits associated with the process: the high level of growth in the economy, and the funds that had been allocated for education, welfare, transportation, and immigrant absorption. The pictures of the various peace ceremonies with President Clinton and Prime Minister Rabin were also an important part of the message. In keeping with what was said earlier, the Peres campaign talked about the need to achieve both peace *and* security. Nevertheless, most of the claims centered on the success of the peace process. The negative element in the Peres campaign focused on Netanyahu. The major attack on the opposition leader was that he wasn't "fit" to be Prime Minister. The charges centered on Netanyahu's lack of experience and raised questions about his personal integrity.

The Netanyahu campaign also attempted to exploit the resonance of both peace and security. Their major slogan was: "Netanyahu: A Secure Peace." The message was that Netanyahu would move the peace process forward, but at a slower, more cautious pace. For months before the election Netanyahu had been moving towards the center of the political spectrum. His major shifts from previous positions were his proclamations that he intended to honor the Oslo agreements signed by the Rabin government and that he would be willing to meet with Yasser Arafat. Netanyahu attacks on the government centered on three major issues: the "appeasement" of the Palestinians, the failure to prevent terrorism, and charges that the next Peres government would divide Jerusalem. All three of these themes were designed to tap into people's concerns that the Oslo peace process had undermined Israel's security.

The election commercials produced by the two major parties provide a convenient index of their messages. In Israel election ads of all of the political parties are broadcast within a single block of time during the last thirty days of the campaign. The data in table 3.1 show the number of ads each candidate devoted to the ten major substantive issues raised in the election campaign.[10] Whereas the goal of this analysis is to examine the struggle over ideological frames, personal attacks are not included in this list. The last column lists the difference between the proportions of ads devoted to each topic by each candidate. A positive number indicates that it was more a "Netanyahu issue" and a negative number means that it was more a "Peres" issue. The higher the level of difference, the more the issue can be identified exclusively with one campaign.

[10] For details of the coding procedures used in these analyses see the methodological appendix.

Table 3.1 *Issues promoted in the Netanyahu and Peres commercials (1996 election campaign)*

Issue	In Netanyahu Commercials (%)	In Peres Commercials (%)	Difference Netanyahu: Peres
Terrorism, terrorist acts	23.31	6.60	+16.71
Palestinians, negotiations	24.51	36.93	−12.42
Jerusalem (split)	16.34	2.40	+13.94
Golan Heights + Syria	3.12	10.81	−7.69
Settlers, settlements	18.26	17.11	+1.15
Economy, finances	3.84	8.40	−3.76
Religion and state	2.64	2.10	+0.54
Education	4.08	8.70	−4.62
Israeli Arabs	0.48	1.20	−0.72
Immigration and Absorption	3.36	5.70	−2.34
Total	100% (n = 416)	100% (n = 333)	

The two major Netanyahu issues are terrorism and Jerusalem. The numbers provide a graphic illustration that the Likud was interested in emphasizing these topics while the Labor Party attempted to avoid them. While almost 40 percent of the Netanyahu ads dealt with these two topics, only 9 percent of the Peres commercials discussed them. As one might expect, many of the Peres ads that did deal with these topics were designed to defend the Prime Minister from Netanyahu's attacks. Netanyahu's emphasis on terrorism was hardly surprising given the traumatic events of years leading up to the election. This was clearly the strongest component of the Security First frame. Terrorism was also an extremely negative issue that was bound to generate a good deal of "free" coverage. The Peres camp's greatest fear was that there would be another bombing before the election. It never took place, but as discussed below, terrorism became a major issue in the campaign. Netanyahu's decision to focus on the future of Jerusalem was an attempt to raise a new issue onto the agenda. The charge was that if Peres remained Prime Minister he would hand over the eastern part of the city. While there was quite a bit of controversy concerning the future of the

West Bank and Gaza, there was almost universal consensus within the country that Jerusalem would remain the undivided capital of Israel. The slogan "Peres will divide Jerusalem" was everywhere and it constituted an important element in Netanyahu's campaign strategy. Peres attempted to ignore the issue, but in the end was forced to vehemently deny the charges.

One does not find a similarly important "Peres" issue. While Peres devoted proportionately more attention to the peace process with the Palestinians, Netanyahu was clearly not avoiding this issue. The left presented the Oslo accords as a major achievement, while the right attempted to portray the agreement as surrendering to Israel's enemies. Viewing these commercials provides a good illustration of the ongoing competition between the two ideological frames concerning Oslo. The Peres campaign is also more interested in promoting the idea of peace with Syria in their election campaign. There had been an active peace process and significant progress had been made in the negotiations. Netanyahu was opposed to surrendering any land to Syria in exchange for peace, but it seems that he was reluctant to emphasize this in his campaign. While the Peres campaign devoted almost 11 percent of their commercials to the Syrian issue, only 3 percent of the Netanyahu ads dealt with this topic.

One topic was conspicuously absent from the Peres campaign: there was virtually no mention of the Rabin assassination. This was the one negative issue of substance Peres could have used against Netanyahu. Raising memories of the assassination might have also allowed the Peres campaign to remind voters of the Rabin's "legacy of peace." While there are a number of theories about why the Labor Party refrained from using this weapon, a large number of political pundits expressed surprise.[11]

Looking at the top four issues of dispute – terrorism, Jerusalem, negotiations with the Palestinians, and the issue of what to do about Syria – it is clear that the major debate in this election was over the peace process. The Netanyahu campaign wanted to emphasize the dangers and threats associated with the process, while Peres wanted to talk about the opportunities it presented. Given all that has been said till now, this should have worked in Netanyahu's favor: it is easier to promote fear to the news media than hope.

---

[11] One theory put forth was that Peres's advisors were reluctant to "heat up" the campaign due to their lead in the polls. The other was that focus groups with undecided voters had suggested that such an attack would prove counter-productive.

Table 3.2 *"Substantive issues" and "campaign issues": TV coverage of the 1996 elections*

Substantive Issues		Campaign Issues	
Issue	% of items	Issue	% of items
Terrorism, terrorist acts	15.3	Campaign strategies of the parties	55.8
Palestinians, negotiations	22.4	Divisions, conflicts within parties	6.8
Jerusalem (split)	5.3	Surveys, pre-election polls	8.1
Golan Heights + Syria	8.7	Accusations, "bad-mouthing"	13.2
Settlers, settlements	19.7	Speculations (about "deals," nominations)	16.1
Economy, finances	11.2		
Religion and state	4.1		
Education	2.3		
Israeli Arabs	7.4		
Immigration and Absorption	2.3		
Other	1.3		
Total	100% (n = 268)	Total	100% (n = 385)

ELECTION NEWS

Election news in Israel, it turns out, suffers from many of the same problems as were found in other countries. The substance of the political debate is considered less important than the drama of the race. The analysis relates to all election news stories that were broadcast on the two national television stations during the sixty days before the election. The results presented in table 3.2 classify the items into different topic areas.

The first thing to note is that, as in other countries, more attention is given to campaign issues than substantive subjects. Fifty-nine percent of the election news stories dealt with campaign issues. These campaign stories are the same as in other western countries: stories about campaign strategies, sleaze campaigns, deals between the various political parties, polls, stories about television ads, and predictions about the outcome. News dealing with party strategies is by far the largest of the categories.

Table 3.3 *The salience of issues in 1996 election news: first and second months*

Issue	First month (%)	Second month (%)	Difference
Terrorism, terrorist acts	12.12	17.68	+5.56
Palestinians, negotiations	29.29	18.90	−10.39
Jerusalem (split)	3.03	6.78	+3.75
Golan Heights + Syria	18.18	3.04	−15.14
Settlers, settlements	7.07	27.43	+20.36
Economy, finances	14.14	9.75	−4.39
Religion and state	4.04	4.26	+0.22
Education	3.03	1.82	−1.21
Israeli Arabs	7.07	7.92	+0.85
Immigration and Absorption	2.02	2.43	+0.41
Total	100% (n = 99)	100% (n = 164)	

Here, too, then, the need for drama and conflict serves to lower the level of public debate.

There are four major substantive topics for media coverage: the debate over the peace process with the Palestinians; the conflict over the settlements; the dispute over terrorism; and arguments about the economy. Less attention is given to the issues having to do with Syria and the Golan Heights, the Israeli Arabs, the issue of Jerusalem, religion and state, education and immigration. At first glance, one cannot detect any clear-cut winner in the battle over the agenda: there doesn't appear to be a clear preference for either Netanyahu issues or those being promoted by Peres.

This picture changes when one separates the first month's coverage from the second. As discussed, due to the Grapes of Wrath operation, the campaign did not really begin until the second month. In any case, this is when the political ads began to air so this distinction provides a better indication of the impact of the advertising on the electoral agenda. Looking at table 3.3, one sees an important change over the two-month period that worked chiefly to Netanyahu's benefit.

The issues favored by the Peres administration were an important part of election news during the month before the ads began. This was the time when people's attention was focused mostly on the war in Lebanon, although interestingly this never became a campaign issue. The two

Table 3.4 *Rank-order correlations between the parties'*
agenda and television agenda in 1996 election

	TV Agenda First Month	TV Agenda Second Month
Netanyahu Agenda	0.44*	0.77*
Peres Agenda	0.80*	0.56*

* Statistically significant at the 0.05 level.

major issues discussed were the negotiations with the Palestinians and the Syrian issue, both of which were "Peres" issues. The issue of terrorism was further down the list and the subject of Jerusalem was barely mentioned.

There was a dramatic rise in the prominence of Netanyahu issues in the second month of the campaign. There was a significant increase in the number of election stories that dealt with terrorism and almost four times as many stories about the issue of Jerusalem. There was also an important drop in the number of stories about the Palestinians and the Syrian issue.

The most significant change was the increase in election stories about the settlements. Peres was supposed to pull out of part of Hebron before the election and most settlement stories centered on this issue. There was a great deal of tension and debate over this decision and many felt that such a controversial move would provide a considerable amount of ammunition to the opposition. Given the symbolic importance of Hebron, one can understand why the press devoted so much attention to this issue. In the end, Peres decided to avoid the controversy by not withdrawing. The steep rise in the importance of the settlements story is a good example of how events can independently change the electoral agenda. The media follow the drama and in this case it led to Hebron. There is no reason to believe, however, that this provided any advantage to either candidate, because both referred to the settlement issue in their campaigns.

Rank-order correlations were calculated by comparing the order of the issues in each of the television campaigns with the order in which they appeared in the news. We were especially interested in the change between the first and second months of the campaign because, as noted, the election ads only began during the last thirty days. The results are presented in table 3.4.

The results show that during the first month, the correlation between the Peres campaign themes and election news was 0.80 while the corresponding figure for the Netanyahu campaign was 0.44. Some of this difference in the level of success can be attributed to the advantages enjoyed by incumbents. During the second month of the campaign, the correlation for the Netanyahu campaign rose to the 0.77 while the Peres coefficient dropped to 0.56. Thus, once the campaign got started, there was a genuine reversal of fortunes.

There was also a reversal of fortunes in the election. As noted, Peres was leading in the polls until the final weeks of the campaign. In the end, Netanyahu pulled off a come-from-behind victory, winning the election by a mere 30,000 votes, nine-tenths of a percentage point of the total vote. It would be foolhardy to suggest that the change in the political agenda was the only reason for Peres's defeat. Nevertheless, given the extremely small margin of victory one cannot discount the possibility that the change in the election agenda made an important contribution to Netanyahu's success.

Thus, the 1996 election campaign provides some important evidence concerning three major points that were put forth in the theoretical discussion. First, it illustrates why it is often easier to promote a Security frame to the news media than a Peace frame. Images of terrorism proved to be more newsworthy than those associated with reconciliation and this provided Netanyahu with important advantages. Second, it again demonstrates how changes in the political environment can have an important impact on the role the news media play in such contests. After the Rabin assassination, many believed it would be years before the right wing would be able to mount an effective challenge to the Peres government. However, the re-emergence of terrorism brought the Security First frame back with a vengeance. Finally, this research provides another illustration of the PMP cycle. The change in the political environment (return of terrorism as an important issue) led to a change in media performance (increasing focus on terrorism as a campaign issue) that may have led to a major change in the political environment (the election of Netanyahu as Prime Minister). It is interesting to note in this respect that although Netanyahu attempted to use the same campaign strategy in 1999 against Ehud Barak, the news media were unwilling to cooperate. The terrorism theme failed to resonate, in part because it was a period of relative quiet.

In many ways the election of 1996 was the first open contest between the two major frames about the Oslo peace process. The playing field was leveled somewhat because journalists were more willing to hear what Netanyahu had to say within the context of an election. The opposition was given a chance to take initiatives rather than simply wait for a change in climate. True, the news media were still more interested in style than substance, but the candidates were given a certain amount of space to argue over the issues. Therefore, one could argue that the role the news media played in the election debate over Oslo was far superior to the role they played in between the elections.

IN SUM . . .

Three major points emerged in this chapter. First, the news media are a poor forum for public discourse over political issues. The rules of access and the norms of debate are mostly designed to ensure a good show rather than an intelligent exchange of views. Every discussion is knowingly transformed into a shouting match. This problem may have especially severe consequences when dealing with the issues of peace and war. Passions run extremely high on these topics and the stakes are correspondingly high. The risk of violence is never far from the surface and the news media have a professional interest in bringing it out. This was certainly the case in the initial debate over Oslo; the media were, in many ways, a major source of incitement.

The second point is that the news media not only lower the level of the debate over peace, they also narrow it. One of the chief victims of these routines were the Arab Knesset members, whose views were considered too radical for serious consideration. At the same time the opposition to the Oslo peace process also suffered from news routines. Due to their lack of media status, they were often forced to choose between either turning radical or being shut out of the discussion. They were placed in an especially difficult position after the assassination of Yitzhak Rabin. The universal adoption by the Israeli media of the Incitement frame made it impossible for them to mount a serious defense of their position. The media's performance during this political wave was just as simplistic and one-sided as it had been during the many terrorism waves that preceded (and followed) that historical event.

Finally, the research carried out with regard to the elections in 1996 once again demonstrates that threats are almost always considered more newsworthy than opportunities. Netanyahu was much more successful in placing terrorism on the electoral agenda than Peres was in talking about peace. This finding provides a helpful integration between two streams of research. One of the major reasons why negative campaigns are so popular is that they provide journalists with the drama they need. This same principle also helps explain why it is easier to promote the need for security than to talk about the benefits of peace. Threats are concrete, specific, and immediate while the benefits of peace tend to be abstract, general, and distant. The "best" news always focuses on conflict, whether it comes to election campaigns or peace processes.

CHAPTER 4

The Palestinians and the Israeli media

The British comedy group Monty Python used to perform a comedy sketch about a group of elderly gentleman sitting around a coffee table talking about how difficult their childhood had been. The first talked about living with his family in a small shack in the middle of the woods. The second laughs and says something like: "A shack, we only wish we had a shack, we all lived in one room the size of a closet." The third laughs yet again: "A closet, why we dreamed about living in a closet, we had to live in a shoebox." Well, when it comes to the political actors and their relationship with the Hebrew news media, we've now come to the shoebox.

The Israeli press has always related to the Palestinians as enemies. As in any other country, the news slot reserved for enemies centers on the amount of threat they pose and on what the country is doing to minimize that threat. The news media also serve as an important forum for expressing public hatred towards enemies and for reflecting and reinforcing common stereotypes. Sources or journalists who are suspected of sympathizing with enemies are likely to come under intensive attack. The denigration of CNN reporter Peter Arnett, who was stationed in Iraq during the Gulf War, is a well-known example of this phenomenon.

Nevertheless, the political environment has an important influence on the negativity of enemy images. The news media become the most ethnocentric in the midst of violent conflict. Enemies appear especially cruel and vicious when they are killing our people. Emotions run high during such confrontations and media images and rhetoric amplify those feelings. This point was made abundantly clear in the analysis of news coverage associated with the terrorist attack at Beit Lid. More evidence along these lines will emerge when the discussion turns to the role of the news media in the Second Intifada, which broke out in the fall of 2000.

The more interesting question is whether a peaceful environment can make a difference. Do media images of the enemy improve when there is an active peace process? Given what we know about the news media and about human nature, one would assume that negative incidents would leave a more lasting impression than positive ones. Images of buses blowing up are more difficult to forget than signing ceremonies. Nevertheless, the initiation of a peace process should lead to changes in news about the enemy. As the relations between two sets of political leaders improve, this should also have an effect on the interactions between journalists and sources from the other side.

The case of the Oslo peace process provides an important opportunity to examine these questions. As discussed, Prime Minister Rabin faced a number of difficult challenges in his attempts to convince the public that the PLO could be a partner for peace. Years of suspicion and hatred do not simply disappear. Collective memories of the victims remain powerful obstacles to change, especially when people continue to die. Rabin himself had an extremely ambivalent attitude towards Arafat and made no secret of it.

The Israeli news press had a similarly conflicted attitude towards the Palestinians. On the one hand, the ongoing negotiations and the peace ceremonies brought an entirely new dimension of coverage. For the first time Israelis were seeing Palestinian diplomats and not only Palestinian terrorists. There was also a growing attempt to develop Palestinian sources that could provide information about their own perspectives on the peace process. While Palestinians had always maintained a certain amount of contact with the Israeli press, the inauguration of the peace process led journalists to establish new routines to ensure a steady flow of information. Reporters were suddenly talking to people whom they had only heard about in the past. Thus, the fact the initiation of a peace process leads to the creation of new news slots has a significant influence on the sources that are used.[1]

Nevertheless, the Palestinians were still considered adversaries and some remained bitter enemies. While the Oslo peace process did bring about some important changes in Israeli media coverage of the Palestinians, many basic norms and routines remained in place. The press, especially the more tabloid press, remained a bastion of ethnocentrism. News stories continued to talk to "us" about "them." The Jews in Israel

---

[1] Weimann (1994) describes a similar process concerning the peace process between Israel and Egypt after President Sadat's historic visit to Jerusalem.

speak to each other in Hebrew about the Palestinians and the Palestinians talk to each other in Arabic about the Israelis.

The purpose of this chapter is to examine how Israeli journalists construct news about Palestinians, and whether this process changed because of the peace process. As always, the answers to these questions can be found by examining the values that govern the interactions between Palestinian sources and Israeli journalists and the resulting news content. Just as the Israeli government and the opposition were attempting to use the media to promote their views to the Israeli public, so was the Palestinian leadership.[2] The relationship between Hamas and the Israeli press was more complex but as part of the Palestinian opposition they too had to take the Israeli press into account. Here, too, one finds that the often-changing political environment had a major influence on all of these relationships and on media images of the other side.

THE PALESTINIAN LEADERSHIP AND THE ISRAELI PRESS

The historical enmity between the Israelis and the Palestinians is by far the most important factor explaining the difficulties the Palestinians face in promoting their positions to the Hebrew press. Cultural assumptions about enemies are difficult to change, as are the journalistic values and routines that mirror and strengthen those assumptions (Bar-Tal and Teichman, in press; First 2000, 1998; Liebes, 1997). The PLO was for many years considered the most viscous of Israel's enemies, and Arafat was the most hated enemy leader. While there have been important changes in Israel with regards to both of these assumptions, remnants of this past will continue to influence news coverage for many years to come.

It is not unusual for political movements to attempt the transition from violent challengers into responsible actors. Looking at the case of the Palestinians provides some useful insights about the role of the news media in such changes. In the early years many Israelis rejected the very term "Palestinian," preferring to think of that people as simply "Arabs." As detailed below, most of the news stories in those years appeared within the context of stories about other Arab countries. The dramatic terrorist attacks carried out by the PLO in the 1970s forced Israel and the world to relate to the Palestinians as important and independent players in the

---

[2] It is worth noting in this regard that the interviews with the Palestinians were carried out during the same period as those conducted with the Israelis (1995–96).

conflict. It is unlikely that the PLO would have achieved such a high level of international status without the use of terrorism. At the same time, the images associated with that violence remained an indelible part of Israel's collective memories.

Until there was a genuine peace process in place, there was very little direct contact between the PLO and the Israeli press. PLO leaders refused to give interviews with Israeli journalists because such contact would be seen as indirect recognition of the Zionist enemy. The Israeli government also prohibited any contacts between Israeli citizens and the PLO, and for many years it was forbidden to interview any Palestinian leader on Israeli television and radio. Israelis were only allowed to hear from local officials, Palestinian prisoners, or ordinary citizens. While some material could be taken from foreign press services, the general norm was to avoid giving the PLO any publicity. The PLO was framed almost exclusively as a terrorist organization.[3]

Many would argue, however, that one of the most important turning points was the Madrid peace talks, which took place in 1992. Although Israel insisted that the Palestinian representatives be considered part of the Jordanian delegation, it was the first time there were real negotiations going on between the two sides. It was also abundantly clear that the Palestinian delegates were in fact representing the PLO. It was the first time the Israeli press was covering the PLO as a negotiating partner rather than as a terrorist organization. Madrid was also an important turning point in terms of the willingness of the Palestinian leaders to deal with the Israeli media. One of the Palestinian interviewees referred to both of these changes.

> In my opinion the point at which the change began was Madrid, not Oslo. Before the Madrid conference the attitude of the Palestinian leadership [located in Tunisia] towards the Israeli press was negative and there was also considerable reluctance on the part of the Palestinian leaders in the occupied territories to work with the Israeli press. The Israeli press was politically antagonistic then. The atmosphere between the two sides was bad . . . But after the Madrid conference there began a gradual change in this area . . . I believe there was a positive change in the work of the Israeli media, they became more credible . . . [In addition] The Palestinian leadership in Tunisia was interested in receiving legitimacy from Israel and

---

[3] Exceptions to this rule might include the Lebanese War in 1982 and the First Intifada, which began at the end of 1987 (Cohen and Wolfsfeld, 1993).

therefore they tried to get to the Israeli hearts and minds and to the
Israeli politicians through the Israeli news media. (O19; February
19, 1995)

The election of the Rabin and the breakthrough at Oslo led to further
changes in the interactions between Israeli journalists and the Palestinians. The PLO leadership was now eager to talk to Israeli journalists, and
the feeling was mutual. Journalists covering Arab affairs who had to depend on secondary sources for so many years were suddenly flying to
Tunisia to meet with the top of the PLO leadership, including Arafat himself. A television reporter talked about the changing relationship after
the initial breakthrough at Oslo.

> I was always able to write. But today I can get a much wider variety
> of sources and first sources. Ten years ago I had to talk to in-
> termediaries and now I can talk to the people themselves . . .
> They're much more open now, you can get to them . . . Who would
> have believed that Chawatmeh [leader of the Palestinian Front for
> the Liberation of Palestine] would give an interview to the Israeli
> press? (O40; February 2, 1995)

The increasing willingness of Palestinians to gain access to the Israeli
news media should be understood within the general context of their
dependence on Israel. As the occupying force, everything that Israel
does has an immediate and massive impact on the lives of the Palestinian
population. Critical decisions were being made in Israel about pulling out
of Palestinian cities, the release of thousands of Palestinian prisoners, and
the ongoing problem of "closures," where Palestinians were prevented
from coming into Israel to work. Interviews that were carried out with
Palestinian leaders at that time reveal that many saw the Hebrew media
as a critical tool for influencing Israeli public opinion and political elites.
It is true that many of the Palestinians we spoke to were more likely
to have contact with the Israeli media, so these informants may not be
completely representative. Nevertheless, there are several indicators that
many Palestinian leaders attribute a great deal of importance to the Israeli
news media.

One such indicator is the extent to which the Palestinian leadership
monitors the Israeli press. The routine monitoring of the Israeli news
media goes back many years. The Jewish press served as both a strategic
tool and as a barometer of success for the Palestinian resistance. Arafat
apparently likes to tell some of his confidants that by reading Ze'ev Shiff,

a well-known Israeli military correspondent, he became convinced that Israel would invade Lebanon in 1982. Monitoring the Hebrew media was also important during the years of the (First) Intifada in order to assess the impact of the uprising on public opinion in Israel. Many Palestinian political organizations and news media hire professionals to translate and summarize the news and editorials from the major media in Israel. Not surprisingly, there is no similar practice within the Israeli news media. As often happens, the flow of information is mostly from the powerful towards the weak. The asymmetry in political and economic power means that Palestinians depend on Israel much more than Israelis depend on the Palestinian authority.

After Oslo, Palestinian leaders were even more anxious to use the Israeli media as a tool of influence. A Palestinian academic with good ties to the Palestinian leadership put it this way:

> The media influences Israeli public opinion. Israeli public opinion influences the media and the Israeli government. Thus, we have a complete circle: Israeli public opinion, the Israeli media, and Israeli policy. This circle is all connected, therefore the Palestinian public and the Palestinian leadership cannot influence government policy without having an influence on Israeli public opinion and the Israeli media . . . The media have tremendous power on Israeli attitudes. (O29; February 12, 1995)

The Palestinian leadership also uses the Israeli media to send messages to their own population. Many Palestinians living in the territories watch Israeli programming in Arabic that is broadcast on both television and radio. This led to a surprising amount of competition among Palestinian leaders who wanted to be interviewed on these programs. One Palestinian journalist was bitter about the fact that their leaders seemed more interested in appearing in the Israeli media than in the Palestinian press. Several also expressed concern that this provided the Israeli press with the power to provide political advantages to those Palestinian leaders who received coverage. As one of those interviewed put it:

> The media turns certain people into recognized people. People see them and hear them without any connection to what they say, thus when the name is raised people accept it naturally. The Israeli media, and especially the television in Arabic, is seen and heard in every Palestinian house and that makes it the most important tool possible for every person that has political ambitions . . . After a

while people forget that they saw them on a hostile media, they just remember they saw them. (O30; February 5, 1995)

As the Palestinian and other Arab broadcasting systems became more developed, this particular need may have diminished.[4] However, leaders who hope to have a broader influence in the area still have an interest in appearing on Israeli news.

STRUCTURAL AND CULTURAL BARRIERS TO THE PALESTINIAN MESSAGE

The Palestinian leadership was attempting to promote three major messages during this initial stage of the Oslo process. The first was that they had made an historic compromise in the interests of peace. The compromise involved recognizing Israel's right to exist, giving up the armed struggle against occupation, and working with Israel to halt terrorism. The second message was more defiant and thus more worrisome to Israelis. It was that the struggle to end the occupation would continue – assumedly through diplomatic means – and would eventually lead to a Palestinian state with Jerusalem as its capital. The third message was that the Palestinian population was suffering and something had to be done to ease their plight. The lack of jobs and money, the constant closing of the territories, and the ongoing harassment and humiliation associated with occupation were a direct threat to the peace process. Palestinians wanted to convince the Israeli public and the world of the need to alleviate this distress and to move forward towards a final settlement.

The difficulties the Palestinians faced in transmitting these messages were both structural and cultural. The cultural barriers are more obvious, but it is also important to consider some of the structural impediments. The Palestinians' lack of resources and media skills would be fairly high on their list of difficulties. The Palestinian authority is poor and it is understandable that building essential services would be given a higher priority than public relations. There are very few people who make their living as spokespeople, and even fewer that have the necessary knowledge and experience to deal with the Western press. Israeli and foreign journalists are constantly complaining about how difficult it is to get

[4] One of the most important developments in this area was the emergence of Al-Jazeera television broadcasting out of Qatar (Makovsky, 2001). This station became one of the most dominant and credible communication channels in the Arab world, especially after the outbreak of the Second Intifada and the US attacks on Afghanistan and Iraq.

information or even reactions from the Palestinian authorities. One of the Israeli journalists claimed that the Palestinian skills and resources in this area resembled those of the Jewish community at the time of the British mandate.[5]

Some of these difficulties can be related to what happens when a closed society attempts to communicate with an open one. The authorities' attempts to keep careful control over information, fears of reprisals for speaking without permission, and a lack of experience in dealing with a free press make it hard for such entities to promote their frames to the western media. A journalist responsible for covering the rest of the Arab world said the problems dealing with the Palestinians were similar to what he and his colleagues had experienced in many Arab countries. These leaders use their own press as a propaganda tool and find it difficult to adjust to a more critical form of journalism.

An interesting fact that emerged from the journalists was how seldom Arafat himself gave interviews to the Israeli press. While he was apparently quite willing for his underlings to do so, he deals almost exclusively with the foreign press. One journalist argued that this was because Arafat does not really trust the Israeli media to pass on his message as he intended it. Another reason, the reporter claimed, was that Arafat did not want to give his opponents more ammunition by appearing too close to Israel. In any case much of what he says in the foreign press will be quoted in the Israeli media, so there are many advantages to taking this indirect route.[6]

It is also important to remember that Palestinians who want to speak to the Israelis have to overcome language barriers. While many Palestinian leaders do speak Hebrew, few speak it eloquently. This makes them sound less intelligent and sophisticated when they are being interviewed on Israeli television and radio. Speaking Hebrew can also lead to disapproval within their community. A Palestinian leader talked about this issue:

> I speak in Hebrew when I want to pass on messages to the Israeli people. Because it is difficult for me to pass my message in Arabic. My message won't be received properly. So I use Hebrew, although

---

[5] It is ironic that many Israelis believe that the Palestinians are far better at public relations than Israel. They believe that the international press always favors the Palestinians over Israel. The actual situation is much more complicated. If the Palestinians do enjoy any advantages with regard to the international press, it is more likely related to them being seen as victims than as a result of any public relations skills.

[6] One might ask why Arafat's lack of contact with the Israeli press has never become a public issue. Perhaps the Israeli media's inability to get to Arafat is seen as a professional failure and this explains journalists' reluctance to publicize it.

> I get a lot of criticism from other Palestinians that I'm talking too much in Hebrew . . . Some of our leadership doesn't really have command of Hebrew, they can't really express themselves in that language and express their position, and despite that they give interviews and talk in Hebrew. So even though they have strong arguments their message is weakened because of the language. This is a very important reason a good part of the Palestinian leadership refrains from speaking to the Israeli press. (O29; February 12, 1995)

Israeli editors are also reluctant to use translators and thus they prefer to interview Palestinians who can speak Hebrew. As always it is the weak that must find a way to adapt to the needs of the powerful.

The problems of inter-cultural communication, however, go far beyond problems of language. The building of media frames, it was argued, is based on journalists attempting to find a narrative fit between incoming information and existing frames. The ideological frames that the Palestinians were attempting to promote to the Israeli news media simply do not exist within the Israeli consciousness. There are elements within the Israeli left that have a certain amount of sympathy for the plight of the Palestinians and the Arab minority within the country supports most of the Palestinian positions. Nevertheless, the Hebrew media employ exclusively Israeli frames of the conflict. The Security First and Peace frames represent attempts to solve problems facing Israel, not the Palestinians.

Many in Israel, especially at the beginning of the process, still considered the PLO a terrorist organization dedicated to the destruction of the state.[7] Others were willing to give Arafat and the PLO a chance to "prove that they had changed." The difficulties the Palestinian leadership was likely to face in their struggle for legitimacy within Israel were already apparent at the first signing ceremony held on the White House lawn. There was a tremendously fierce debate in the press about how Rabin could shake Arafat's hand after Israel had suffered from so many years of Palestinian terrorism. No similar debate emerged when it came to shaking King Hussein's hand, even though the wars with Jordan had led to far more Israeli deaths. King Hussein was seen as a legitimate statesman while Arafat was still considered at best a reformed terrorist.

The Palestinians interviewed were all very conscious about the cultural problems associated with dealing with the Israeli press. The Israeli media were considered hostile, ethnocentric, and condescending. Comments

---

[7] This attitude again became prevalent after the outbreak of the Second Intifada, when elements of the PLO returned to the use of terrorism.

along this line included: "The Israeli press is concerned with Israeli interests not those of the Palestinians," "I can't get my message across because the media is for the Jews," "I would like to have an objective picture in which the Palestinians are treated like human beings," or "Even if there's peace, the Israelis will still think they're special." While most believed that the image of Palestinians had improved since Oslo, it was still a long uphill battle before they could hope to achieve respect and legitimacy.

One of the major channels for passing on Palestinian messages were the Israeli journalists who covered the Arab beat. Every Israeli news medium has at least one journalist who is responsible for covering Arab affairs. Many of these reporters spent their army years in intelligence, where their knowledge of Arab language and culture were a critical asset. It is not surprising therefore that many of their most important sources come from the military. Nevertheless, many of these same journalists were quite sympathetic to the Palestinian plight. They spent a good deal of time interacting with Palestinians and thus are in a better position to understand that people's perspective.

There are important differences among these Arab affairs reporters and there is no doubt that this has an important influence on their stories. Given what was said earlier, it is no surprise that most of the less ethnocentric reporters work for the elite newspaper *Ha'aretz*. This is the only news medium in Israel that makes a serious commitment to in-depth coverage of the Palestinian issue. Although the newspaper does not have any reporters who are Palestinian, the editors make a point of covering the issue from a number of perspectives that are ignored by the other media.

Some of these reporters have very different views than their colleagues about journalism ethics. Fighting against injustice, they argue, does not end when one crosses the border. One of these reporters was particularly emphatic about this point, arguing that journalists have a moral obligation to deal with the injustices of occupation.

The relationship with the territories is a colonial one, so every journalist sees himself as a messenger of his government. That's first of all illicit. You shouldn't be anybody's messenger. I can't deny that I was always opposed to the occupation, I can't hide that . . . The other reporters – actually with good intentions – come for a day, see a few towers in the center of town, see a road or two with asphalt and say: "Wow! There's improvement!" So everyone says

I'm negative because I go to the refugee camps and see that nothing has changed. I'm shocked by what I see, I'm really shocked. (O37; March 31, 1996)

Part of this dispute among reporters has to do with how much one should depend on Palestinian or Israeli sources in building stories. Those who believe that the press should adopt a more critical role complain that their colleagues rely too heavily on the sources within Israeli intelligence and the security forces. Other journalists are more suspicious of the Palestinians and accuse their more leftist colleagues of a lack of objectivity. Several were especially critical of Amira Hass, the journalist from *Ha'aretz* who purposely chose to live in Gaza at the time in order to understand the Palestinian perspective. This interviewee talked about the normative differences between himself and those journalists who were more sympathetic to the other side.

I'm not going to go and live in Gaza and I'm not going to help Palestinians get licenses. That's not my role as a journalist. My role is to travel to Gaza and see what is really happening, but I don't put my personal involvement into my work. But, my job is certainly to find out if the Palestinian authority is not functioning and if there is criticism of it, than I certainly should do that. (O38; April 4, 1996)

The Palestinians who were interviewed were very aware of the differences between Israeli journalists. Some of the differences they attribute to the reporters themselves, and some to the editorial policy of the various media. Those who were interviewed talked about journalists who "support the peace process and those who don't," "those who are 'objective' and those who aren't," and "those who support the occupation and those who don't." Some of the less sympathetic journalists are even suspected of working for the Israeli security forces. Naturally, the amount of cooperation Palestinian sources are willing to give Israeli reporters is directly related to such perceived differences.

The important lesson from all this has to do with the relationship between sensationalism and ethnocentrism. The willingness of the editors of *Ha'aretz* to employ sympathetic journalists is based on their belief that their audience is interested in learning about the other side's perspective.[8] The more popular newspapers, on the other hand, insist on

---

[8] An alternative explanation is that *Ha'aretz* includes such reports because it is simply a more leftist newspaper. This point will be discussed further below.

providing the mainstream view of the political world. Quality newspapers tend to introduce the readers to a wider spectrum of views about the issue. Editors and owners from the popular news media defend themselves by arguing that they are merely supplying people with the stories they want. There is some truth to this justification. The ethical question is whether the news media also have a professional obligation to inform and educate. I shall return to this issue in the concluding chapter.

In sum, the interviews with the Israeli journalists and their Palestinian sources lead to three major conclusions. The first is that the ongoing peace process did improve the image of the Palestinians in the Israeli press. The fact that the Palestinians were being interviewed as diplomats and negotiators is an important example of such a change. The second finding is that, despite such changes, the Hebrew media still exhibit a generally hostile attitude towards the Palestinians. Palestinians are still framed as enemies and the major reason for media attention is because they represent a serious threat to Israel. Finally, the interviews also point to some differences among the Israeli media in their overall orientation towards the Palestinians. The elite newspaper *Ha'aretz* appears to be more open to input from the Palestinians than the popular news media. The next analysis provides a more direct test of these ideas.

CHANGING IMAGES OF THE ENEMY

An extensive content analysis was conducted to look at the Palestinian image in Israel's print media. The analysis looked at fifty days of newspaper coverage about the Palestinians that appeared during four different years: 1965, 1985, 1995, and 1997.[9] The years were chosen both to provide an historical perspective and to examine changes that were related to the inauguration of the Oslo peace process and the election of Prime Minister Benjamin Netanyahu. The year 1965 represents a period before the PLO was created and the year 1985 represents a full two years before the outbreak of the Intifada. As Oslo was initiated in September of 1993, the data from 1995 provides some evidence about the Palestinian image after the early euphoria had worn off. In 1997, the Labor government was replaced by a more right-wing administration led by Prime Minister Netanyahu. Given the change in atmosphere the period chosen allows for sufficient distance to examine some more enduring changes in the Palestinian image.

[9] For details see the methodological appendix.

A major thesis of this work is that the news media tend to reflect and reinforce changes in the political environment. This proposition refers to both long-range changes as well as more immediate variations in climate. It was argued that changes in news slots represent an important mechanism for explaining this dynamic. The inauguration of a peace process indicates a reduced level of political enmity and this should also lead to a less demonized image of the enemy in the press. In addition, the growing political recognition accorded to the Palestinians should be reflected in a similar rise in the groups' media status in Israel. Thus, the first question to be examined is whether or not the improvements in the relations between the sides have led to positive changes in the media image of the Palestinians.

It is helpful to think about different levels of media legitimacy for political challengers. The worst fate is to be ignored, to be considered irrelevant to the political process. Thus, the first goal for weaker adversaries is to achieve *standing* in the news media (Gamson and Wolfsfeld, 1993). It is important to be recognized as an important force, even if it means being considered a dangerous force. A higher level of legitimacy would to be considered *negotiating partners*. The fact that one's leaders are willing to negotiate with the enemy automatically grants the other side a certain amount of legitimacy. News stories about such negotiations serve to reinforce this change in image because diplomacy is much less threatening than violent conflict. The highest level of media legitimacy is one in which the media provides supportive coverage which reflects some of the ideological frames being promoted by the group.

Changes in the images of the Palestinians are investigated by dividing the news stories from the four time periods into five general news slots. The first category looks at those items in which the Palestinians are discussed within the context of another news story, usually having to do with other Arab countries. It was assumed that this type of coverage was especially common in early years, before the Palestinians received sufficient standing to be considered a separate group. The second category contains all news stories that relate to the Palestinians as a threat to Israel. The most common of these stories are those that deal with either the possibility of violence, actual violence, or what the Israeli authorities are doing to prevent Palestinian violence. The third category contains news stories about the peace process, or (in earlier years) the possibility of a peace process. The fourth category includes any stories that relate to the internal affairs of the Palestinians. This would include news about internal politics and general stories about Palestinian society. The willingness

Table 4.1 *Newspaper coverage of Palestinians by topic and year*[a]

			Topic			
Year	General Arab	Security	Peace Process	Internal Society	Victims	Total (Number)
1965	49%	32%	0%	13%	7%	72
1985	20%	53%	17%	4%	7%	91
1995	13%	30%	38%	14%	5%	235
1997	14%	34%	23%	18%	11%	183

[a] Based on sample newspaper stories appearing on first four pages of *Yediot Ahronot* and *Ha'aretz*. Differences in percentages are due to rounding.

of a news medium to publish such stories suggests a somewhat less ethnocentric approach to the other side. The fifth and final class of stories is the most sympathetic to the Palestinians. These are the articles that deal with Palestinians as victims. These pieces usually focus on either injustices related to Israeli occupation or the poverty of those living in refugee camps. The changes in the distribution of each class of stories are presented in table 4.1.

The first pattern to note is the differences between 1965 and 1985. Almost half of all the news stories about the Palestinians in 1965 related to them as secondary actors. Twenty years later only 20 percent of the stories fell into this category; the Palestinians were now considered important enough to justify an independent news slot. The types of stories that increased during that time were stories having to do with the threat posed by the Palestinians and those having to do with earlier attempts at peace. The increased activism of the PLO and other Palestinians groups during this period pushed Israel and its media to recognize them as independent challengers. On the other hand, one does not find a significant rise in the overall number of articles written about the Palestinians.

The most significant rise in the amount of media attention takes place in the next ten years: there are two and a half times more stories published in 1995 than there were in 1985. The evidence also confirms that because of the initiation of an active peace process, there is a rise in the use of more promising news slots. There was a serious drop in the proportion of stories written about the threat posed by the Palestinians and an increase in the percentage dealing with peace. Some might argue that this was a rather trivial finding: it is hardly surprising that there are more news stories about peace when there is an active peace process going on.

It is important to remember, however, that many of these stories dealt with negative aspects of the peace process. In addition, I would argue that these results provide a useful illustration of how changes in the political environment lead to important changes in news routines. While one should not confuse the creation of news slots with the construction of media frames, there is a relationship between the two phenomena. In 1965 there was, for the most part, only one dominant ideological frame in Israel concerning the conflict: a Security frame that focused on Israel's ongoing struggle with her Arab neighbors. Twenty years later Israel had already signed a peace treaty with Egypt and the Palestinians had become a political force. Now there was an additional frame available for dealing with the Palestinians – the Peace frame. This provided leaders, citizens, and journalists with an additional frame for dealing with the conflict. Media frames, it will be remembered, attempt to tell us what is at issue. In the early years the question was whether Israel would survive the threat posed by the Arab countries. By the 1990s, the issue was whether or not Israel could have peace with her neighbors. This is a very different type of question, and is well reflected in the change in news slots.

Progress in the peace process led to more peace stories being published. It is also important to keep in mind that the Rabin government was one of the first that had a genuine *interest* in promoting the Palestinians as serious partners for peace. The interviews with his advisors reveal that an important part of this strategy was to supply the news media with materials that would increase the amount of support for peace. This helps explain why 1995 was the only year in which peace stories outnumbered security stories. Prime Minister Netanyahu was much less enthusiastic about the Oslo process and this too appears to be reflected in the general division between peace and security stories in 1997.

The fact that Israelis were exposed to a smaller proportion of threatening stories about the Palestinians presumably led to a more conducive political atmosphere for making further progress. If one accepts the fact that negative images raise the level of hostility between populations, it is reasonable to also suggest that the reverse is true. It is admittedly much more difficult to erase the scars left from years of conflict. Nevertheless, the softening media image of the Palestinians during these years may have at least something to do with the fact that a growing number of Israelis were willing to consider territorial concessions for peace (Arian, 1995; Shamir and Shamir, 2000). It is also worth reiterating that the

Palestinians we spoke to also felt that their media image had improved over the years. Such a feeling on their side could also contribute to a more positive atmosphere. If so, such an influence would be another example of the PMP cycle. Progress on the peace front led to less severe images of the Palestinians, which may have led to a more conducive atmosphere for promoting peace.

The results presented in table 4.1 also suggest that the coverage of the Palestinians grew somewhat less ethnocentric over the years. There was a significant increase in the number and percentage of stories dealing with the internal affairs of the Palestinian society. There were almost five times as many stories in 1995 than there were ten years earlier. A similar number was found during 1997, when Prime Minister Netanyahu was in power. Once again this does not mean that these were necessarily "positive" stories about Palestinians. At the very least, however, this change in focus does provide a more multidimensional image of that people. It also represents an *editorial change* that cannot be directly linked to the major events associated with the peace process. The increasing willingness of the Israeli press to cover the internal affairs of the Palestinians indicates a higher level of political standing for that population.

On the other hand one does not find a systematically higher level of sympathy for the plight of the Palestinian people. Only 5 percent of all news stories about the Palestinians that appeared in 1995 framed them as victims. This is very similar to the proportion of stories produced thirty years earlier. In is interesting that there is a rise in these types of stories during the Netanyahu years, but the overall trend is extremely stable. The extremely small number of news stories that represent the Palestinians as victims demonstrates the tremendous barriers that group faces in promoting their frames to the Israeli press. It is one thing to talk about the possibility of peace, it is quite another to sympathize with an enemy. Such stories are especially problematic when Israel is being held responsible for the victimization of that people. News stories that focus on the plight of the Palestinians *are* very common in the western press, a fact that often angers many Israelis (Wolfsfeld, 1997a). Thus, despite some important changes in the way the Israeli media cover the other side, overt sympathy for the Palestinians remains mostly out of bounds.

The analysis also employed another indicator of Palestinian media status. Coders were asked to assess the extent to which Palestinians were identified as the first source for a news story. The original list of choices included a variety of possible sources that was then divided into three

Table 4.2 *Newspaper coverage of Palestinians by source and year*[a]

| | Source | | | |
Year	Israeli	Palestinian	Other	Total (Number)
1965	56%	19%	26%	27
1985	64%	21%	15%	87
1995	55%	39%	6%	247
1997	62%	32%	6%	169

[a] Based on sample newspaper stories appearing on first four pages of *Yediot Ahronot* and *Ha'aretz*. Differences in percentages are due to rounding.

overall categories: Israeli, Palestinian, and other. In keeping with what was said earlier, it was assumed that the Palestinians' rising level of political standing would be reflected in an increasing tendency to use Palestinians as sources. The results are presented in table 4.2.

The findings confirm the rise in the status of Palestinian sources. In 1965 and 1985 about 20 percent of these news stories were based on Palestinian sources. In 1995 the figure was closer to 40 percent, although there was somewhat of a drop in 1997, during Netanyahu's reign. Bear in mind that the analysis deals only with news stories *about* the Palestinians, not about the peace process as a whole. The fact that such stories still depend more on Israeli sources once again demonstrates the fundamental ethnocentrism of the news media.

Thus the content analysis provides empirical support for the ideas that emerged in the interviews. First, the rise in Palestinians' political standing has led to rise in their media standing. This is born out by both the rise in the number of news stories that relate to them as independent actors and the extent to which the Israeli news media turns to them as sources. Their image had also become somewhat less threatening since the inauguration of the peace process. The initiation of a peace process not only provided an important new context for covering the Palestinians, it also appears to have led to an increasing willingness to deal with internal issues.

The analysis also illustrates that there are important limits to this progress. The security frame remained a central element in news about the Palestinians. Israelis still regarded the Palestinians as a serious threat

Table 4.3 *Newspaper coverage of Palestinians by source and newspaper*[a]

	Source			
Newspaper	Israeli	Palestinian	Other	Total (Number)
Yediot	67%	22%	11%	172
Ha'aretz	54%	38%	8%	358

[a] Based on sample newspaper stories appearing on first four pages of *Yediot Ahronot* and *Ha'aretz*. Differences in percentages are due to rounding.

and this is clearly reflected in the media. This is especially evident when one remembers the fact that a collection of articles about a terrorist attack is likely to have far more impact than a similar number of articles about peace negotiations. The Israeli press also had extraordinarily few stories about Palestinian suffering. This is especially revealing given the prominence of this theme in the world media. One can only speculate whether a greater emphasis on this aspect of the conflict might have also contributed to the cause of peace. At the very least, the Israeli public would have been less surprised when the Second Intifada broke out in the fall of 2000.

As noted, the final point that emerged from the interviews concerned the difference between newspapers. It was claimed that *Ha'aretz* was more open to Palestinian input than the more sensationalist newspapers, and had a less hostile attitude towards them. The content analysis allows us to also look at this issue more directly. If the claims about openness are true then one would expect *Ha'aretz* to publish more stories about the Palestinians and to be more willing to use them as sources for such stories. The comparison between *Ha'aretz* and *Yediot Ahronot* is presented in table 4.3.

The results confirm the difference between the two papers. First, there are over twice as many news stories about the Palestinians in *Ha'aretz* than in *Yediot Ahronot*. Even more importantly *Ha'aretz* is much more likely to use Palestinians as major sources for these news stories. While *Yediot Ahronot* only turns to Palestinian sources in 22 percent of these stories, *Ha'aretz* does so in 38 percent. Nevertheless, one should not exaggerate this divergence. Israelis are still the major sources for news stories about the Palestinians in both newspapers. *Ha'aretz* may have

Table 4.4 *Newspaper coverage of Palestinians by topic and newspaper*[a]

	Topic					
Newspaper	General Arab	Security	Peace Process	Internal Society	Victims	Total (Number)
Yediot	25%	39%	22%	10%	5%	199
Ha'aretz	16%	33%	27%	16%	9%	381

[a] Based on sample newspaper stories appearing on first four pages of *Yediot Ahronot* and *Ha'aretz*. Differences in percentages are due to rounding.

adopted a less ethnocentric approach to the Palestinian story, but it is still a newspaper written by and for Israelis.[10]

This pattern also becomes apparent when looking at some of the differences in the subjects the two papers choose (table 4.4). Some notable differences between the two papers are apparent. The most important have to do with the higher number and proportion of *Ha'aretz* stories dealing with Palestinian internal affairs and with their problems. One finds over three times as many of these types of stories in *Ha'aretz* (thirty-three) as in *Yediot* (nine). On the other hand even *Ha'aretz* only devotes 9 percent of their coverage to the plight of the Palestinians. While this is slightly better than the 5 percent published in *Yediot*, the other's suffering is certainly not a major focus of their coverage. Here too, the Security frame remains the most popular category of news stories.

It is only fair to note that these findings do not represent a complete test of the hypothesized relationship between sensationalism and ethnocentrism. The problem is that *Ha'aretz* is also the more liberal paper, and it is difficult to know whether the more open approach to the Palestinians is better attributed to political bias. Interviews with the journalists at that paper also reveal that editors at *Ha'aretz* made a conscious decision to support the Oslo peace process. The dovish stance also comes out very clearly when one examines the distribution of views appearing on the opinion pages of the paper.

[10] As discussed, one is more likely to find sympathy for the plight of the Palestinians in the editorial section of *Ha'aretz*. One finds there are two writers (Amira Hass and Gideon Levy) who regularly write about this issue and a number of others who occasionally do so.

I would argue that both of these factors have an influence on the final product. The commitment to a higher quality of journalism is inherently less ethnocentric. Thus, one of the central features of all elite newspapers is that they devote more space to foreign news. The assumption is that readers have a certain amount of knowledge and interest in what is happening in the rest of the world. This orientation should also lead to a greater willingness to learn about the "other side" in a conflict. The fact that the paper also takes a more dovish position on the Arab–Israeli conflict serves to reinforce this tendency.[11]

The results of this content analysis provide then some helpful insights into some of the historical changes that have taken place concerning Palestinian images in the Israeli media. They suggest that changes in the political environment have indeed led to variations in how that group was covered. The Palestinians had achieved a higher level of media status, and the initiation of a peace process had created a less threatening news slot for coverage. Nevertheless, the Palestinian threat to Israel's security remained the major filter for news coverage. It was also extremely rare to find news stories that deal with the plight of the Palestinians. The attitude of the Israeli media towards the Palestinian people in the 1990s was quite in keeping with the political climate of the time. There was a certain willingness to consider the possibility of peace but very little trust or sympathy for the other side.

NEW ENEMIES REPLACE THE OLD

The opposition movement Hamas has been a part of this discussion from the very beginning.[12] This tells us something important about how Hamas and the Islamic Jihad movement used terrorism to establish themselves as serious players.[13] There were three "movers and shakers" during the period under study: the Rabin/Peres governments, the Palestinian authority, and Hamas. What distinguished Hamas from the other two was

[11] Fortunately, there is an additional method for examining the effects of sensationalism. The news media environment in Northern Ireland, I intend to argue, is much less sensationalist than that of Israel. As further elaborated in chapter 6 this serves to reduce the likelihood of the news media playing an inflammatory role in that conflict.

[12] Readers interested in learning more about Hamas should refer to Hroub, 2000, and Mishal and Sela, 2000.

[13] For the sake of simplicity, I will refer only to Hamas, which was the most visible of the two movements. There is no reason to believe, however, that the relations between the Israeli news media and the Islamic Jihad movement were any different.

its lower level of standing and resources. Despite this, the organization dominated the political agenda for an extended period, forced all of the other players to alter their plans and policies, and played a major role in bringing down the Rabin/Peres government. The news media were not responsible for all this, but they did serve as an important catalyst for turning terrorism into political influence.

It is important to begin by examining the unusual relationship between the Israeli press and Hamas. In many ways it can be considered a sordid affair. The two sides come together to meet basic needs. Both feel guilty about the relationship and the truth is that neither of them even likes the other. But the costs of ending the relationship somehow seem greater than maintaining it.

The attitude of the Israeli press towards Hamas is similar to their former attitude to the PLO. Hamas is considered the enemy and there is a national consensus that all members and sympathizers should be considered terrorists. The guiding assumption for virtually all Jews in Israel is that Hamas's goal is to destroy the state of Israel. The press is concerned exclusively with assessing the nature and extent of the threat. There have never been any negotiations with Hamas, so there is no alternative frame available. Terrorism is big news and most Israeli journalists believe that it would be wrong to apply any restraints on their coverage. Their job is to report what happens, or what *could* happen, without concern for political consequences. As one journalist put it, the relationship between Hamas and the Israeli media is one of mutual exploitation.

> Everyone here has an interest in passing on their message to the media, the message they want. The media for them is a tool. We have almost a permanent procedure for every attack that occurs. The terrorists call here and explain what they did and we even interview them. It's a matter of a communication channel. They want to pass on a certain message, so they use us to pass their message on, and we use them for journalistic information. It's mutual exploitation of the same means. (O28; April 4, 1996)

The truth is that all relationships between sources and journalists consist of mutual exploitation. Journalists are more likely to *think* about such dilemmas, however, when covering the enemy. Media frames of the enemy are also much less ambiguous. The fact that the reporter quoted above tells us about what happens when the "terrorists call here" illustrates how well defined the frame is for such actions.[14] The template already exists; journalists and editors merely fill in the details about where, when, how, the number of casualties, and which groups are considered responsible. It is also important to remember that there would be no reason at all to interview members of the Palestinian opposition without these attacks. Whenever there were extended periods of time without terrorism, Hamas disappeared from the political screen. The attacks serve as an extremely effective means of raising the group's visibility in the media and in the domestic and international political environment.

While the Israeli media's attitude towards Hamas resembles the prior situation concerning the PLO, there are important differences. The norms and rules were much more restrictive in past years and the idea of interviewing a PLO leader after a terrorist attack would have been inconceivable. In many ways this is a positive development, for the Israeli public is provided with a much richer set of information. One cannot ignore, however, the fact that this new openness is part of a more general trend to provide drama and entertainment. As several Palestinians noted, the emphasis on terror and violence came at the expense of more moderate voices within the Palestinian community.

The attitude of Hamas towards the Israeli press is also ambivalent. Many leaders are extremely reluctant to initiate contacts with the Israeli press, for such an act is seen as tacit recognition of Israel. One of the most significant differences between the research interviews with the Palestinian leadership and those with Hamas was the extent to which ideology dominated the discussions. Questions about the movement's relationship with the Israeli media, about media strategy, and about media images of the Palestinians inevitably invoked ideological responses about the ongoing struggle against Israel. It is impossible, from a Hamas perspective, to distinguish between attitudes towards Israel and attitudes towards the Israeli media. Consider how one of the Hamas members described the role of the Israeli press:

> The Israelis know what the Palestinian message is and what the Palestinians are going through, but they prefer to purposely ignore it in order not to bring about a change in Israeli perceptions of

[14] Some readers might raise similar questions about my own use of the word terrorism. I consider terrorism to be the most accurate term to describe acts of violence that target civilians. Similar acts against soldiers should, on the other hand, be considered guerilla warfare.

the Palestinians, so the Israelis won't start relating to us like human beings that have rights, and that's something that mars the Zionist dream. They know everything, the Israeli security services [Shabak], the Israeli researchers, and the military officers all know what the Palestinian people are going through, but they try to prevent the deprivations and suffering of the Palestinians, and what the Israelis have done to us, to get to the Israeli people. The Israeli media play a major and even pacesetting role in this; they are the major tools for executing this policy. (O28; February 10, 1995)

Despite this antagonism, Hamas wants to send messages to the Israeli people and this requires a certain amount of contact with the Israeli media. There are a few unofficial spokespeople who are given the responsibility for dealing with the Israeli and international press. They rarely initiate contacts with the Israeli press but are often willing to talk to reporters when they are approached. It is assumed that such spokespeople are not members of the combat division of Hamas, but have some knowledge about what is happening in the movement. Nevertheless, many people we spoke to spent at least some time in either Israeli or Palestinian prisons both before and after the interviews.

The need for Hamas and the other opposition movements to gain access to the Israel press rose with the establishment of the Palestinian authority. Whereas the Palestinian press is carefully controlled and censored by the Palestinian authorities, the Israeli press offered one of few means of communicating with the world. This is especially true when it comes to human rights violations or attempts by Arafat to shut down oppositional news media. Arafat is apparently very sensitive to any negative publicity about his administration that appears in the Israeli press.

The Israeli news in Arabic also allowed Hamas leaders to send messages to their own people. One of those interviewed argued that the Israeli press had more impact on Palestinian opinions than their own press.[15] Here, then, is another irony about relations with the media during the peace process: the Israeli press serves as an important outlet for Israel's fiercest opponents. This brought at least one Hamas interviewee to express a grudging admiration of the Israeli media.

[15] Here, too, the emergence of Al-Jazeera had an important impact on these relations (see footnote 4). This provided Palestinian opposition leaders with a much more effective means of circumventing the official Palestinian press. The outbreak of the Second Intifada also led to a decline in the credibility of the Israel press because many Palestinians felt that the Hebrew media had mobilized for the cause against them (Rubinstein, 2001).

I, as part of the Palestinian opposition, didn't find any Palestinian media through which I can send my opinions and my outlook to the Israeli and Palestinian people . . . We're always reminding the Palestinian press when we argue with them that they should learn from the Israeli press how to cover news and events and to give expression to all opinions. (O17; June 8, 1995)

Nevertheless, he goes on to say that the Israeli press is much more accurate when covering Israeli society than when dealing with the Palestinians. The Israeli opposition claims that the Israeli media gets it wrong on both counts: it treats the right wing too negatively, and the Palestinians too positively. The Israeli government and the Palestinian leadership have their own views on this subject. Media bias is always in the eyes of the beholder.

It is important to emphasize that the interviews did not reveal a single, unified attitude towards the Israel press. Although we were undoubtedly speaking to the more moderate elements in Hamas, some were extremely antagonistic while others were more pragmatic. Most, however, saw the use of the Israeli media as a "necessary evil," and believed that the Hebrew press was a useful but tainted tool.

TERRORISM AND THE MEDIA FROM A HAMAS PERSPECTIVE

The most important thing to understand about the Hamas commitment to the armed struggle against Israel is that it does not center on media considerations. This does not mean that they are unaware of how the media amplifies the impact of such acts. But the strategic decision to use violence as a means to fight Israel comes from the outrage against the occupation and all it entails. One of the people associated with Hamas provided vivid expression to these feelings.

I can tell you that the Israeli occupation, the oppression, Israeli terrorism and crimes against the Palestinian people that have gone on for the twenty-seven years of murderous occupation, you can easily compare to what the Jews underwent in the days of the Nazis. The Jews murder us every day a hundred times, they murder us slowly, and therefore this is the Palestinian holocaust . . . The Israelis have turned us into caged animals. When a Palestinian decides to blow himself up in Tel Aviv he does so because the alternative is no better. What do I have left as a Palestinian in life? Only suffering, depression, daily humiliation, repression, and daily murder. That reality is a thousand times worse than death. In the end, whoever carries out suicide missions only loses one thing: the desperation, the suffering, and the pain that the Israeli occupation brings to him and to his family. (O20; February 10, 1995)

The Palestinian people, they argue, have no other weapon against the Israelis. This is how another Hamas activist puts it:

You have to pay attention to the fact that when the [First] Intifada started Hamas didn't use these weapons and especially not suicide bombers. That shows you that Hamas used all of the other possible means to accomplish its goals. But when all the other means failed, Hamas was forced to use this tool. The Intifada started as a popular, nonviolent protest. Afterwards we moved over to stones and bottles and violent confrontations with the army, but when that didn't work the move towards weapons and suicide bombers was inevitable. Because the Israelis thought that through repression, killing, and arrests, that could suppress the popular uprising of the Palestinian people. Therefore the military actions are the height of protest action and if the situation continues to get worse in Gaza, the attacks will continue, because there is no alternative. (O23; June 8, 1995)

It is critical to remember that terrorism is seen first and foremost as a means of fighting against Israel. The actions are not carried out for purposes of publicity. The publicity serves to increase the impact of these acts, but the use of violence for political struggle goes back long before CNN. Terrorism also occurs in countries without a free press. Nevertheless, the Hamas leaders we spoke to are very aware of the impact of media coverage. They also realize that without such acts they would be ignored. This is how one of them described it:

The enemy can sometimes serve us indirectly. We don't have any large news institutions that will publicize and cover the things that we're interested in . . . So in the end, the Hamas actions force the media to report and relate to the activities and positions of the movement. I want to use the military actions to prove my abilities on both the local and regional level. The Israeli press helps with this. Therefore, through my military action I am trying to pass a message that Hamas is a central force among the Palestinians and it is impossible to ignore it. (O25; June 8, 1995)

The news media become the great equalizer. It allows those without political standing to achieve standing. Unfortunately, the only way for such groups to gain access is to carry out outrageous acts of violence. The greater the drama produced, the greater the media coverage. The greater and more sensationalist the media coverage, the more likely it is to have an influence on the peace process. This is another example of the politics-media-politics cycle. Consider the chilling analysis offered by one interviewee when asked about whether he believed that the Hamas actions had an influence on the Israeli–Palestinian negotiations.

There's no doubt. The military actions of Hamas played a central role in the negotiations with Israel . . . For example when Hamas was kidnapping soldiers to release the Palestinian prisoners, this helped those carrying out the negotiations to put pressure on Israel by showing how important the release of prisoners is among the Palestinians. Therefore, the claim of the Palestinian authority was that if Israel would release the prisoners, then Hamas wouldn't have any reason to kidnap soldiers . . . Kidnapping is the most painful means possible in Israeli society. When you kill a soldier, you kill him once. In a kidnapping the soldier dies every day a hundred times. Therefore, the Hamas actions and the media coverage it generates don't just affect the negotiations themselves; they also affect policy and the general atmosphere in the area. (O17; June 8, 1995)

Hamas also takes the Israeli media into account in their planning of an operation. The same interviewee who talked about the kidnapping described this process.

The military actions of Hamas are carried out by the Az Aldin Elkasam unit. After every action of those units always comes a press release on the action carried out, explaining their claims or their demands. Before carrying out every action they prepare a press release including films and pictures about what needs to be shown or explained. Thus, the media dimension is very important in this context. (O17; June 8, 1995)

The Hamas leaders are not only fighting for standing within Israeli society and the international community, they are also fighting for standing among the Palestinians. They are competing with Arafat and the PLO for leadership of the Palestinian people. Surveys suggest that the Palestinians living in the territories were, at the time, divided about the use of terrorism against Israel.[16] Many in Hamas believe, however, that the use of such actions in Israel increases their status among their people.

> The average Palestinian believes that Hamas is capable of carrying out things that no one else succeeded in doing. Therefore, it only increases the status of our movement. The Israeli army is still in Gaza, they even kill Palestinian police officers, the suffering of the Palestinian people continues and therefore the Hamas actions represent the cumulative anger of the Palestinian people against Israel, especially because of the deep disappointment from the results of the Oslo agreement. (O23; June 8, 1995)

It is a mistake to see terrorism as a publicity stunt. It is rooted in desperation and a deep-seated anger against a more powerful force. The media increase the effectiveness of such actions by amplifying the message to the point where none of the parties can ignore it. It is understandable that those who carry out such acts will do everything in their power to ensure that they get the maximum amount of coverage for their actions.

The Hamas message

At this stage in Oslo Peace process, the leaders of Hamas were sending a very different message to the Israeli people than the PLO leadership. As one Palestinian leader put it: "We [PLO] are sending a message of peace, while they [Hamas] are sending a message of war." The Hamas people we spoke to put it differently. There were telling the Israelis that Hamas could not be ignored, the only way to send that message, they contend, is through military actions:

> The military actions are just a means of getting the message across to the Israeli society to get the minimal conditions of Hamas. Our message is clear. The military actions come in order to pressure the Israeli decision makers to pay attention to what we say and to hear our opinions and our demands. We want Israeli citizens to come to a conclusion that there will be no peace without negotiating with the Hamas movement. (O25; June 8, 1995)

As noted, most Israelis believe that the major goal of Hamas is to destroy the state of Israel. It is hardly surprising, then, that this movement

---

[16] Surveys show a dramatic increase in the amount of support for the "armed struggle against Israel" after the outbreak of the Second Intifada. For a list of surveys carried out among the Palestinians see the website of Palestinian Center for Policy and Survey Research (http://www.pcpsr.org).

has little success in promoting their frames to the Israeli press. Hamas rarely deals with the issue of Israel's right to exist in public interviews, preferring to focus on the evils of Israeli occupation. The very use of the word "occupation" serves to obscure their position on this issue for it is not clear if they are referring to the occupation of the territories taken in 1967 or all of what is now considered Israel. One of the more moderate leaders of the movement provided a more detailed view:

> I'm willing, as a representative of Hamas, to come to any agreement with the Israelis about an Israeli withdrawal from the West Bank, East Jerusalem, and the dismantling of the settlements, and holding elections. Then there will really be two states for two people. On this basis I'm willing to have with you *hudna* [Arabic word that refers to a ceasefire as the prophet Muhammad would have with those who fought with him]. Among the Palestinians there is a very wide consensus around this demand. Hamas will not recognize Israel as an existing state but will have a *hudna* with her for say, twenty years. (O36; February 27, 1995)

It would be probably have been hard to find Israelis who even knew about this idea at the time. Even if they did know about it, Israelis would have rejected it. Nevertheless, considering the tremendous amount of publicity given to the movement, one would expect some attention to the Hamas position on this critical issue. Interestingly, Hamas and Islamic Jihad did declare a three-month *hudna* in the summer of 2003, which was the first serious ceasefire to be initiated since the outbreak of the Second Intifada in the fall of 2000. One problem with coming into the media from the back door is that journalists are interested in what you do and not in what you say.

The Hamas movement is only newsworthy as a terrorist organization. Coverage of Hamas was centered on the likelihood of terrorism, the terrorist acts themselves, the consequences of terrorism, and what the Israelis and Palestinians were doing to stop it. Any contacts between Israeli reporters and the Hamas leaders naturally center on this issue and any other views or actions are left on the editorial floor. Everything is seen through the editorial prism of terrorism. Hamas is a religious movement but this is only relevant in terms of how such fanaticism leads to suicide bombers. Hamas also carries out many educational and social services in the territories. Here too the only reason for the Israeli media to cover this aspect of the organization is if it can be linked to the overall effort against Israel.

As discussed above, the Hamas people we spoke to believe that the Israeli media are tools for carrying out the policies of the Zionist state. The negative image of the Palestinians is seen as an important component of that policy.

> The black image of the Palestinians in the Israeli press is inseparable from the Zionist policy against the Palestinian people. They want to instill in the young generation of Zionists a horrible picture of the Palestinian in order to justify the murderous actions they carry out against us. They want to wipe the Palestinians out of the collective consciousness and memory of the Jewish people, just as the Americans did to the Indians, so it won't trouble their conscience. (O20; February 10, 1995)

The members of Hamas with whom we spoke seemed to have conflicting views about how they were treated in the Israeli press. Some statements showed anger about the Israeli media propagating the image of Hamas as a terrorist movement. Other comments were more detached, suggesting that Hamas does not care what Israelis think about them. An editor of a Hamas newspaper gave a good example of the latter type of comment.

> Israel and Hamas are in a state of war. Therefore I don't expect the Israeli press to praise their enemies or to describe them objectively. The same is true about the Islamic press. The Islamic press for example doesn't use the expression "state of Israel." I'll never use that expression, but rather the Israeli invaders and occupiers or the Israeli entity. Similarly I can't say that the Prime Minister of Israel said so and so, rather I'll use expressions like the head of the Zionist entity or the terrorist Rabin. Therefore I am not surprised and don't expect anything different from the Israeli press when it describes the actions of the Islamic movement. There is a war between the two sides and it is a normal situation of mutual degradation. (O17; June 8, 1995)

The Israeli journalists who cover the Palestinian beat generally conform to Israeli public opinion on the issue of Hamas. After Oslo there was a tendency to portray the PLO as the moderates and Hamas as the new enemy. Those who attempted to present a more complex picture found themselves running into problems with their editors. One of the more leftist journalists described some of these pressures.

I have tens of examples where they cut out things that I write. There was once a sermon in a Mosque where the Imam said: "They say that we hurt Jews because they're Jews, and it's not true. We're not racists, we only hurt those that occupy us." So they [the editors] took that out of my story. In my newspaper it's the desk editors, I mean it's an internalization of the general attitude in the society. The official line is: "We'll present the positive things about Arafat, we'll represent the PLO as all right, and we'll present the Hamas as not all right." (O26; March 31, 1996)

Here, too, there is a certain amount of variance among the journalists we spoke to concerning coverage of Hamas. Nevertheless, due to the hostility towards Hamas within Israel, the range of opinions is much narrower. It is one thing to be suspected of sympathy for the Palestinian people, it is quite another to give aid and support to terrorists dedicated to the destruction of the state.

It is also difficult to separate professional considerations and political ones. Because Hamas is only newsworthy as a threat, journalists can only compete with one another by finding evidence of such a threat. As in any good horror story, the aim of such reporting is to frighten people. This entails finding the most radical speaker possible or filming the scariest part of any gathering. Typical pictures of Hamas rallies center on the burning of Israeli flags and young men in white gowns vowing to become human bombs.[17] This pattern was part of the coverage of the Palestinian leadership, but at the time it was balanced by more routine news coverage dealing with negotiations and diplomacy. This search for frightening material can be illustrated by listening to one journalist explain why they report on Hamas even if such coverage may serve to increase the movement's standing.

We are working for the public's right to know. That's the principle that guides us. Not who it serves or doesn't serve. If Hamas says, for example, that the Jews are pigs or pigs' feces, and things like that, then the public in Israel should know what these people think about them. Does that mean that you are serving their [Hamas's] interest? There's a very fine line here. If there are very serious anti-Semitic manifestations within the Hamas and the Islamic Jihad

---

[17] This should be seen as a cooperative production, for some of this theater is no doubt *intended* to scare Israelis. One can only wonder if those who organize these events rush home to watch the show on the Israeli news.

movements, if there are anti-Semitic publications, that's a reason not to publish them? Because it might serve their interest? . . . In these kinds of things you should present them without a lot of interpretation, let the thing speak for itself. Of course we try to ensure that it will remain in the boundaries of good taste. (O27; May 6, 1996)

As with any enemy, the Israeli media image of Hamas is a simplistic one. It is a frightening terrorist organization whose only goal is the destruction of Israel. Given the circumstances, this was about the "best" coverage the political opposition in the territories could achieve. Hamas could exploit their status as spoilers to increase their internal and external political standing. The only alternative was to be condemned to obscurity. This is exactly what happened to Hamas during the often long periods between terrorist attacks. The movement simply disappeared from the Israeli arena. As far as the Israeli press was concerned, the movement no longer existed. Unless Hamas was going to pay the entrance dues, it would be left outside.

LESSONS ABOUT ENEMIES IN THE NEWS MEDIA

The ways in which the news media relate to the enemy is an important element in any attempts at reconciliation. The more threatening the images of the enemy, the less likely the public will be willing to move forward. It is true that a successful peace process is not solely based on questions of mutual trust. Cold calculations about national interests also play a part in leaders' considerations. Nevertheless, in democracies the amount of political latitude leaders have for making concessions is directly related to public perceptions about enemy intentions. As the news media are the central source of information about the other side, they can play a critical role in defining such perceptions.

As emphasized, media frames of the enemy are constructed within a particular political context. It is important to examine both long-term and short-term changes in the political climate in order to understand how media images can vary. There were two major historical changes that took place during the period that was examined in the content analysis. The first was the growing recognition that the Palestinians must be recognized as a separate people and as independent actors. This change in political status led to a significant change in media status such that the Israeli news media devote much more time and space to the Palestinian story. The second change centered on the peace process that began during the Madrid talks in 1992 and received its greatest boost at the time of the Rabin government. The initiation of that process provided the Israeli media with a completely new framework for dealing with the Palestinians. For the first time the Israeli public was continually exposed to intelligent, reasonable Palestinians who offered at least the possibility of peace between the two peoples. Thus, by the 1990s, there were two competing media frames of the Palestinians that complemented the two broader cultural frames. The threatening image of the Palestinians served to reinforce the Security First frame; the major issue was how Israel could best protect itself from its enemies. The less threatening images of diplomats, on the other hand, served to augment the Peace frame, which suggested that peace was not only worthwhile, but also possible.

It was never, however, an even competition. As has been repeatedly said throughout this study, threats and violence will always be more newsworthy than peace and reconciliation. This fact provided important incentives and advantages to those opposed to peace. Hamas and Islamic Jihad were extremely successful at bringing back the old image of the Palestinian terrorist. Although the Israeli media did make some early efforts at differentiating between the various groups, the previously discussed case of Beit Lid demonstrates just how quickly such distinctions can disappear. It should also be remembered that the competition between the two approaches begins with the Security First frame well in front. Years of distrust and hate are extremely difficult to change and each new outbreak of violence and death leaves a fresh set of scars. The durability of the Security First frame can be attributed to the simple fact that fear is a more primal emotion than hope. This explains why fear is such a central component of all news, especially sensationalist news. A peace process is extremely fragile and so are the media frames that can be used to promote it.

The Hebrew news media are constructed for Jewish Israelis and are inherently ethnocentric in orientation. Even the quality newspaper *Ha'aretz* exclusively employs Jewish journalists to write about Palestinian affairs. This newspaper was somewhat more open to the Palestinian sources, but the amount of space devoted to that group's problems remained extremely small. The public deliberation over what to "do about the Palestinians" remains an essentially internal debate about what "we" should do about "them."

The most the Palestinians could hope for in those circumstances was to convince the Israeli press that peace is possible. This, in turn, is only likely to take place when all of the planets are lined up together. It depends on having an Israeli government actively promoting peace, the opposition from both sides refraining from any violence, and an atmosphere in which the concessions being offered appeared reasonable to most Israelis (and Palestinians). Should any of these factors fall out of place, the Israeli news media quickly return the default mode for covering the enemy. This is exactly what happened in the fall of the year 2000, with the outbreak of the Second Intifada. This deterioration will be discussed at length in chapter 7.

This chapter began by asking whether or not an active peace process improves media images of the enemy. The answer to that question is "yes, however . . ." One does find certain improvements, especially because of the change in news slots. The increase focus on "the peace process" as a major issue introduced an alternative template for covering Palestinians. There was also an increasing willingness to treat Palestinians as independent actors and to allow them to speak. The process did not, however, have much of an effect on the willingness of the Israeli press to deal with the plight of the Palestinians. In addition, the security threat remained the central element of that story, especially because Palestinian terrorism continued to plague the relations between the two sides.

It might well be argued, however, that the peace process with the Palestinians is not necessarily the best case to examine these issues. This process was, after all, continually plagued by violence and never enjoyed a high level of political consensus within Israel. Which brings us to look at the role of the news media in the very different peace process that took place between Israel and Jordan.

CHAPTER 5

The media and the Israel–Jordan peace process[1]

This chapter departs from the previous ones in three important ways. First, the peace process between Jordan and Israel was very different than Oslo. It was shorter, more congenial, and ultimately more successful. Second, the fact that a formal peace agreement was signed between the two countries allows us to explore the role of the news media in building peace after such accords have been signed. Finally, this part of the study also includes evidence taken from a very different type of media environment. Collaboration with a Jordanian counterpart provided important insights about the values and routines that were adopted by the Jordanian journalists during this period and about changes in coverage of Israel.

As always, it is important to begin this analysis by considering the political environment surrounding the peace process. Jordan and Israel have always had a rather complex and unusual relationship that differs from Israel's relations with other Arab states or peoples. Although the countries fought two wars against each other (1948 and 1967) and a war of attrition in the period 1968–70, both maintained back-door communication and cooperation channels, especially during times of crisis. Each country had its own reasons for maintaining this tacit understanding.

Jordan's attitude towards Israel can be better understood within the context of Jordan's regional and global priorities (Abu-Odeh, 1999). Historically, Jordan and its Hashemite leadership have successfully adapted to the need to coexist with two important movements in the modern Middle East – Islamism and Zionism – both of which have engaged in occasional armed conflicts or longer-running verbal battles with Jordan.

[1] The research for this chapter was carried out together with Rami Khouri of the *Jordanian Times* and Yoram Peri of Hebrew University. It was funded by the Turner Fund for Peace through the auspices of the Truman Institute of the Hebrew University.

The more serious modern threats to Jordan have emanated from other sources, especially Communism, Nasserite pan-Arabism, Ba'athism and other leftist movements that challenged Jordan's role in the Arab East Mediterranean region.

Israel's attitudes towards Jordan are also complex. Jordan shares the longest border with Israel and its military forces were the closest Arab forces to Israel's major cities. Until 1967, Jordan also controlled the eastern part of Jerusalem, which prevented Jews from gaining access to the Western Wall. On the other hand, Israel always saw Jordan as the most moderate of her Arab neighbors and as a political and geographic bulwark against her more extreme enemies such as Syria and Iraq. Israelis also had a remarkably favorable opinion of the late King Hussein. The King was considered an extremely charismatic leader who exuded trust and a genuine desire for peace.

The Palestinian issue has always played a major part in Israel–Jordanian relations. Massive numbers of Palestinian refugees fled to Jordan during the wars in 1948 and 1967, a fact that had a devastating impact on the country. In the 1970s and 1980s the Jordanian leadership feared that an Israeli plan to transfer Palestinians from the West Bank to the East Bank would result in Jordan becoming a Palestinian state, at the expense of the Hashemites and the interests of Transjordanians. This helps explain why the large number of Palestinians living in Jordan has been a source of both conflict and cooperation between the two countries. The fact that so many Jordanians are either Palestinian or related to Palestinians means that every Israeli and Palestinian clash inevitably leads to an increase in tension between Israel and Jordan. At the same time both Israel and Jordan often feel threatened by dynamic manifestations of Palestinian nationalism and self-determination.

All of which brings us to the process that culminated in a peace treaty between Israel and Jordan in October of 1994. Here, too, it is impossible to separate the ups and downs of the Israel–Palestinian conflict and the relations between Israel and Jordan. It was the initial breakthrough at Oslo that provided the impetus for Israel and Jordan to initiate serious negotiations. These talks were exceedingly rapid and cordial, in part because there were few territorial issues to resolve. The mood at the signing ceremony was euphoric as King Hussein, Prime Minister Rabin, and President Clinton all expressed hopes that the agreement would facilitate a period of reconciliation between the two peoples.

The surrounding political environment for this agreement was very different in the two countries. In Israel there was an enormous amount of support for the agreement in Israel. Whereas the Knesset was completely split over the Oslo accords with the Palestinians, the Jordanian agreement passed by a vote of 92 to 3. The level of elite support in Jordan was considerably lower. Although King Hussein was able to use his prestige and power to mobilize support for the accords, a number of political parties and institutions were opposed to making peace with Israel. This opposition in Jordan became even more prominent when the Israeli–Palestinian peace process ran into troubles. The establishment of a right-wing government that followed the election of Israeli Prime Minister Netanyahu in May of 1996 served to galvanize the opponents in Jordan. The relatively short period of time between the optimism associated with the signing in the fall of 1994 and the pessimism that marked the Netanyahu period (1996–99) provides an excellent case for examining how quickly the environment can change and with it the nature of media coverage.

Thus, the political environment in Israel was conducive to peace, while the Jordanian environment was more negative. Based on this alone, we would expect the leadership in Israel to find it easier to promote peace than the leaders in Jordan. However, as discussed, the media environments in which journalists work also influences the construction of news about peace. What proved interesting about this case was that in both countries factors in the media environment pulled coverage in very different directions than those that characterized the political environments.

THE MEDIA ENVIRONMENT IN JORDAN

The most important differences between these two media environments concern the amount of government control. The Jordanian news media have traditionally presented government viewpoints on domestic and foreign issues, although they have enjoyed more pluralism in news reporting and opinion/analysis since 1989. The government has always owned and managed the television, radio and news agency services, all of which see their role primarily as presenting the government viewpoint on public issues. The official press has limited credibility, suffers from erratic standards and low levels of training, and has seen some of its audience drift away to more credible or entertaining commercial media in recent years. Nevertheless it still has a fairly wide audience because of the fact that it announces official news and covers local events.

The Jordanian government traditionally guided the editorial coverage of privately owned publications, by requiring them to obtain a government-issued license that could be suspended or revoked if publications technically broke the law or veered too far from the state line. There are four Arabic-language dailies today, an English daily and a weekly, and around fifteen weekly newspapers, which are largely ideological or purely profit-motivated.

As noted, strict government controls of the press have been liberalized somewhat since 1989, due to domestic demands for more freedom and also to the impact of competition from satellite television channels and other sources of news that the state could not control. The state has taken scores of journalists and publications to court in the past nine years, but in many cases the courts have decided in favor of the press and against the state. Thus a new balance of power, freedom, rights and responsibilities is slowly being established in Jordan between the private press and the state. The privately owned print media continue to offer a wider range of dissenting opinions than the state-owned media.

Another important factor to understand about the media environment in Jordan concerns the Press Association. This organization joined the other professional associations in criticizing the peace treaty with Israel and continually threatens to punish journalists who "normalize" relations with Israelis. If a Jordanian journalist goes to Israel to cover a story, he risks being thrown out of the organization and thus not being able to work in that profession. On the other hand, it is worth noting that many consider the Press Association a relatively weak body with only a minimal amount of professional impact or standing.

Thus, while the Israeli news media are closer to what one would find in most democracies, the Jordanian model is more of a hybrid between a developed and developing state. While the press in both countries has become more independent over the years, the change in Jordan is both more recent and more moderate. In addition, while the emphasis on drama is an important consideration for all news media, it appears to be a more central factor in explaining the construction of news in Israel. As we shall show, these differences had an important impact on the construction of news about peace in the two countries.

The discussion will be divided into two major sections. The first attempts to explain the coverage of Israel in Jordan and the second part deals with news about Jordan that appeared in Israel. As before, the findings are based on two methodologies: in-depth interviews and content analyses.[2] The first method provides evidence about the values and

---

[2] For details beyond what is presented in the text, see methodological appendix.

routines journalists employ for covering the "other side," while the second tells us about variations in coverage between countries and over time.

THE COVERAGE OF ISRAEL IN JORDAN

The first stage of the research in Jordan involved interviews with editors and journalists who were responsible for constructing news stories about Israel. These sessions were held in 1997, when the peace agreement between the two countries had already been in place for over two years. The interviewer was himself a senior journalist in Jordan with many years of experience in both the print media and television.[3] This not only enhanced the value of these sessions but also ensured that his sources would be more open in discussing their professional dilemmas in covering Israel.

The political environment concerning Israel was fairly negative at the time of the interviews. Benyamin Netanyahu had already been elected Prime Minister, and there had been increasing anger within the Arab world about (what they saw) as Israel's belligerency towards the Palestinians. King Hussein, however, was still committed to the peace process and prohibited any overtly aggressive news stories about Israel. Thus the Jordanian journalists found themselves working under a number of cross-pressures in covering Israel. On the one hand, they were attempting to reflect the mostly negative attitude of their audience. At the same time, the government expected them to help in promoting the peace process. One columnist and editor described these pressures as follows:

> We tend to get conflicting pressures from different sources in society; the government mildly pushes us to promote peace and normalization with Israel, while the opposition, professional associations, and parts of the public at large pressure us against normalization of ties with Israelis. We have to be careful because in some cases the professional unions will expel members for dealing with Israelis, and this could mean the loss of a job. We do feel the pressures for and against normalizing ties with Israel, but we also devise ways to deal with them. (J9)

The professional norms of Jordanian journalists, then, call for meeting the needs of their audience without overly antagonizing the government.

---

[3] I am referring to my fellow researcher: Rami Khouri.

The safest strategy in this situation is to stick to a dry, factual reporting of events, a point that will become clearer in the content analysis. There can be little doubt, however, that if it were not for these government limitations, the coverage of Israel would have been even more negative. Indeed, some journalists see their coverage as part of the more general struggle against Israel. That same editor put it this way:

> We cannot treat Israel like Nigeria or South Africa or some other foreign story. People in Jordan want to see and to show the negative aspects of Israel, because the conflict is not settled yet and people use their perceptions of Israel as a means of fighting Israel. Many distorted facts form the basis of commentaries about Israel in the Arabic-language press, which simply confirms the public's willingness or even its desire to see the negative side of Israel. (J9)

Similarly, the editor of a weekly newspaper put it even more bluntly:

> The full scope and complexity of Israeli society are not adequately represented in our paper, because we prefer to cover the negative aspects of Israel, we avoid using positive news, and sometimes we even exaggerate a little bit about aspects of Israel, like portraying the far-right fringe extremists in Israel as part of the mainstream. (J4)

These last quotes demonstrate that one cannot understand the construction of news about enemies without taking into account *both* the political and the media environments. The fact that many of the events associated with the Netanyahu period were negative, and that the mood had turned pessimistic is one part of the story. However, it is the professional norms and routines that determine how journalists turn these inputs into news stories. Jordanian editors were constantly trying to produce a product that enjoys the maximum appeal to their anti-Israel public without overly antagonizing the pro-peace government.

Which brings us back to the major questions raised in the last chapter: did the establishment of a peace process have significant and lasting influence on media coverage in Jordan? A content analysis was carried out on a sample of newspaper articles that were published in two different Jordanian newspapers. The newspapers selected from Jordan were *Al-Ra'i* and *Addustour*, respectively with majority and minority government shareholdings. Both are full-size, serious dailies that diligently reflect government thinking in their editorials and official news coverage. Nevertheless, they also provide a wide variety of pro- and anti-government views in their op-ed pages and cartoons. *Al-Ra'i* has traditionally been seen as the semi-official newspaper of the government while *Addustour* has a more independent, pro-Palestinian reputation.

Three periods were chosen in order to examine the influence of changing political climate on media coverage. The first period – from October 1992 to September 1993 – was a time before there were any negotiations between Israel and Jordan. The second year – from October 1994 to September 1995 – was chosen to represent the "peace year." The peace agreement between the two countries was signed on October 24, 1994 and thus this was an exceptionally positive time for Israel–Jordanian relations. The third and final period ("post-peace agreement") ran from October 1996 to September 1997, after Prime Minister Netanyahu had taken office. As noted, this was a time of increasing tension between the countries, in part because of Israel's ongoing conflict with the Palestinians. Fifty dates from each year were randomly selected and all articles in each country that dealt with the other side were analyzed.

A coding sheet was developed that looked at two major variables: the general topic area of the news story and the overall valence (evaluative direction) of the story. Based on an extensive pretest, it was found that the stories could be divided into six topic categories that were applicable in both countries: stories having to do with the peace process and/or normalization between the two countries; political and economic meetings/relations; multilateral relations (Jordan/Israel and others); the foreign policy of Jordan/Israel; security issues related to Jordan/Israel; and the internal affairs of the other. This division into topics was intended to provide evidence about the prominence of various news slots over time and political circumstance.

The stories were also divided into three evaluative categories in order to gauge the overall valence of the story: positive, neutral, and negative. Making such distinctions in content analysis is never easy, but coders in both countries were given instructions that increased the reliability of the coding. They were asked to consider the perspective of the average Jordanian or Israeli. Was the news story they had read more likely to leave a more positive impression about the other country, a more negative one, or neither? If the answer was neither, or if they were at all unsure about the answer, they were asked to code the story as neutral.

It was understood that this measure would only provide a rough estimate concerning the valence of news stories about the other side. Negative stories concerning violence, for example, are likely to have more impact than negative stories about a problematic meeting between Israel and

Table 5.1 *Coverage valence of Israel in Jordan during three time periods*

	Overall Evaluation			
Period	Negative	Neutral	Positive	Total
Pre-Peace Agreement	56	126	16	**198**
(1992–93)	(28.3%)	(63.6%)	(8.1%)	
Peace Year	45	224	96	**365**
(1994–95)	(12.3%)	(61.4%)	(26.3%)	
Post-Peace Agreement	121	144	15	**280**
(1996–97)	(43.2%)	(51.4%)	(5.4%)	
Total	222	494	127	**843**
	(26.3%)	(58.6%)	(15.1%)	

Jordanian leaders. On the other hand, the power of a negative and positive story was partially reflected in the number of different articles that appear about it. Thus, while this indicator is not intended to be a definitive measure of the media image of the other, it does tell us something about the overall tone of such coverage and how it changed over time.[4]

The analysis starts by looking at the proportion of negative, neutral, and positive news stories that were published during the different periods. We assumed that the coverage would be notably more positive during the peace year, when the political climate was so positive. The more interesting question was how far Israel's image would retreat after this initial burst of enthusiasm. If peace did have a lasting effect, we would expect to find images to be less negative after peace than before. As can be seen in table 5.1, this is certainly not the case.

These findings suggest that the formal inauguration of peace had no lasting effects on Israel's media image in Jordan. As expected, there was a significant increase in the amount of positive news about Israel during the euphoria of 1994–95. The proportion of positive stories rose from 8 percent to 26 percent and the proportion of negative stories dropped from 28 percent to 12 percent. This is indeed a serious change. A closer look reveals that a good deal of this change took place in the first few months during the more celebratory stage. King Hussein and Prime Minister Rabin worked closely together during those months to initiate as many events as possible. The goal was to promote the new peace to

---

[4] Further details about the content analysis can be found in the methodological appendix.

both populations. The proportion of negative stories about Israel and the peace process already began to rise during the second part of that period.

More importantly, none of this positive outlook carried over into the Netanyahu year (post-peace agreement). If anything, the situation was even *worse* than it was before peace was inaugurated. The proportion of negative stories about Israel rose to an extremely high 43 percent. These results make clear that the effects of the political climate on media coverage also take place within a more controlled media environment. The fact that Jordanian journalists reflect the prevailing political atmosphere also came through in the interviews we conducted. A television manager and reporter put it this way:

> The importance of stories from Israel fluctuates according to the news and the mood of the day. I remember when the peace agreement was signed we planned to do some cooperative television work with Israelis, such as parallel documentaries and joint programs; this was one of the fruits of peace. We started working together in 1996, but then we stopped after the Jerusalem tunnel incident, Abu Ghneim (Har Homa) and other such events angered us. Our judgment changed about working with Israelis when their policies turned aggressive, especially after Netanyahu's election. (J6)

Thus the fact that King Hussein and Yitzhak Rabin signed a peace treaty did little to improve the basic attitude of the Jordanian press towards Israel. It is also possible that the fact that Israel's media image got even worse can be attributed to dashed expectations. The two leaders may have made a strategic mistake in placing such a large emphasis on the benefits that would come with peace. In subsequent months, the conventional wisdom was that Jordanians were "disappointed" that they never saw the "fruits of the peace." In any case, the most direct reason for this reversal was the extremely negative reaction in Jordan to Netanyahu's policies concerning the Palestinians.

It is also worth taking note that most news stories about Israel fall into the neutral category. It is at least possible that this is one of the ways Jordanian editors deal with the cross-pressures described earlier.

Finally, there is another insight to be learned from table 5.1 that will become even more important when the discussion turns to the Israeli media. Israel was and remains an extremely important news story in Jordan. Israel is considered a major threat to Jordan and the Palestinians and this leads to a high level of media attention. It will be remembered that a total of 150 identical dates were chosen in each country. In Jordan this led to a total of 837 news stories about Israel. In other words, there are an average of five and a half stories about Israel on any given day in the two newspapers that were studied. This is a remarkable amount of attention that both reflects and reinforces the salience of Israel within the political culture of Jordan.

CHANGES IN NEWS SLOTS

It was argued earlier that one of the reasons it is so difficult to promote peace to the news media has to do with definitions of newsworthiness. The emphasis on drama, it was claimed, means that editors will be more interested in conflict stories than those that deal with cooperation. In addition, the fundamental ethnocentrism of most news media means that journalists will have little interest in learning about the internal affairs of the other side. There is little reason to believe that the initiation of a peace process should change this basic dynamic in the long run. One way to explore this issue is to examine the effects of peace on the prominence of various news slots. This allows us to move beyond questions about general tone of the news and deal with the more specific issue of what was actually covered.

One of the first things that emerged from this analysis was the extremely small percentage of news stories in Jordan that dealt with the internal affairs of Israel. Despite the enormous amount of attention devoted to dealing with Israel, less than 1 percent of all news stories dealt with this topic. We also found no change in this situation after the inauguration of peace between the two countries. This finding is a perfect illustration of the overall ethnocentrism of the news media.[5] It is also an accurate reflection of how Jordanian journalists use the media as a tool of conflict. Thus, for many years the Jordanian press would not even use the word "Israel."

This problem of ethnocentrism also emerged in the interviews that were carried out prior to the content analysis. Even those Jordanian journalists who supported the peace process with Israel were unable to modify basic definitions of newsworthiness. Here are the comments of a senior Jordanian journalist (and government employee) responsible for television coverage:

---

[5] It is also worth noting that very few Jordanian journalists have any working knowledge of the Hebrew language.

Israel gets more than enough coverage in the Jordanian media, but the coverage is one-dimensional, mainly linked to the Arab–Israeli issues; we do not provide our readers with sufficiently deep or wide coverage of Israeli society as a whole. We need to understand Israelis better, if we want the peace process to succeed. (J1)

Despite the basic ethnocentrism of the news media, one would still expect the initiation of peace to influence the prominence of various news slots. Thus, the very fact that journalists are assigned to cover negotiations should provide leaders from both sides with an opportunity to convey encouraging information about the process. The initiation of cooperative efforts between former enemies should also provide a new angle for news coverage. We decided to look at this issue by asking two questions. First we wanted to know how much positive and negative news was generally associated with different news topics. The assumption was that certain topics were more likely to bring negative news about the other side than others. We calculated a rough "valence score" based on the percentage of positive stories appearing about a certain topic minus the percentage of negative stories. Thus a positive score indicates that news stories in a particular category were more likely to paint the other side in a sympathetic light while negative scores suggested more hostile images.[6] In table 5.2 we present the valence of each of the various news slots and the changes in prominence of each topic over time. The extremely infrequent category of internal affairs was removed in order to simplify the table.

The first thing to note is that the most frequent category has to do with Israel's relations with others (multilateral relations). It is also the most negative slot for news about Israel. Looking over the actual headlines, one finds that the vast majority of these stories have to do with the on-going Israeli–Palestinian conflict. This did not come as a surprise. Given the centrality of the Palestinian issue within Jordan, it is only natural that a good deal of the news about Israel revolves around this conflict.

---

[6] These valence scores were created in order to reduce the overall number of tables. In addition, due to the rather small numbers of articles in some of the categories, it was decided not to detail the changes in valence over time for each category. This would have been especially problematic with regard to the Israeli data, where the overall number of stories is even smaller. Here are the actual percentages of negative, neutral, and positive stories associated with each news slot: Multilateral Relations (35.7/57.6/6.8), Peace Process Normalization (34.6/50/15.4), Diplomatic and Economic Relations (9.9/61.3/28.7), Israel's Foreign Policy (12.5/77.8/9.7), Security Issues (6.9/62.1/31).

Table 5.2 *Valence of Jordanian news slots about Israel and prominence during three periods*

	News Slots					
Valence Scores Period	Multilateral Relations −28.9	Peace Process and Normalization −19.2	Diplomatic and Economic Relations +18.8	Israel's Foreign Policy −2.4	Security Issues +24	Total
Pre-Peace	125	30	15	22	2	**194**
Agreement	(64.5%)	(15.5%)	(7.7%)	(11.3%)	(1%)	
(1992–93)						
Peace Year	86	118	109	23	20	**356**
(1994–95)	(24.2%)	(33.1%)	(30.6%)	(6.5%)	(5.6%)	
Post-Peace	100	80	57	27	7	**271**
Agreement	(36.9%)	(29.5%)	(21%)	(10%)	(2.6%)	
(1996–97)						
Total	**311**	**228**	**181**	**72**	**29**	**821**
	(37.9%)	**(27.8%)**	**(22%)**	**(8.8%)**	**(3.5%)**	

The ongoing confrontation between the Israelis and the Palestinians provides two of the most important criteria for news: drama and relevance. The most dramatic aspects of this relationship also tend to be the most negative.

The second most prominent topic for news about Israel had to do with the peace process between the two countries and the issue of normalization. One is struck by the surprisingly negative valence of this category. Looking at the actual numbers behind the score one finds that there are over twice as many negative stories (79) than positive stories that fall into this category (35). Thus, there is nothing inherently optimistic about this news slot. While it is true that the prominence of this topic provided important opportunities for the pro-peace government in Jordan, it also provided opportunities for those opposed to the process, including some of the journalists. Because so many Jordanians are opposed to normalization with Israel this category turns out to be one of the more negative areas of news.

Nevertheless, as discussed earlier, pessimistic stories about a peace process are better than negative stories that focus on conflict. News items that deal with tensions between the two countries are less likely to rouse passions than pieces that report on violent confrontations between Israel and the Palestinians.[7] Jordanians are unlikely, for example, to take to the streets because of a dispute over trade agreements. The change in political context that is associated with a peace process does have an influence on "what is at issue." A debate about whether or not to make peace or to normalize relations with Israel is quite different than a dispute about how to defeat her.

The most positive news slot with a significant number of news stories has to do with the ongoing meetings and economic relations between the two countries.[8] As can be seen there is a dramatic rise in these types of stories during the peace year. The two governments no doubt promoted many of these items in an effort to convince the Jordanian people about the benefits of peace. This again demonstrates how a change in the formal relations between the two countries created news slots that were unavailable in the past. Journalists adapt themselves to such changes by developing new routines for covering such stories. As can be seen, however, two years later these types of news stories became less frequent.

They also became decidedly more negative (not shown). The proportion of positive stories about these topics dropped from 41 percent during the peace year to 12 percent during the Netanyahu Year; the proportion of negative stories rose from a mere 3 percent to 26 percent. The reasons for these changes were made clear in the interviews with Jordanian journalists. First, cooperation between the two countries was no longer considered novel, especially when compared to the increasing tensions between Israel and the Palestinians. Second, positive stories about such cooperation were considered less appropriate given the change in the political climate. Negative stories about the relations between the two countries were more likely to resonate with an increasingly hostile Jordanian public.

In sum, the evidence provides little evidence that the inauguration of peace between the two countries had any lasting influence on Israel's image in the Jordanian media. Although there was a dramatic improvement during the first year of peace, the press again became antagonistic after Netanyahu was elected to office. Indeed, if not for government controls,

---

[7] Needless to say, it was just such stories that became the major focus for Jordanian news coverage after the outbreak of the Second Intifada.

[8] The "Security" category has an even higher valence score, but very few news stories fall into this grouping.

the Jordanian press probably would have been in the vanguard of those trying to derail the peace process. This latter point suggests a disconcerting inconsistency between the desires to achieve peace and to maintain freedom of the press: a truly free press in Jordan might have made peace between the two countries that much more difficult.

The one important exception to this generally negative conclusion has to do with the creation of news slots that were unavailable before the inauguration of peace. The nature of the Jordanian debate about Israel did change and this is well reflected in journalistic routines. While the creation of such slots does not ensure positive coverage of the other side, they could lead to a certain change in the public's frames of reference.

THE COVERAGE OF JORDAN IN ISRAEL

As discussed, the political environment surrounding the peace process in Israel was very different than the situation in Jordan. There was an extremely high level of consensus surrounding the accords. Officials from the government who were interviewed at the time talked about how much easier it was to promote the Jordanian process than Oslo (Wolfsfeld, 1997b). It was also clear that Israeli journalists were only too happy to participate in the festivities.

Thus, peace with Jordan began from an unusually positive position. The major question however remains the same. Did the inauguration of peace with Jordan have a significant and lasting impact on media coverage of that country in Israel? The findings with regard to this question can be found in table 5.3.

The results suggest that if the peace process did have any effects on media coverage, they were small. In many ways the most striking finding concerns the *lack* of news about Jordan in Israel. The same sample of 150 days led to almost five times as many stories in the two Jordanian newspapers than appeared in Israel. This asymmetry in the importance each side attributes to the other is reinforced when one looks at the placement of the news stories in the two countries (not shown). Whereas a remarkably high 47 percent of all stories about Israel appear on page 1 of the Jordanian newspapers, only 13 percent of the stories about Jordan were placed on the front page in Israel. Israel is an important story in Jordan; Jordan is a marginal story in Israel. There is no indication that peace had any influence on this difference.

The reasons for Jordan's lack of salience in Israel's media environment are instructive. Traditionally Syria and Egypt were considered more

Table 5.3 *Coverage valence of Jordan in Israel during three time periods*

Period	Overall Evaluation			
	Negative	Neutral	Positive	Total
Pre-Peace Agreement	19	7	9	**35**
(1992–93)	(54.3%)	(20%)	(25.7%)	
Peace Year	21	20	51	**92**
(1994–95)	(22.8%)	(21.7%)	(55.4%)	
Post-Peace Agreement	20	8	16	**44**
(1996–97)	(45.5%)	(18.2%)	(36.4%)	
Total	**60**	**35**	**76**	**171**
	(35.1%)	**(20.5%)**	**(44.4%)**	

powerful and more hostile, and the confrontation with the Palestinians has dominated coverage for quite some time. Thus, the lower the threat, the less the media covers an enemy. It is interesting that the dominance of the Palestinian story *increases* the importance of the Israeli story in Jordan and yet *lowers* the salience of Jordan in Israel. One of the Israeli political reporters put it this way:

> The Palestinian issue is so acute that it drowns out everything else. In the Egyptian coverage there is an additional dimension because they see themselves as mediators concerning the Palestinian issue. Therefore it is only natural that the Egyptian coverage is more extensive. The Jordanian story is more on the margins, even though there is more empathy for the Jordanians, there's nothing to do. (J18)

This lack of interest is also reflected in the assignment of reporters. Most of the news organs have one specialist in Arab affairs who deals with all of the parties involved. Thus, unless something unusually newsworthy takes place in Jordan, there is no reason to divert attention from the usual stories. Even when these journalists are convinced that certain events justify a story, they find it difficult to sell it to their editors. A good example was provided by one of the Israeli reporters working for one of the national radio stations. In August 1996 there were two days of localized riots over the cost of bread in Kerak and other areas in south Jordan. One would have thought that this would have been a major story, yet the journalist had trouble convincing his editor to allow him to report on it. In a commercial media environment, professional definitions of newsworthiness take precedence.

One also finds little evidence that the formal establishment of a peace had much of an influence on the overall tone of coverage. It is true that as expected the image of Jordan in Israel is generally more positive than Israel's image in Jordan. There is also a dramatic increase in the number of stories about Jordan during the peace year, and 55 percent of these pieces are positive. The coverage during the post-peace agreement period, on the other hand, looks only marginally better than what was published before the peace process. There are still very few stories, and there are still more negative stories than positive ones. The fallback is not as severe as in Jordan, but given the very small number of articles, it is unlikely that such changes would have much of an impact on public images.

There is another interesting finding that emerges from comparing these results to what was found in Jordan. The proportion of "neutral" stories is much smaller in Israel than it is in Jordan. It is possible to come up with three reasonable explanations for this difference. The first has already been discussed: Jordanian journalists may adopt a more neutral style of reporting in order to deal with conflicting pressures they face from the government and the public. The second is that the Israeli media environment is more sensationalist than the one in Jordan and this leads to a greater emphasis on drama. The third explanation brings us back to Jordan's relatively low media status in Israel. Given that lack of interest only events that are especially positive or negative will pass the strict threshold of newsworthiness. Routine events, which are more likely to be neutral, are simply not covered.

The interviews with the Israeli journalists provide additional insights into this process. It is true that the amount and quality of access improved considerably after the establishment of peace: reporters could now contact Jordanian officials directly rather than depend on secondary sources. Yet, not a single one of the Israeli news media stationed a permanent correspondent in Jordan. After waiting fifty years for the opening of the borders between the two countries, there appears to be little need for an extended stay. Coverage of Jordan became episodic, and often negative. This type of coverage is typical of the ways in which the news media cover the political periphery (Van Dijk, 1996; Wolfsfeld, Avraham, and Aburaiya, 2000).

Consider, for example, the two most important news stories about Jordan that appeared in the Israeli press in 1997 – the last year that was studied. One, in March of that year, concerned a Jordanian soldier opening fire and killing seven Israeli schoolgirls who were on a class trip to a "peace park," which had been dedicated in honor of the agreement. The second took place in October and centered on a botched attempt by Israeli intelligence to kill a Hamas leader (and a Jordanian citizen) living in Amman. The second incident led to crisis between the two countries that also received a considerable amount of coverage.

There is an important lesson here concerning the role of the news media in efforts at building peace after the hoopla associated with signing ceremonies has died. Such ceremonies may mark the final dramatic act available for leaders to promote. After that, media attention will only be diverted if trouble should break out. Thus, the long-term picture for peace may be as bad as what was found in the short term: negative news about the other side will still be considered more newsworthy than positive news.

The power of such values becomes even more apparent when one considers that many Israeli journalists wanted to publicize more positive stories about Jordan. Many of them even went so far as to justify Jordan's complaints against their own country. This is an important lesson for those who see political bias as the primary variable explaining news coverage. When journalists are forced to choose between political considerations and professional ones, the latter normally win out. The fact that Israeli journalists want to promote better relations between the two countries is far less important than their need to produce interesting news stories. Their editors quickly put reporters who forget these principles in their place. Consider, for example, the comments made by of one of the newspaper reporters who covered the Arab beat:

> I would like to put in items about Jordan. There are wonderful acts by the King; the King gives wonderfully pro-Israeli speeches, very strong ones. I write about that but it doesn't get into the paper. The deputy editor vetoes many pro-Israeli stories about Jordan; they don't interest them [the editors]. Stories about Jordanian anti-Semitism will get in. (J16)

CHANGING NEWS SLOTS FOR JORDAN

Which brings us to the issue of news slots. The first thing to note is that, as in Jordan, the proportion of stories about the internal affairs of

Table 5.4 *Prominence of Israeli news slots about Jordan during three time periods*

	News Slots					
Valence Scores Period	Peace Process and Normalization +50.2	Meetings and Economic Relations +58.3	Multilateral Relations −44.5	Jordan's Foreign Policy −5.3	Security Issues −62.5	Total
Pre-Peace	3	3	8	12	6	**32**
Agreement	(9.4%)	(9.4%)	(25%)	(37.5%)	(18.8%)	
(1992–93)						
Peace Year	40	18	13	7	4	**82**
(1994–95)	(48.8%)	(22%)	(15.9%)	(8.5%)	(4.9%)	
Post-Peace	5	15	10	3	6	**39**
Agreement	(12.8%)	(38%)	(25.6%)	(7.7%)	(15.4%)	
(1996–97)						
Total	**48**	**36**	**31**	**22**	**16**	**153**
	(31.4%)	**(23.5%)**	**(20.3%)**	**(14.4%)**	**(10.5%)**	

the other side remains extremely small: less than 6 percent of all news stories that appeared in the two Israeli newspapers dealt with such topics. While this is a somewhat higher *proportion* than in Jordan, given the extremely small *number* of articles, very few Israelis are likely to notice them. This finding again demonstrates the inherent ethnocentrism of the news media.

Despite this, the formal inauguration of peace did have a notable effect on the prominence of certain news slots. The same analysis was that was carried out with regard to the Jordanian news was also carried out in Israel. The results are presented in table 5.4.

The first thing worth noting concerns the valence associated with each topic. The most negative context for news centers on two topics: Jordan's multilateral relations and security issues related to Jordan. This is understandable as both subjects are directly linked to the ongoing Arab–Israeli conflict. The findings also show that the most positive news slots have to do with the peace process and with the meetings and economic relations between the two countries. Thus one can say that we have two major slots for news about Jordan: the more negative slots that deal with confrontation and the more positive ones that deal with areas of cooperation.

The findings in this table again illustrate the influence of political context on the prominence of the various news slots. The inauguration of peace increased the prominence of two topics: those directly associated with the process and those having to do with the ongoing relations between the two countries. It is these stories that provided the basis for the increase in positive media attention during the peace year. Once the peace with Jordan was signed, however, there was no process. This is not a trivial finding because the issue of normalization remained an important (and controversial) topic in Jordan. For Israel, questions about peace with Jordan were resolved, for Jordan they were not.

A more encouraging finding concerns the proportion of stories dealing with meetings and economic cooperation. Here the number of news stories dropped only slightly between the peace year and the Netanyahu period, and this became the most prominent category for news about Jordan. Prime Minister Netanyahu had a definite interest in showing that despite his generally skeptical attitude towards the Palestinians, he did want to solidify the peace with Jordan. Arranging meetings with Jordanian leaders and talking about possible areas of cooperation between the two countries provided a useful means of achieving this goal. Had peace never been signed between the two countries such initiatives would have been impossible.

The results from Israel then are somewhat more encouraging than in Jordan, but still mixed. The more encouraging finding is that Jordan's media image started out more positive, improved after the formal establishment of peace, and suffered less of a setback when relations between the countries took a turn for the worse. One also finds that the establishment of relations created news slots that were more conducive for building peace between the two countries.

The importance of this change is limited, however, by the small number of news stories about Jordan. The peace process also did not lead to any increase in media interest in the internal affairs of Jordan. Open borders mean very little when journalists have no professional interest in crossing them.

IN SUM . . .

What are the lessons from all of this? The first is that even when things are pretty good, they're not so great. The Israel–Jordan peace process was probably one of the most amicable peace processes that has ever taken place. Yet, even here one finds little evidence that either set of news media made a lasting contribution to leaders' attempts to bring about reconciliation between the two peoples.

It is true that the reasons appear to be different in each country. In Jordan, after a temporary improvement linked to the signing of the accords, Israel's ongoing conflict with the Palestinians again soured the atmosphere. The lack of any significant change in Israel is better related to the fact that peace is boring. The absence of a credible threat from Jordan meant that there was little reason to cover it. These differences only demonstrate how difficult it is to promote peace to the news media on a sustained basis. The default mode of operation for the press is to cover tension, conflict, and violence. Any willingness to divert from this value is temporary and conditional.

The analysis of changing news slots in the two countries afforded a somewhat different perspective on this issue. The establishment of ongoing and formal relations between the two countries did alter the focus of media attention, providing leaders with important opportunities for the promotion of peace. At the very least, news stories about high-level meetings and economic cooperation suggested that peace was possible. The findings in both countries suggest that there was an important change in the prominence of constructive news slots. In this way the news media do not merely reflect the change in political context, they helped define it.

The interviews carried out in the two countries also provided valuable insights into the norms and routines journalists employ to cover each other. Such practices are clearly rooted in the political and media environments in which these journalists operate. In Jordan, the journalists found themselves caught between a pro-peace government and a population that remained hostile towards Israel. In addition, many of the journalists themselves had serious reservations about the peace process and many believed that the news media should be used as a weapon. Thus, Jordanian journalists who were interviewed believed that ideological considerations were an important and legitimate element in the construction of news. The fact that there was partial government control over the news media prevented the situation from being even worse.

In Israel the political environment was more conducive to peace, but the media environment was less so. It is true that Israeli journalists were just as enthusiastic about peace with Jordan as the rest of the public. Here again, however, when journalists were forced to choose between commercial and ideological considerations, the former won out. Whatever sympathy they had for Jordan, it did not justify any change in definitions of newsworthiness. The fact that the Israeli media do not have a single correspondent permanently stationed in Amman is particularly telling. In addition, although one cannot completely discount the influence of ideology on the construction of Israeli news, political bias is considered professionally incorrect.

It would seem, then, that only when all the political and professional planets are lined up can one expect the news media to play a constructive role in a peace process. The next chapter will be devoted to discussing just such a situation.

CHAPTER 6

The media and the struggle for peace in Northern Ireland

The time has come to move away from the Middle East to another part of the world. The theoretical principles outlined in the beginning of this work should also explain the role of the news media in other peace processes. Indeed, one of the most important elements of the model attempts to clarify how variations in the political and media environments influence that role. Examining the various stages in the Oslo peace process and the peace process with Jordan demonstrates how changes in the political environment influence the media's behavior. The case of the Northern Ireland peace process provides an even broader perspective. For here one can look at the impact of changes in both the political and the media environments.

The analysis will focus on the period surrounding the Good Friday agreement, which was signed in April of 1998. As noted in the introduction to this work, the interviews were carried out in the spring of 1999. A total of twenty interviews were carried out with political leaders, their advisors, and with a wide range of journalists working in Belfast.[1]

It is helpful to begin by considering some of the similarities and differences between this process and that of Oslo. Similarities include the fact that both conflicts have a long and bloody history and that religious differences play an important part in the ongoing confrontations. In addition, each set of negotiations was long and difficult and opponents in both regions have used terrorism in an attempt to halt the processes. It can also be said that news media in Northern Ireland and Israel are both, for the most part, free from government control.

---

[1] I also returned to Belfast in the summer of 2001 and conducted more informal talks on the situation.

There are also some important differences between the two conflicts. One of the most important contrasts is that the conflict in Northern Ireland is more of an internal dispute between two groups living within the same community. The major confrontation centers on whether that community should remain part of the United Kingdom (as favored by the Protestant Unionists) or become part of Ireland (which is the position taken by Catholic Nationalists). The people share a common language and, for the most part, vote in the same elections. The Israelis and the Palestinians, on the other hand, lived as completely separate communities until 1967. They speak different languages and live in very different cultures. In addition, the ultimate goal of the Oslo process is to create two separate political entities that can coexist in peace, while in Northern Ireland the aim is to live together.

In the present analysis the most important differences have to do with the political environment and media environments surrounding the two peace processes. The leaders promoting peace in Northern Ireland were able to mobilize a broader level of elite consensus in support of their policies. The political environment was also calmer in Northern Ireland during this period. Although there were a number of important crises associated with the implementation of the Good Friday agreement, they were less numerous and severe than those associated with the Oslo accords.

The media environment in Northern Ireland was also more conducive to peace. Citizens from both sides of that conflict use the same news media and, as argued in chapter 1, this leads the press to play a more constructive role. The most important news organs in Northern Ireland are also less sensationalist and this had a similar effect. The fact that the ongoing coverage of the process is less emotional meant that the news media were less likely to inflame public passions.

This does not mean that the media played an ideal role in Northern Ireland. Many of those interviewed raised a number of complaints against the press. Unionists who were opposed to the Good Friday agreement believed that media bias prevented any serious deliberation about the risks and costs associated with the process. One also heard from many different groups concerns about the growing tendency towards "sound bite news" among journalists in Northern Ireland. The difficulty leaders faced in attempting to send complex messages in twenty seconds or less paralleled those found in other Western countries.

Nevertheless, when one compares the role the news media played in Northern Ireland and in Israel, one finds a world of difference. The discussion below attempts to describe some of those differences and explains some of the reasons for them.

THE POLITICAL ENVIRONMENT

The building of a wide consensus in support of the Good Friday agreement was a long and difficult process. Many of the parties involved had been through a large number of previous attempts that had ended in failure. The most recent example was the Anglo–Irish agreement signed in November of 1985, which had been rejected by all of the Unionist parties. It was clear that only an agreement enjoying a wide spectrum of political support would have any chance of succeeding. Leaving out parties associated with the various paramilitary groups would be especially dangerous, for this would increase the likelihood of violence.

The international commission headed by George Mitchell worked for over two years on the agreement. In Mitchell's book, *Making peace* (1999), he talks about how difficult it was to keep all of the various groups at the same table. His efforts eventually proved successful and the Good Friday agreement received more support across the political spectrum than any previous attempt. Not only was the agreement supported by the major parties from each camp (the Ulster Unionist party and the Social Democratic and Labour party), it was also endorsed by the political parties associated with paramilitary groups (Sinn Fein, the Progressive Unionist Party, and the Ulster Democratic Party). The only major groups to oppose the accord were the Democratic Unionist Party (DUP) and the United Kingdom Unionist Party (UKUP).

The level of political consensus was reinforced by the decision to carry out a national referendum on the Good Friday agreement in both Northern Ireland and Ireland. The accord received 71 percent support in the North and 94 percent in the South. This was a critical turning point for the peace process. The very fact that the plan had been put to a democratic vote placed those who would continue to oppose the agreement at a considerable disadvantage. The peoples of Northern Ireland and Ireland had spoken; even those who lost were expected to respect that decision.

It is worth noting in this regard that no such referendum was ever held in Israel. Many of the opponents to the Oslo peace process argued that the Rabin government had never been given a mandate to recognize the PLO or to give up territories. They argued that neither of these policies had been put forth in Rabin's election campaign, and thus the government had no legitimacy. This claim became a common theme for opposition

Table 6.1 *Estimates of elite and public consensus surrounding peace processes in Israel and Northern Ireland*

Indicator	Israel	Northern Ireland
Percentage of Legislative Members Supporting Agreements[a]	51%–55%	75%
Percentage of Support for Agreement Among Public[b]	32%–44%	56%–73%

[a] The Israel figure is based on first and second votes in the Knesset on Oslo agreements. The Northern Ireland figure is based on the number of representatives elected from parties who supported the Good Friday agreement (additional details in footnote 2).
[b] The Israel figure is based on seventeen monthly polls of the Jewish population carried out by Tami Steinmetz Center for Peace Research at Tel Aviv University (additional details in footnote 3).

posters and bumper stickers. A referendum on the Oslo peace process might have undermined such a claim, especially if it received a sizable majority.

A rough summary of the relative levels of political consensus in the two countries can be found in table 6.1. The first measure is based on the number of political representatives who supported the various peace agreements. The Israeli tally includes the Knesset votes on both the first and second agreements with Palestinians. As discussed, the Oslo B agreement barely passed (61 votes for and 59 against), while the first Oslo agreement received somewhat more support (61–50). The Northern Ireland figure is based on the results of the elections to the Northern Ireland Assembly that were held in June, 1998. Although these party leaders did not actually vote on the Good Friday agreement, they were all active during the campaign over the referendum. The figure of 74 percent is based on the proportion of representatives who were elected from those parties who supported the agreement.[2]

The estimates concerning the amount of public support also come from two different measures. The Israeli figure is based on an ongoing

[2] The political parties in favor of the agreement in Northern Ireland included the Ulster Unionist Party (28 representatives), the Social Democratic and Labour Party (24), Sinn Fein (18), The Alliance Party (6), The Northern Ireland Women's Coalition (2), and the Progressive Unionist Party (2). Opposing the agreement were the Democratic Unionist Party (20), The Northern Ireland Unionist Party (4), The United Unionist Assembly Party (3), and the UK Unionist Party (1). There were also a number of other political parties in favor of the yes-vote who did not win any seats in the Assembly (Unionist Democratic Party, the Greens, Labour Coalition, and the Workers Party).

survey conducted by the Tami Steinmetz Center for Peace Research (1996) at Tel Aviv University examining public opinion about the Oslo peace process. It is based on a total of seventeen surveys conducted between June of 1993 and October, 1995 (when the Oslo B agreement was signed).[3] The Northern Ireland figures are based on polls carried out by the *Irish Times* (1998) during the referendum campaign.

Although these figures cannot be considered perfect measures of political consensus, they do provide a general sense of the political climate in the two countries. As discussed, the differences in consensus among the political elite are especially likely to have an impact on the role of the news media. The political parties in Israeli were completely divided over Oslo, which came as no surprise to those familiar with the political history of that country. The level of elite support in Northern Ireland, on the other hand, was much higher and included almost all of the major political parties. It is important to bear in mind that this high level of support for the peace process is a relatively new phenomenon: only a few years earlier the political environment in Northern Ireland was similar to that in Israel.

The evidence gathered from the interviews carried out in Northern Ireland demonstrates the impact this changing level of consensus had on the local news media. One of the most meaningful insights relates to how assumptions about political consensus influence the language and tone of news reports about the peace process. In the past journalists in Northern Ireland were much more cautious, because any implicit support for the peace process would bring charges of bias or even disloyalty. The more polarized a society, the more likely journalists are to come under attack. When all of the major political forces are pointing in the same general direction, it makes it easier for journalists to frame news stories accordingly. One of the newspaper reporters talked about this change:

> The other thing I've noticed is that, well, the media, you know there was almost a discomfort of even using the term peace process for a long time, because a lot of Unionists wouldn't accept it was a peace

---

[3] The average level of support among all of these surveys was 37.6 percent, with an average of 23.8 percent saying they were undecided. If the Arab citizens of Israel (almost all of whom supported the Oslo accords) had been included in these surveys the average amount of support would have probably have risen to about 45 percent. This is still far from a consensus. In addition, previous research suggests that the Hebrew press mostly ignores the Arab population in Israel (Avraham, Wolfsfeld, and Aburaiya, 2000; Wolfsfeld, Avraham, and Aburaiya, 2000). The voting figures from the Knesset include both Jewish and Arab representatives.

process, it was a surrender process, or an appeasement process. I feel more comfortable using it now because the Ulster Unionists have embraced it to a degree, are starting to take ownership of the peace process. But up until '96, the Unionists saw the peace process as a conspiracy by the Republicans to lure them into a united Ireland. (NI7, April 13, 1999)

This observation, and others like it, illustrate that the political change preceded the changes in media coverage. The Ulster Unionists' willingness to accept this particular peace process was based on a long and difficult process of negotiation and political maneuvering. As the political climate began to change journalists felt "more comfortable" adopting the Pro-Peace frames that had previously been considered controversial. The reactions journalists receive from their audiences tell them whether their stories fall within the realm of contemporary political consensus.

Nevertheless, when the media do adopt a Peace frame it can have a significant impact on the political process. One of the most significant examples of this influence was when the Unionist paper the *Ulster Newsletter* and the Nationalist *Irish News* published a series of common editorials in favor of the peace process. As the political camps began to move closer on the peace process, so did the newspapers. The culmination of this cooperation was the fact that both papers asked their readers to vote yes in the referendum. A British official claimed that the *Newsletter*'s endorsement was especially important for the process.

The fact is that the *Ulster Newsletter*, which in the past was a decidedly pro-Unionist newspaper, not a moderate Unionist newspaper, but I would say actually a newspaper that was to the right of center within the Unionist community, it actually advocated a yes-vote in the referendum. It kind of led the way and at a time when it wasn't at all clear which way the Unionist community was going to go on this . . . the paper was prepared to take a lead role in advocating endorsement of the agreement. (NI6, April 13, 1999)

I would argue that this is an excellent illustration of the PMP cycle of influence. Changes in the political environment (opposing political parties converging around the peace plan) led to changes in media norms and routines (more pro-peace stance) that then led to further changes in the environment (rising legitimacy of peace process among Unionists). If this official is correct, the *Newsletter* played a critical role in moving the peace process forward.

The fact that the peace process was no longer considered controversial allowed all of the news media to take an active role in promoting it. An analysis of editorials appearing in the Nationalist newspaper the *Irish News* and the Unionist paper the *Belfast Telegraph* provides striking evidence about the extent of this support.[4] This analysis was intended to provide a parallel to the evaluation of the editorials about the Oslo process that was discussed in chapter 3.[5] As will be remembered, the newspaper editorials in Israel provided a good forum for debate. In the case of Northern Ireland, twenty-two events were chosen that run from the violence associated with an Orange March in July of 1997 to the Hillsborough Declaration in April of 1999.[6] The period includes a large number of events that took place both before and after the Good Friday agreement was signed in April of 1998. A total of 147 editorials were examined.

The final tally for the *Irish News* shows a remarkable 64 editorials in support of the peace process, 5 that express a more ambivalent attitude, and only 1 that was opposed to the process.[7] The distribution of opinion of the *Belfast Telegraph* is equally one-sided: 62 editorials in favor, 18 ambivalent, and again only 1 expressing opposition to the process. This finding is especially surprising given that these editorials were written during a number of periods of violence, when the process appeared to be in danger. Editors in Northern Ireland apparently felt little need to provide a balance between proponents and opponents.

It could be argued that this is one area in which the Israeli news media play a more positive role than in Northern Ireland. As discussed, the editorial section of the newspapers in Israel provided a rigorous debate over the pros and cons of the Oslo peace process. In Northern Ireland,

---

[4] The major reason for selecting the *Belfast Telegraph* (rather the *Newsletter*) as the Unionist newspaper was that it has by far the largest circulation. Rolston estimated its readership at 500,000, which is three times the audience of either the *Irish News* or the *Newsletter*. This tells us something about the potential impact of such a paper on the political climate. The *Newsletter* is, however, a more purely Unionist newspaper and thus an analysis of its editorials might have produced somewhat different results.

[5] There were, however, a number of differences between the two analyses. The editorials in Israel were written by a variety of different writers and this allowed for a greater range of views. By contrast, most of the editorials in the two Northern Ireland newspapers – the *Irish News* and the *Belfast Telegraph* – represented the official position of those newspapers. There were also fewer editorials written after each event, which is why it was decided to examine editorials from a larger number of events in Northern Ireland.

[6] The twenty-two events are listed in the methodological index, pp. 242–3.

[7] The inter-coder reliability of the category assignment was over 90 percent.

on the other hand, the papers provided little room for those opposed to the process. Part of the reason has to do with format: the editorials in Northern Ireland represent the official positions of these papers; there are very few "op-ed pieces." However, the climate of consensus in support of the process also has an influence. The newspapers would be reluctant to publish such pro-peace editorials if they believed it would alienate a substantial part of their readership.

There is also good reason to believe that this same bias in favor of peace carried over into the news section. It is helpful to look at coverage from three different events in order to demonstrate how pro-peace values are translated into news stories.[8] One of the incidents is more minor, while the other two represent major events in the history of the peace process. The smaller event involves a series of murders of Catholics by Loyalist paramilitaries that took place in late January of 1998. The two major events were the signing of the Good Friday agreement itself (April 11, 1998) and the coverage given to the terrorist attack at Omagh on August 17, in which twenty-nine people were killed and over 200 were injured.

The news stories published about the January murders are revealing for they provide insights about professional norms for dealing with sectarian violence in the period leading up to the agreement. As in the Middle East, many of these terrorist acts are designed to derail the peace process, and thus editorial decisions about how to frame such events are of critical importance. In Northern Ireland one finds that both Nationalist and Unionist papers take a similar approach to these murders.

On the front page of the Nationalist *Irish News* is the headline: "Loyalists gun down Catholic workman" (January 24, 1998).[9] There is also a sub-headline that reads: "Victims shot in head as killing spree continues." This is the lead story and is accompanied by a number of other articles that deal with the angry responses of leaders from across the political spectrum. On January 26 there is an emotional interview with the workman's widow on page 1 with the headline: "He kissed me goodbye and said 'I love you' like he always did, and then he was gone".

---

[8] Unfortunately, despite a number of efforts, it was not possible to obtain archival material from television broadcasts. However, looking at sectarian newspapers provide a stricter test of the argument, for this is where one would be most likely to find anti-peace news articles.

[9] Readers should note that the use of capitals when quoting from the headlines is in keeping with what appeared in the news stories.

There is nothing surprising about this coverage and it runs along similar lines to what one would find in other countries.

Far more revealing is the attitude of the Unionist papers. Given the fact that the victims came from the "other side," one might have expected a more subdued or defensive type of coverage. This is certainly not what one finds. The *Belfast Telegraph* published a special issue with a major headline filling the entire first page: "THE PAIN GOES ON" (January 24, 1998). A picture of the victim, his name, and a brief description of the event also appear on the front page. Other headlines are equally forceful: "HORROR ON OUR DOORSTEP" (p. 3), "AGONY OF THE INNO-CENTS" (p. 4), "SICK WORDS OF JUSTIFICATION" (p. 6 – referring to a statement released by the Ulster Freedom Fighters). Most remarkable of all is the organizing title linking the various articles throughout the issue: "Terror on our Streets." The decision to relate to members of Union paramilitaries as terrorists is profound. It is impossible to imagine a similar description in either the Israeli (Hebrew) or Palestinian press.

The language used in the Unionist *Ulster Newsletter* is somewhat less charged, but the overall message is the same. The first day's front-page headline talks about "Mystery of New Killing" which the sub-headline reads: "Pipe-layer murdered after UFF calls Halt" (January 24, 1998). The story itself presents a sympathetic portrait of the victim and his family. A more forceful call against violence appears in the Monday paper (January 26) after five people were killed. As part of their cooperation, the *Newsletter* and the *Irish News* put forth an initiative asking members of both publics to sign a petition condemning the violence and supporting the peace process.

"TELL THE KILLERS IT'S TIME TO STOP"
The *Newsletter* and the *Irish News*, the newspapers which together represent both sides of the divide, today call on the people of North ern Ireland to send a clear message to the gunmen: IT IS TIME TO STOP THE SENSELESS KILLING. (*Newsletter, Irish News*, p. 1)

One of the more interesting aspects of this initiative is the fact that leaders from both sides of the fence supported the initiative: the Mayor of Belfast, Nationalist Alban Maginness, and his Unionist deputy, Council-lor Jim Rodgers. The news article emphasized this point by underlining that part of the story. This helps demonstrate how a high level of political consensus can have a direct effect on the media coverage.

It should be kept in mind that all of this was taking place three months before a final agreement was reached. This was a critical juncture for the peace process and continued violence would have impeded any advancement. It is clearly impossible to isolate the impact of the media from all the other forces that were brought into play. What is clear is that the news media from both sides of the divide were a central agent for placing those who use violence beyond the pale.

It is less surprising to find pro-peace coverage when the Good Friday agreement was signed. The Nationalist *Irish News* is the most enthusiastic about the agreement and it is often difficult to distinguish between the news reports and the editorials. The April 11 issue that was published the day after the signing contains a huge headline that reads: "Today is only the beginning, it is not the End" (p. 1). The lead paragraph reads as follows:

A NEW beginning arrived for Northern Ireland today after US President Bill Clinton, British Prime Minister Tony Blair and Taoiseach Bertie Ahern secured a peace deal – despite last minute Unionist jitters. (p. 1)

The next major story about the agreement reads:

First Brick in peace wall

The far-reaching and radical proposals contained in yesterday's agreement has the potential to transform relationships within these islands and start to build lasting peace in Northern Ireland. (p. 3)

Here are some of the other headlines from that issue of the *Irish Times*: "Parties unite in welcome for pact" (p. 4); "Prayers are answered" (p. 4); "The long wait, the long Good Friday" (p. 5). There are also a number of pieces from the victims perspective. "Noreen [whose husband was killed] welcomes news" (p. 6); "Mother [whose son was killed] optimistic for future" (p. 6); "Family hopes guns fall silent" (p. 6). "Parry Family [whose son was killed] 'delighted' at deal."

There are two major stories in the *Irish Times* that provide the position of those opposed to the agreement. The first reports on the reaction of MP William Thomson from the Ulster Unionist Party (UUP), who despite his party's position was against the agreement: "Thompson vows to defy deal" (p. 3). The second story appears on page 7 and provides the more severe reaction of DUP leader Ian Paisley: " 'Assembly of treachery' says Paisley."

The coverage in the Unionist *Belfast Telegraph* runs along similar lines. It too emphasizes positive aspects of the agreement. Such historical moments represent one of the few times when hope becomes more newsworthy then fear. The major headline for April 11 reads: "Destiny Day" (p. 1). The front page also contains a rather large and moving picture of two women – one Protestant and one Catholic – praying at their respective churches. The caption reads: "UNITED IN PRAYER FOR PEACE." An editorial in support of the agreement also appears on the first page: "After the bloody days that the people of Northern Ireland have experienced for more than a generation, today is truly Good Friday. The other headlines are somewhat less enthusiastic than those that appeared in the *Irish News*: "A FIRST LOOK AT THE BLUEPRINT FOR PEACE" (p. 3); "Gunmen are still poised for action" (p. 4); "LET'S HOPE IT'S FOR REAL – Optimism rises on city's streets" (p. 6).

The coverage in the *Ulster Newsletter* is the least positive of the three newspapers. This is in keeping with what was said earlier about this being the more partisan of the two Unionist newspapers. Those opposed to the Good Friday agreement are given more space. The front-page headline reads as follows: "TRIMBLE FACING REVOLT." The second page is somewhat more encouraging: "Burden of sad history 'lifted at last.' " Many of the remaining stories are more technical in nature; the *Newsletter* adopted a less enthusiastic tone than the other two papers. This is consistent with the rather hesitant endorsement given in an editorial that appears on page 6:

> The hard work is only beginning
>
> A TENTATIVE agreement may have been reached in our long drawn-out Northern political process, but only the most politically naïve and those unfamiliar with life in the Province will be convinced that it will deliver a lasting peace to our divided community. (p. 6)

Thus the eventual – and critical – decision of the *Newsletter* to support the Good Friday agreement took some time to develop; it was far from inevitable.

In general, though, one finds that the news stories about the agreement are very pro-peace. One of the most striking facts about the interviews carried out in Belfast was the universal belief that the news media were actively promoting the Good Friday agreement, especially in the period leading up to the referendum. This pleased some and displeased others but no one questioned the fact that the press was pro-peace. None of those interviewed could think of a single journalist who was opposed to the peace process. A reporter for one of the radio stations was asked whether there was something inherently unfair about the way the media related to the opposition.

> Unfair to an extent, there's no doubt about that both governments [Ireland and Britain] are pushing the pro-peace line and I think that no matter who you are you can't fail but want that line to work. Everybody has that sense of wanting it to work so badly that you feed into it. But I believe also that in Northern Ireland you would fail abysmally unless you take both sides . . . everything is sensitive and you've got to balance everything. (NI1; April 14, 1999)

This helps explain the frustration of those who were against the Good Friday agreement. The Democratic Unionist Party, led by Dr. Ian Paisley, was the most outspoken about media bias. They argued that they were not being given a fair share of time and space to explain their positions.[10] A spokesperson for the party described the difficulties in swimming against the media stream.

> They want the world to be soft and easygoing and people to talk and we all sit around the table and everybody's good friends and pals and love, peace, and harmony breaks out and everything's wonderful, and this man [Paisley] comes along and says, "Wait a minute! That's not right. It's not right to kill people . . . We're not going to suffer this." And you know, right's right and wrong's wrong. And this man upsets them and he stirs things up and he's a thorn in the side of the establishment. I mean, they would love Ian Paisley not to be there. They would love the DUP not to be there. (NI10; April 14, 1999)

Editors in Northern Ireland did make room for other voices, but one does get a sense that it was an uneven playing field. When there are so many forces working to promote the peace process, media values and routines serve to marginalize those who oppose it.

One of the most telling demonstrations of the influence of consensus on media coverage comes from the coverage of the terrorist bombing at Omagh, which took place in August of 1998. This was the most destructive attack ever carried out in Northern Ireland and produced a

---

[10] It is worth noting that research carried out by Fawcett (2002) came to the conclusion that Sinn Fein and the Democratic Unionist Party have become the most successful at modernizing their approach to political communication. Thus, while the DUP may have an uphill battle to wage, they may be better equipped than the larger parties at waging it.

huge political wave. Twenty-nine people were killed and over 200 were injured. While no group claimed responsibility, most suspected that the Real Irish Republican Army (RIRA) carried it out in an effort to stop the peace process.

Based on the experience in Israel, one would have expected this bombing to have been a major setback for the peace process. The response within Northern Ireland was exactly the opposite: it provided a major impetus for the pro-peace forces. The news media played an important role in constructing and amplifying this reaction. The front page of the *Belfast Telegraph* provides an important illustration of this difference in coverage. At first glance the news stories look familiar; as in Israel one finds the faces of the victims staring out at the reader. The meaning that is attributed to this event however is very different. In the middle of all of those pictures one finds the following message:

> Let our entire community unite against this evil. Let us commit ourselves to peace and peace alone. Let us back the forces of law and order. Let us resolve to build a new future together, unionist and nationalist alike. Let this be our sincere and lasting tribute to the victims of Omagh. (August 17, 1998, p. 1)

One finds a similar tone in the other two newspapers. The *Irish News* also has pictures of the victims on the first page accompanied by a message from British Prime Minister Tony Blair: "We must defeat evil" (August 17). The message talks about the importance of continuing the peace process so that evil will not secure its objective. The main editorial published in the *Newsletter* makes a similar point: "The bombers wanted to divide us. Today we stand united by grief" (August 17, p. 6). The Peace frame continued to be emphasized in the editorials that were published afterwards. In the days following the Omagh attack, the *Irish News* printed nine editorials in favor of continuing the peace process, and the *Belfast Telegraph* published three with the same position. There was not a single editorial in either of these papers suggesting the process should be slowed or halted. The DUP was calling for just such a move, but it was not given any editorial space to express these views.

The comparison with the case of Beit Lid – which was discussed in chapter 2 – is striking. Many in Israel saw the terrorist attacks as proof that the Palestinians could not be trusted and that the only reasonable course of action was to halt the process. That wave provided an important opportunity for the right-wing opposition to promote their anti-Oslo frames to the Israeli news media. As discussed, the Israeli press amplified this mood by denigrating Arafat and the Palestinians.

This is an extremely powerful demonstration of the influence of political consensus on the construction of media frames. In Israel, the ongoing competition between the Security First and Peace frames meant that every act of terrorism evoked the Security frame. Indeed, Prime Minister Rabin himself employed that frame after such attacks by promoting his plan for "separation." In Northern Ireland, on the other hand, the wide consensus in support of the Peace frame meant that it was even applicable in the wake of a terrorist attack such as Omagh. In the Israeli case the natural inclination was to halt the process, while in Northern Ireland the natural reaction was to accelerate it.

Another reason for the unity after Omagh can be attributed to the fact that the explosion killed people from every camp. Whereas most previous attacks had been directed at either Protestants or Catholics, the shock waves from this attack ran through both communities. One of the senior journalists talked about this factor.

> You had members of the Gaelic Association, you had members of the DUP, you had members of the Ulster Unionists, you had women out buying clothes for their children going back to school, Catholics, Protestants, you had people from the Irish Republic, you had people from Spain killed there. It was a bomb that touched everybody's life in some way . . . That bomb was pretty unique in the sense that it was a bonding bomb. It actually drew people closer together. (NI11; April 15, 1999)

As noted, there were those in the DUP who attempted to promote a different frame about Omagh. Similar to the claims made by the opposition in Israel, they argued that the attack proved that the IRA would never respect the cease-fire. Representatives of the opposition appeared on a number of talk-shows and the like, but here too they felt sorely outnumbered. As one of their key spokespeople put it: "the press bought into this process before the referendum, they bought into at the Assembly elections, and they bought into it at Omagh" (NI10; April 14, 1999).

A leader from Sein Fein was especially emphatic about the role of the media after Omagh. He argued that the brunt of the rage was targeted at that Real IRA. The news media in the South, for example, printed a full-page photograph of the alleged head of that organization. This led to a boycott and the man apparently lost his business. This same source claimed that the press coverage also had a more significant impact on the peace process.

> Of course one of the things that all of the media wave or media stuff gave is it became very difficult for anybody to oppose the Good Friday agreement, particularly from within Republicanism or Nationalism. So a lot of people I know who are very anti-agreement but not necessarily pro-armed struggle just went into hiding for like a week or two weeks . . . because people would say, "Well, it is the agreement or it's over." So I think the media very definitely did the opposite of inflaming the conflict. It genuinely and probably very consciously worked overtime to make conflict, in terms of military conflict, all the more difficult. (NI3; April 13, 1999).

This leader also believed that media's reaction to Omagh might have also played a role in the Real IRA's decision to declare a ceasefire after that attack.

It was argued earlier that the Israeli news media tended to blur the distinction between the Palestinian authorities and the rejectionists, especially after terrorist attacks. In the case of Omagh the role of the news media was exactly the opposite. It created a bond, albeit temporary, among the pro-peace groups from both camps. A clear distinction was being made between Sein Fein and the terrorists. Such a distinction can be an important tool in the process of reconciliation.

It is important to take note of the fact that the media's emphasis on the Peace frame is in some ways a relatively new phenomenon in Northern Ireland. As discussed, changing media frames are rooted in changes in the political environment. As pointed out by McLaughlin and Miller (1996), the traditional media frame for dealing with such attacks had focused on the need to find a solution to terrorism. This is similar to the Security First frame used in Israel in that it generally opposes making any concessions to the "enemy." Indeed, the same Anti-Terrorist frame became the dominant creed after the outbreak of the Second Intifada. When violence racks any society most efforts focus on restoring law and order rather than on finding a political solution. A good deal of the research dealing with the media in Northern Ireland was very critical of this bias (for a review see Cottle, 1997). The local and British news media, it was argued, were nothing more than a government mouthpiece propagating the anti-terrorist theme.

Some might argue that the Northern Ireland news media continue to echo the government line. It's just that most official sources are now promoting a different frame about the conflict. One is reminded here about the comments quoted earlier when a journalist talked about "both governments pushing the pro-peace line." Britain, Ireland, and many other forces within Northern Ireland all devote a massive amount of resources – including public relations efforts – to ensure the success of the Good Friday accords. It is much easier to "manage the news" when the most powerful actors are all pointing in the same direction.[11] While leaders such as Ian Paisley enjoyed some of the benefits of the Anti-Terrorist frame in earlier years, they now find themselves in an uphill battle to promote their less popular frames to the media. Given the results of the referendum, those opposed to the Good Friday agreement should be entitled to about 30 percent of the public space devoted to this issue. There is little evidence that they received this amount of access.

The political environment surrounding the Northern Ireland peace process was also calmer than in Israel and this too had an influence on the role of the media. In Israel, news stories about violence constituted a major part of the Oslo coverage. Not only was there a much higher level of terrorism but, as discussed, the internal protests were both massive and violent. Most of the opposition to the Good Friday agreement, on the other hand, was verbal. There certainly was violence, especially during "marching season," and people from both camps were killed. The political atmosphere, however, was generally less heated and emotional than in Israel.

This is not meant to imply that that the Northern Ireland peace process was smooth. There were bitter arguments along the way and many deadlines passed without agreement. There is also no guarantee that the peace process will continue. Nevertheless, the fact that all of the major paramilitaries operating in Northern Ireland declared a cease-fire and the relatively low level of protests provided leaders with an extremely conducive environment for negotiation. This climate also allowed news stories about the peace process to focus on negotiations rather than on violence.

All of these factors are strongly connected with one another. The high level of elite consensus surrounding the agreement provided a sense of unity that made violent dissent more difficult. This was especially true after Omagh, due to the intensive reaction of leaders and the media. The relatively low level of violence led to a relatively calm environment

---

[11] I want to thank my Northern Ireland colleagues Liz Fawcett and Greg McLaughlin for emphasizing the importance of government spin in this process.

for negotiating peace that also had an important impact on the tone of coverage. In short, nothing succeeds in the media like political success.

THE MEDIA ENVIRONMENT

The role of the press in the Northern Ireland peace process was also influenced by the nature of the local media environment. There were two aspects of that environment that are directly related to the theoretical arguments made in chapter 1. First, most media are shared between the rival communities. Second, the media environment in Northern Ireland is characterized by a relatively low level of sensationalism. Unlike the variables that have been discussed till now, these are more enduring factors and thus political leaders have less direct control over them. Fortunately for the authorities promoting the Good Friday agreement, these factors also worked in their favor.

The fact that so many Protestants and Catholics get their news from the same media appears to be especially significant. The greatest overlap in audience composition takes place with regard to television and radio. According to Tim Cooke (1998) two daily television news programs – Ulster Television's *UTV Live* and BBC Northern Ireland's *Newsline* – account for a combined audience share of about 70 percent. The only way to maintain such large audiences is to adopt a political perspective acceptable to both sides of the conflict. Owners, editors, and journalists all have a clear commercial interest in appealing to as wide an audience as possible.

There is more separation among newspaper readers but one also finds a significant amount of overlap within this audience. The *Irish News* and the *Newsletter* are more sectarian, but the *Belfast Telegraph* prides itself on attracting readers from both communities. The less partisan *Telegraph* has by far the largest audience, with almost three times as many readers as the other two papers (Rolston and Miller, 1996). Rolston (Rolston and Miller, 1991) states that the proportion of Protestant and Catholic readers is similar to that which exists in the general population.[12] The British press also attracts a wide readership from both communities.

Thus, while the news media are not completely shared, it is certainly more communal than in other conflicts. Cooke (2003) also notes this

---

[12] The figures are based on a somewhat dated readership survey from 1988. An estimated 61 percent of the readers were Protestant and 32 percent were Catholic. The proportion in the population was about 57 percent Protestant and 37 percent Catholic at the time.

difference in his own article about the role of the news media in this peace process: "Northern Ireland does not fall victim to one of the difficulties apparent in some other divided societies – that of a media divided by language and speaking to only one side in the conflict" (p. 4). This fact, that the many of the news media in Northern Ireland target people from both sides of the conflict, has a major impact on coverage of the process.[13]

The ability to bridge the gap begins at the hiring stage. Northern Ireland has an extremely strict Fair Employment Commission, which insures that all companies, including the news media, employ people from both communities. Although this cannot prevent all forms of discrimination, it does ensure that every news organization has both Protestants and Catholics working together. One also finds people from both communities working in the more partisan newspapers. A leader from Sein Fein talked about the overlap.

> For example I think the new editor of the [Nationalist] *Irish News* may have worked for the [Unionist] *Telegraph* at one stage . . . like you wouldn't go into the *Irish News* and go, "Yes, there are all Nationalists," and go into the *Telegraph* and, "They're all Unionists." It's not like that. And of course, the difference is because here it's much more difficult to assess ethnic differences, whereas it wouldn't be so different where you are from, and the other thing it's not polite. In middle-class circles, which are of course where the newspapers circulate, it's not polite to ask somebody's religion. (NI12; April 13, 1999).

The fact that ethnic differences are not obvious is one of the reasons there are shared media in Northern Ireland. In the Middle East, the large linguistic and cultural gap that divides Israelis and Arabs is also reflected in their separate news media. With all their differences, people living in Northern Ireland have much in common and this facilitates movement between the two societies. This mixing of the populations also makes it easier for reporters to gain access to sources from both communities. None of the journalists who were interviewed had any problems interviewing people from either side.

---

[13] Alan Bairner (1996) makes exactly the opposite claim about the media in Northern Ireland, arguing that the fact that so much of the press is partisan reinforces the divisions in the area. The disagreement between us has to do with the difference in perspective. In this article the emphasis is on the comparative perspective. When one compares the situation in Northern Ireland to that which exists in most other conflicts, one finds more political overlap in the composite of the audience.

Here, too, one finds that the role the media play in conflicts can only be understood by looking at the larger social and political context in which they operate. The narrowing of the divide between the major antagonists made it easier for the news media to bridge that gap. At the height of the "troubles" journalists found it more difficult to create any news stories that would be considered fair to both sides. Part of the process of any reconciliation is to build a set of terms and concepts that will be acceptable to all sides. A Northern Ireland university professor who has studied these issues talked about this change.

> Years ago that's where you would've seen differences [between the newspapers from the two communities], you know. Like, for example, say the mid-eighties, when the *Newsletter* constantly fumed against the Anglo-Irish agreement, refused to call it the Anglo-Irish agreement even. What did they call it then, the Anglo-Eire Diktat, whereas the *Irish News* was much more positive about that. (NI12; April 16, 1999)

As noted, the Unionist *Belfast Telegraph* makes a concerted effort to attract Catholic readers. A number of those interviewed referred to it as a Unionist paper "with a small 'u.'" One of the journalists who writes for the paper talked about how assumptions about the audience influenced coverage.

> I'm working for a paper that has mostly got a Unionist readership, but is cross-community, has a Catholic readership, so it is the only main paper in Northern Ireland that can boast a sizeable section of its readership coming from the two communities, although, we're still predominantly a small "u" Unionist paper . . . So, you know, you're trying to straddle two communities, it's very difficult with the *Telegraph*. You know, if you're with the *Newsletter* or the *Irish News* you can just do whatever the hell you want and you're not going to offend your readers. (NI7; April 13, 1999)

It is never easy to find common ground between hostile groups. It is far easier to produce news stories that echo local myths and prejudices. Many journalists in Northern Ireland are forced to make that extra effort in order to attract a larger audience. This is perhaps the only example where the commercial interests of the news media actually *benefit* those attempting to promote peace.

It is hard to overestimate the impact of this difference on the construction of news about peace. When there is a large amount of overlap within the audience, there is no clear enemy to write about; definitions of "us" and "them" become less clear and distinct. The need to end the conflict and violence becomes a common problem for the entire community.

The media environment in Northern Ireland is also more conducive to peace because journalists have adopted a less sensationalist approach to covering the conflict than in Israel. The BBC tradition of public broadcasting remains an important influence on all of the electronic media and this raises the level of discourse. There is a major emphasis within this tradition on two important values: distance and restraint. While drama still plays an important part in the constructing of news in Northern Ireland, these values serve as important counterweights.

There are tabloid newspapers that are popular, including those based in London that are called the "Sunday papers." But it is the three regional newspapers – The *Irish News*, the *Telegraph*, and the *Newsletter* – that provide the most extensive print coverage of the peace process and they are not sensationalist in nature. Although the *Telegraph* and the *Newsletter* do sometimes use large headlines, the reporting is not overly dramatic. There almost seems to be a division of labor in which citizens turn to the tabloids for entertainment and the more serious news media for information.

The most important evidence about the differences between the media environments in Israel and Northern Ireland comes from the interviews with the political leaders and journalists in the two countries. As discussed, such interviews are the optimal method for understanding the professional values and routines that distinguish each culture and how they influence the political process. Every single Israeli leader and spokesperson interviewed referred to the sensationalism of their news media and the problems associated with this inclination. The leaders in Belfast, on the other hand, had quite a bit of respect for their own media, especially in this area.

This sense that the Northern Ireland news media were generally serious and responsible could be found across the political spectrum. A UUP Assemblyman, for example, talked about how lucky they were not to have "too many tabloid journalists" whose major goal is to "stir up trouble." One finds a similar sentiment from a Sein Fein representative, who thought that the more restrained tone of coverage in Northern Ireland might be related to the fact that it was a relatively religious culture.[14]

---

[14] It is interesting to note in this context that none of the religious newspapers in Israel are sensationalist.

He talked about the differences between local coverage of the conflict and the type that appeared in the English newspapers.

> I think one of the things you find is that one of the differences between journalists in England and journalists here or journalists who have lived here for some time and journalists who come from the outside is journalists here are much more tuned into the sensitivities of reporting a conflict and reporting all of the death and tragedy and therefore much more careful. This makes sensationalizing very difficult. Now it still happens with the Sunday tabloids but it makes it much more difficult, whereas when you're coming over from England and maybe to a lesser extent when you're coming from Dublin, it's much easier to want the big, simple, sexy story and to be really blasé about trying to access it and kind of trampling over people's feelings. (NI3, April 13, 1999)

A similar message comes from the journalists themselves. Many of the reporters interviewed talked about the dangers of irresponsible reporting. One journalist was both vivid and succinct: "sensationalism can cost lives." A good example of this concern is that editors in Northern Ireland think very carefully before sending reporters to cover street violence. This is apparently a professional norm that has developed over time due to the negative impact cameras can have on such incidents. A correspondent for one of the radio stations talked about this change in policy.

> Initially any street violence, any civil disorder at all, we would have had a reporter out on the scene reporting there . . . As the situation developed further and the media, I'm not speaking just purely about our station but more generally, accepted and realized that people were playing to the camera, they backed off. I mean there have been nights when there's been quite a lot of violence; a high level of violence compared to the start of it, and nobody's gone. It's just been a case of ongoing violence, don't exacerbate the situation by being there, you know, let them sort out whatever they can as best they can, but don't give them the oxygen of publicity to further hurt and insult the opposite side. (NI1; April 13, 1999)

Israeli reporters would argue that this is self-censorship. The public has a right to know what is happening, and journalists have a duty to tell them. The difference in the two sets of values centers on whether or not journalists should be concerned with the social and political consequences of their reporting. The working assumption in Israel and many other countries is that a press can only remain independent if it reports on everything regardless of the outcomes. One could easily defend each of these approaches. What is clear, however, is that the choice of one model over another can have a significant impact on the role the news media play in the escalation of violence.

None of this is meant to suggest that the press in Northern Ireland is devoid of many of the ills that plague the media in other countries. The political leaders and the journalists themselves complained about "sound-bite news" and how difficult it was to have serious ideological discussions. A representative from the DUP also criticized the media's preference for news from paramilitaries. He argued that the smaller PUP received more coverage than his own party because they posed more of a threat:

> [it's] because they're an armed terrorist group. That's it, there's no doubt about that. If you've got guns in this country, you're important. It doesn't matter how many votes you get or many people you help in a year. If you got a gun you're important. We can't threaten anybody. (NI10; April 14, 1999)

These remarks sound similar to the ones that were expressed by non-violent groups in Israel. The news media in Northern Ireland still look for drama and this can create serious problems for those who are unwilling to produce it.

In general, however, political leaders and spokespeople in Northern Ireland feel less pressure than in Israel to use extremist language and tactics in order to gain access to the media. This is a critical difference between the two political cultures. One of the greatest dangers of sensationalist media is the pressure they place on actors to employ extremist rhetoric and actions. It is only fair to say, however, that such variations may also have to do with the two political systems. The institution of primaries in Israel has increased the need for Israeli politicians to obtain the maximum level of exposure in the media (Peri, 2004). The strong political party system in Northern Ireland serves to lower the incentives for grandstanding.

A less sensationalist media creates a more conducive atmosphere for the promotion of peace both within and between different political camps. A more restrained media environment can lead to a more moderate political environment. To a large extent journalists operate the volume controls for public discourse. The level of amplification is directly related to the norms and routines adopted by journalists. They can either turn the volume knob up or down and this will have a direct impact on everyone involved.

The concern about sensationalism expressed by many of the journalists in Northern Ireland may also be related to their enthusiastic support of the peace process. It is clear to them that sensationalist news coverage has the potential for inflaming an already dangerous situation. While some might object to such a partisan approach, one can certainly appreciate journalists' desire for peace. One of the most respected journalists in Northern Ireland put it like this:

> I'm unapologetic in saying I want peace. I want an end to all this violence, this war. Now journalists dream, journalists come into journalism to have wars. Many of them want to see themselves as war correspondents. I certainly don't want to be a war correspondent. I've seen it all. I've been to the bomb scenes. I've seen life desecrated, wiped out. I've seen my own local pub and shop at home blow up where my sister worked for many years as a student. I saw young Michael Donnelley killed at a petrol pump serving petrol. I saw the bomb attack on those premises. I've seen dozens and dozens, many of my school friends are dead as result of violence. So I want an end to it all. (NI11; April 15, 1999)

IN SUM . . .

There is good reason to believe that the news media play a rather different role in Northern Ireland than they do in Israel. They were much more supportive of the process and appear to have played an important role in mobilizing public support for the accords. One also gets a sense that the journalists in that conflict were much more conscious of the potential harm they could cause by inflaming the internal debate over the process. The debate held over the Good Friday agreement may not have been a completely fair one, but it was certainly a calmer one.

Looking at political and media context in which the media were operating best explains these differences. The journalists working in Israel were reporting on an extremely controversial agreement and the sensationalist coverage not only reflected that difference, it exacerbated it.

The Hebrew news media also had absolutely no incentive for bridging the gap between Israelis and Palestinians. On the contrary, the Israeli media were a critical vehicle for intensifying the public's fears and hostilities.

All of these patterns returned with a vengeance in the fall of 2000. This is the topic of the next chapter.

CHAPTER 7

The collapse of Oslo and the return to violence

The summer and fall of 2000 will be remembered as a dreadful turning point in Middle East history. In July of that year President Clinton convened a summit at Camp David with Ehud Barak and Yasser Arafat with the goal of concluding a final settlement between the two sides. The talks ended in complete failure with each side blaming the other. Tensions continued to rise after the collapse, culminating in the outbreak of the Second Intifada in September of that year, bringing hundreds of deaths and thousands of wounded on both sides. Israelis and Palestinians who had hoped for an end to the conflict found the clock turned back to an era of hopelessness. The level of hate and anger between the two peoples reached new heights and those who had promoted the Oslo peace process looked, at best, fools.

The underlying logic of the Oslo process was that trust could be built in stages. Compromises that would have seemed impossible in 1993, it was thought, would become less difficult after the two sides had learned to cooperate. That is certainly not what happened. There was quite a bit of cooperation between the two sides and a certain amount of progress was made over the years. Nevertheless, each step towards a final settlement became increasingly painful and frustrating for both parties. Each accused the other of violating signed agreements and neither was convinced of the good intentions of the other. Pushing the peace boulder up the hill only became more difficult as the two sides approached the summit. Unfortunately, nothing in the Middle East stays in place for long. When uphill progress was no longer possible, the boulder quickly fell back down the hill, destroying everything in its path.

The question for this work concerns the role of the news media in this process. In keeping with the major thrust of this work, the argument is that the media are not the major reason for such difficulties, but they did make things worse. Given a problematic political environment surrounding peace, the editorial process is more likely to lead to hostility than to trust. Even news about peace is ultimately news about conflict. While the news media are extremely poor tools for the promotion of peace, they become especially efficient tools for engaging in war. This contrast becomes clear when one compares the ongoing news coverage of the Oslo peace process with their coverage of the Second Intifada. The fact that the Intifada erupted immediately after the Camp David Summit allowed for an especially powerful demonstration of this point. Many of the same journalistic values and routines that made it difficult to believe in peace provided Israelis and Palestinians with overwhelming evidence of the need for war.

It is important, however, to begin with a few observations about the Israeli media's coverage of the Oslo peace process in the years immediately preceding the Camp David summit.

THE MEDIA, PEACE, AND THE NETANYAHU ERA

As discussed in chapter 3, one probable reason for Benyamin Netanyahu's victory in 1996 was his ability to raise the media prominence of the Palestinian threat to Israel's security. As Prime Minister, Netanyahu continued this same theme by continually accusing the Palestinians of violating the agreements that had been signed. The denigration of Arafat was a major and ongoing theme of Netanyahu's communication strategy. One of the radio reporters who spent a tremendous amount of time with the Prime Minister echoed what many others said.

> The Prime Minister and his people were extremely successful in undermining Arafat's position, in uncovering Arafat's face as he [Netanyahu] wanted it uncovered: that Arafat is not credible, that he doesn't honor the agreements, that he can't change the Palestinian charter, and all that . . . That's his mantra. It doesn't matter what you ask him [Netanyahu]. You ask him, "What's the weather?" and he'll tell you, "The weather will be better when Arafat keeps his word" . . . There's nothing to do, he has succeeded in inserting the message. (CD37, April 15, 1998)

Netanyahu constantly stressed two major differences between his approach and that of those who had preceded him. First, he wanted to "lower Palestinian expectations" about what they were going to get from Israel. Netanyahu claimed that Rabin and Peres had been too willing to make concessions to the other side. Second, he was going to demand "reciprocity": Israel would only keep its agreements if the Palestinians started doing the same. The Palestinian leadership grew increasingly angry about these ongoing attacks. An example of these sentiments can be found in comments made by a Palestinian negotiator in a magazine interview:

> "That's the difference between Netanyahu and Yitzhak Rabin," says the colonel, who has been involved in the peace talks since August 1993. "Rabin fought us fiercely at the negotiating table, but outside the room he described us as partners. He was courageous, so we could be too. But this person shakes our hand inside, then goes out and throws accusations at us." (Kerhner, 1999, p. 23)

The most severe crisis during this period took place in September of 1996. The Mayor of Jerusalem decided to create a new opening in an existing tunnel under the Temple Mount. Palestinians reacted with violence, and for the first time opened fire on Israeli troops. As one would expect, there was extensive coverage of these events, and this wave provided Oslo opponents with more ammunition against the Palestinians. The fact that the previous government had provided the Palestinians with weapons proved to be an especially potent accusation.

Despite all this, Netanyahu was still interested in making progress in the peace process. Indeed, Netanyahu signed two accords with the Palestinians, both of which met with significant opposition from his traditional supporters on the right. The first was the Hebron agreement, signed in January of 1997, which relinquished a considerable amount of control over that city. The second was the Wye agreement, signed in October of 1998, in which Netanyahu reluctantly agreed to withdraw from additional territories. As a result of this agreement, he was unable to hold on to his right-wing coalition and was forced to stand for early elections against Ehud Barak.

Thus it would be a mistake to paint the Netanyahu period in black and white terms. On the one hand Netanyahu had always opposed the Oslo peace process and lost no opportunity in calling Arafat a liar and a cheat. He was also a firm believer in the necessity, and the legitimacy, of building more settlements in the West Bank. Yet Netanyahu felt it was in Israel's interest to continue to negotiate with the Palestinians and to cooperate with them on security issues. Netanyahu believed that peace between Israel and the Palestinians should be based first and foremost on deterrence. Thus he was a major advocate of the Security First frame. One of his primary advisors and spokespeople provides a good summary of Netanyahu's approach to the Palestinians.

> The major question is if you demonstrate power and determination or you capitulate every time they [the Palestinians] do something to you. Because if you start with that, you never finish. So the trick is today, when Israel met all of its commitments and the other side did not do its part and threatens violence all the time, if all of the people stand behind the Prime Minister and say: OK, we stand behind you, stand firm until you succeed, then the Palestinians will quickly come around . . . Whoever deludes himself is an idiot. You have to come to an arrangement that guarantees your security even if the Palestinians don't like it. So we have to demonstrate determination and power and to understand that we need to keep our own interests here; this is not England and France. (CD38, June 29, 1997)

The role of the Israeli news media during this period is worthy of a separate study. In some ways the press became the "watchdogs" for Oslo by constantly criticizing Netanyahu for his inability to move the peace process forward. Many journalists who were interviewed also expressed an intense personal dislike of the Prime Minister, especially because of what they regarded as his ongoing attempts to manipulate the media. Netanyahu also made no secret of his own disdain for the press. At the same time Netanyahu's continual attacks on the Palestinians were still considered front-page news. It should also be remembered that there were many other ministers in Netanyahu's government promoting an even more anti-Palestinian position than the Prime Minister. Any animosity by the press towards Netanyahu was clearly not translated into sympathy for Arafat. As one senior news analyst put it: "We don't believe that Bibi [Netanyahu] wants peace nor that Arafat wants to fight terrorism" (CD31; September 9, 1997).

THE FLOW OF NEWS: WHAT WAS MISSING?

It is also important to think about the more general flow of news during the years leading up to Camp David. The standard values and routines ensured that very little good news about peace would get through. What was *not* considered news was in many ways just as revealing as what was. Perhaps the most important non-stories had to do with the long periods of quiet that characterized a good part of the Netanyahu years and most of Barak's rule. Not surprisingly, there were never any banner headlines announcing the tremendous decline in terrorism: a lack of events can hardly be considered news. One of the major reasons for the drop in violence was the amount of cooperation between the two security forces, but this too was rarely reported.[1] This period of quiet also brought a major boom of investment and tourism to Israel. The Israeli public would have been hard pressed, however, to find any news stories linking such successes to the peace process. Such reporting would have required a much more in-depth, analytical form of reporting. The enduring benefits of peace simply do not produce dramatic events; they are ongoing processes with virtually no news value.

The Israeli media displayed little interest in what was happening to the Palestinians during this same period. As with coverage of Jordan, the fundamental ethnocentrism of the Israeli media prevented most of the public from learning about the growing frustration and anger on the other side. While Israel was enjoying economic success during these years, the economic situation in the territories deteriorated (Roy, 2001). As discussed in chapter 4, the Israel press rarely carries stories about Palestinian suffering. Israel's occupation was, for the most part, invisible. The news media also had no reason to cover the continual building of settlements in the occupied territories. This was a natural, continual process, and unless the Palestinians reacted with violence, there was no event to report. For the Palestinians, on the other hand, the settlers represented a major and concrete threat.

Finally, there was almost nothing in the Israeli press during these years about Israeli violations of the signed agreements. Ron Pundak (2001), one of the original negotiators at Oslo, wrote about some of the most important violations that took place during the Netanyahu period. Israel did not leave all of the territories that were supposed to be transferred to the Palestinians, completed only one section out of four concerning the freeing of Palestinian prisoners, did not undertake the implementation of safe passage between the West Bank and Gaza, repeatedly delayed the building of the airport and maritime port in Gaza, and continually delayed the transfer of monies to the Palestinian Authority.

---

[1] It is worth nothing that besides the usual desire to keep such topics out of the news, both sides had other reasons to keep this cooperation secret. The Palestinian leadership didn't want to be accused of being "collaborators" and the Israeli government wanted to take full credit for the increasing sense of security.

The Israeli press did, however, provide extensive reporting about Palestinian violations. As noted, the Netanyahu government made sure that the media were provided with a steady stream of press releases, speeches and interviews on the topic. Pundak also provided a list of Palestinian violations:

> The Palestinians did not stop the vitriolic propaganda against Israel by radio, the printed press, television and schoolbooks; did not collect the illegal firearms; did not reach an agreement with Israel on the de facto growth of their Police Force; and did not prove that they were wholeheartedly combating fundamentalist terrorism, including the imprisonment of its activists. (2001, p. 4)

Given the prominence of Palestinian violations and the almost total lack of media attention given to their own country's infringements, most Israelis could reasonably conclude that their side was keeping all agreements while the other was violating them.

It is only fair to point out that the coverage in the Palestinian press was probably even more one-sided. The Palestinian press has never enjoyed freedom. In the years before the creation of the Palestinian Authority, there were many newspapers in operation, but they were all subject to strict Israeli censorship (Wolfsfeld and Rabihiya, 1988). Once Arafat took office, the Palestinian media (which quickly included television and radio) became fully mobilized for the cause. Little dissent was allowed: journalists who attempted overt criticism of the leadership were subject to arrest and imprisonment. The Palestinian press became a major instrument for promoting hatred towards Israel. Although the Palestinian people had more than enough reasons for their hostility towards the enemy, the Palestinian media served as an important agent for intensifying that antagonism. The Palestinian press ensured that any blame for their people's hardships be placed squarely on Israel.

Thus, despite the progress that had been made, each side's news media were telling their people very different stories about Oslo and neither version was encouraging. The Palestinian press was telling an ongoing story about Israeli oppression and treachery, and about their own leaders' heroic attempts to bring independence to their people. The Israeli news story was filled with stories about Palestinian violations of the previous agreement and increasing demands for more concessions. The story in the Israeli press was probably less extreme in that it was less blatantly ideological and did include criticism of the Netanyahu government, especially by the opposition. Nevertheless, there was little in either news media that would either increase trust in the other side or convince people that peace was possible.

The complete divergence between the Palestinian and Israeli news media presents a stark contrast from the situation in Northern Ireland, where both sides of the conflict were being told similar stories. It is difficult to overestimate the importance of this factor in determining the overall impact of the media on a peace process. When antagonistic populations continually tell themselves hateful stories about the other, reconciliation becomes almost impossible. Even if everything else was the same, one would have to conclude that this difference alone meant that the Palestinian and Israeli news media will always be more likely to serve as obstacles to peace than those in Northern Ireland.

The difficulty in promoting Oslo in Israel became especially evident during the 1999 election campaign. Netanyahu – despite the fact that he had just signed the Wye agreement with the Palestinians – ran the same anti-Palestinian campaign as he had in 1996. His campaign focused on three major issues: terrorism, security, and the division of Jerusalem (Weimann and Wolfsfeld, 2002). One of his most important messages was that only he could ensure that the Palestinians would keep their promises. Ehud Barak, on the other hand, ran a different campaign than Peres had run in the previous election. While Peres ran on the peace ticket, the Barak message centered on economic issues and on his ability to bring security to Israel. An analysis of Barak's television advertisements reveals that he almost completely avoided talking about the peace process (Weimann and Wolfsfeld, 2002). Thus both candidates emphasized security and the Peace frame was nowhere to be found. This is especially surprising, given the fact that the peace process had in fact been moving forward at the time.[2]

THE ISRAELI NEWS MEDIA AND THE CAMP DAVID SUMMIT

Although Ehud Barak did not run on a peace ticket, once elected he focused almost all of his efforts toward achieving that goal. He first

---

[2] Interestingly, this situation was reversed in the special elections that were held in 2001. Despite the fact that Israel was in the midst of the Second Intifada, both Ariel Sharon and Ehud Barak placed a great deal of emphasis on the notion of peace. Perhaps both candidates were attempting to provide voters with some hope due to the generally dismal situation.

attempted to reach peace with the Syrians and when that failed turned his attention to the Palestinians. The culmination of those efforts took place in July of 2000 when President Clinton convened a summit between Barak and Arafat with the explicit goal of reaching a final settlement between the two sides. The summit began on July 11 and ended in failure on the 25th of that month.

The analysis begins, as always, by examining the political environment surrounding the Camp David summit. One of the major themes of this work centers on the importance of elite consensus on media performance. Given this formula, it is hard to imagine a political leader in a more difficult situation than Barak as he left for Camp David. Barak's political coalition had completely fallen apart in the weeks leading up to the summit, as a direct result of the concessions he was reportedly planning to make to the Palestinians. Three different political parties (Shas, Mafdal, and Yisrael B'Aliya) abandoned his government after learning that the Prime Minister was planning to offer compromises on Jerusalem. The day before his departure for Washington, Barak suffered a humiliating defeat in the Knesset by losing a no-confidence vote. Although he remained in office (the opposition failed to mobilize an absolute majority), the Knesset had made it clear that the Prime Minister was traveling to Camp David without their support.[3]

The resignations of Barak's coalition partners and the defeat in the Knesset had a major impact on the initial news stories about the talks. Consider the main headline in *Yediot Ahronot*, the most popular newspaper in Israel: "To the Summit – Alone" (July 10, 2000, p. 1). This frame was an important organizing device for many other stories in the newspaper that day. Under the clever caption "Alone at the Summit" there are a number of stories portraying Barak as the tragic hero single-handedly attempting to defeat the odds and bring peace to Israel. The assumption is that his only chance of political survival was to bring some type of agreement back from Washington.

The resignations of the various parties from the government also provided an important opportunity for a variety of leaders to publicly attack Barak about his willingness to make compromises to the Palestinians. The fact that these condemnations were coming from his coalition

---

[3] A number of news reports suggested that the Palestinians were also concerned about Barak's lack of political support at home. Thus, on the opening day of the summit Palestinian leader Muchammad Dahlan talked about his concern that the lack of consensus at home would make it almost impossible for the Prime Minister to either come to or implement an agreement (*Yediot Ahronot*, July 11, 2000, p. 7).

partners makes them both more newsworthy and more damaging. Thus the leader of the Russian immigrants party, Natan Sharansky, accused Barak of "polarizing the people" (*Yediot*, July 10, 2000, p. 4). Sharansky also set up a "protest tent," which remained in place during the course of summit, drawing scores of supporters and reporters. This was only one of many such groups, including one which carried out a well-covered hunger strike. Even worse, Foreign Minister David Levy, who ran for election with Barak, refused to travel to the summit, claiming that it would be a disaster for Israel. Barak's political failures were quite real. As always, the role of the news media was to amplify these failures and to provide them with narrative structure.

There is another part of the political picture that also had a major impact on the role of the news media at Camp David. Barak's stated strategy was to offer what he saw as the maximum amount of concessions that Israel would be willing to make for a final settlement. This move would lead to one of two outcomes. The best scenario would be that it would lead to a peace agreement. If not, then at least the Israeli public and the world would know that Israel had done everything it could for peace. In direct contrast to the initial Oslo strategy, it would be either all or nothing. Thus Israel would either have peace or at least have insured that any failure would be blamed on Arafat and the Palestinians.[4] Once it was clear that the summit would fail the Israeli government carried out an extensive campaign to promote this message.

While many in Israel know quite a bit about the political environment of that time, few have given much thought to the role the news media played at Camp David. The construction of the story of Camp David can be attributed to both the political interests of Israeli leaders and the professional routines of the media. A critical reading of the Hebrew press reveals three familiar problems with the news coming out of Camp David: 1) A major emphasis on the costs and risks associated with the negotiations and almost nothing about possible benefits; 2) a predisposition to view the summit as an isolated event with almost no reference to the long-term process; 3) a major stress on Israel's generosity and the Palestinians' intransigence. All of these tendencies can be attributed to the four values for the construction of news discussed in chapter 1: immediacy, drama, simplicity, and ethnocentrism.

---

[4] Barak talked once again about this strategy in an interview given in *Newsweek* a year after the Camp David summit (Weymouth, 2001).

THE COSTS OF PEACE

One of most significant facets of the news about Camp David was the emphasis on the concessions Israel was considering with virtually no discussion of the benefits peace could bring. There are a number of reasons for this tendency, all of which provide insights into the more general problems associated with the long-term coverage of the Oslo peace process. One reason has to do with the underlying inequality inherent in the Israel–Palestinian conflict. Israel holds the almost all of the assets that were being negotiated. The underlying concept of the Oslo process was land for peace. The serious problem in promoting this formula to the Israeli media (and to the Israeli people) stems from the fact that land is concrete while peace is abstract. In the early stages of the Oslo process, the Palestinians were in a position to offer somewhat more tangible concessions, such as cooperation against terrorism. The final talks at Camp David, on the other hand, focused almost exclusively on what Israel would concede.

In addition, this was the first time that an Israeli leader was offering such concessions. The idea that Israel might be giving up the vast majority of the territories, giving up sovereignty over half of Jerusalem (including possibly the Temple Mount), and even giving up some of its own land was indeed dramatic news. In contrast, the idea that the Israelis and the Palestinians might someday sign a peace agreement could hardly be considered a novel idea. The only circumstances in which the news might consider peace newsworthy would be if the two sides had actually come to an agreement. This is what happened during the "peace festival" that was described in chapter 2.

Dealing with an issue such as Jerusalem makes perfect journalistic sense; constructing news about an eventual peace makes no sense at all. News stories about Jerusalem include maps of how the city will be divided, details about the division of responsibilities, and visual images of the areas in question. Equally important, it is an extremely emotional issue which everyone, especially the opposition, is anxious to talk about. The controversy surrounding such concessions provides for dramatic confrontations on every talk-show on both radio and television. There is really nothing, on the other hand, to report about "peace." Although leaders can always provide familiar platitudes about the importance of peace, this can hardly be considered news. There is also nothing controversial about peace itself; nor is there anything to argue about. The heart of such controversies centers on the risks concerning the agreement, not on the ultimate desire to have peace.

The emphasis of the local news media on Israeli concessions was certainly not in Barak's interest, at least at first. One could argue that a certain number of leaks about compromises would have prepared the Israeli public for the shocks that could come. What was clear was that the emphasis on issues such as Jerusalem provided the opposition with important ammunition against the government. Thus, in the middle of the summit, Barak's opponents mobilized one of the largest protests ever held in Jerusalem, when an estimated 200,000 Israelis came out to demonstrate against the division of the city. Major news stories about the "surrender" at Camp David certainly made it much easier to mobilize the masses against the agreement.

Every government negotiating peace faces a similar dilemma. The communication needs for achieving success at the negotiating table are exactly the opposite of those needed to mobilize political support at home (Wolfsfeld, 2003). The home front wants to be assured that its leaders are "winning," that they are succeeding in obtaining the maximum number of concessions from the enemy while paying the smallest possible price. The major message is that of steadfastness. In the negotiations themselves, on the other hand, success depends on convincing the other side that one is willing to compromise. The only way to deal with this contradiction is to keep the talks secret. There can be little doubt that one of the reasons for the success of the initial breakthrough at Oslo was that neither side had to constantly defend themselves against charges that they were giving away too much to the other side.

The attempts to keep the talks at Camp David secret were only partially successful. The most newsworthy leaks about concessions seriously undermined Barak's argument that he was not going to cross Israel's "red lines." Such reports automatically placed the Israeli delegation on the defensive at home. As an example, consider the phraseology in the following news story:

> There is a draft, but no agreement. Senior Israeli sources admitted yesterday that Barak had, to all intents and purposes, agreed to the division of Jerusalem between Israel and the Palestinians, such that Arafat will receive sovereignty over several East Jerusalem neighborhoods, and "quasi-sovereignty" over the Moslem holy places on the Temple Mount. (*Ma'ariv*, July 25, 2000, p. 2)

Concessions in the interest of peace are something that leaders are forced to *admit*. This can certainly not be considered good news for Israel: Giving up territory implies failure. The Israeli delegation was especially exasperated by those news stories that exaggerated the extent of concessions they were offering. Gilad Sher, one of the top negotiators later spoke publicly about the difficulties they had in denying such stories.[5] Denying such rumors would serve to make the negotiations with the Palestinians more difficult. A failure to refute such stories, on the other hand, would be seen by many as proof that they were true.

The Israeli delegation also attempted to promote the idea that they had forced the Palestinians into making concessions. It was important to demonstrate that Israel was not only giving but also getting something in return. Thus there were unconfirmed reports that the Palestinians had agreed that some Jewish settlements would remain in Israeli hands after the agreement had been signed. The Palestinians, on the other hand, were extremely reluctant to verify any such reports. Saleh Abdel Jawad, a Palestinian political scientist, talked about this aversion in an interview with an Israeli journalist (Hass, 2001). He argued that the Palestinian leadership was so concerned with the political fallout of concessions that they never publicly admitted to what they had offered at Camp David.

Thus in the first days of the summit Barak faced familiar problems in his attempts to promote peace to the Israeli news media. The lack of political consensus concerning Camp David ensured that almost everything that came out of the talks would be considered controversial. It was also clear that it would be impossible to completely prevent leaks about Israeli concessions, and that such stories would be considered big news. This provided the opposition and the public with a continual flow of evidence that Barak was giving in to the Palestinians.

CAMP DAVID AS AN ISOLATED EVENT

The second important feature of Camp David news coverage was the lack of any reference to the past or the future. It was argued earlier in this book that the news media have a great deal of difficulty dealing with long-term processes such as ongoing efforts to achieve peace. Given definitions of

---

[5] Lecture given in a seminar organized by the Jaffe Center for Strategic Research at Tel Aviv University on July 9, 2001. The title of the seminar was: "The Media as Strategy: the Israeli-Palestinian Conflict."

what is considered news, journalists have little choice but to turn such processes into a series of simple, dramatic events. This makes it extremely difficult for citizens to develop the type of long-range perspective that is so critical to any attempt to negotiate peace. In addition, the inability of the press to deal with complex issues inhibits any deeper understanding about the roots of the conflict or about various alternatives for resolving it.

The unwillingness of the Israeli press to place the Camp David events within a more general context was significant. While it had certainly been an extremely difficult and painful path over the years, the Israelis and Palestinians had moved forward and had found a number of areas where they could work together. Yet – apart from some nostalgic references to the previous summit at Camp David between Begin and Sadat – it was almost impossible for citizens to place this particular event within a broader historic context.

Perhaps even more problematic was the media's failure to suggest that negotiations might continue after Camp David. The Palestinians continually stressed the need for a series of meetings, and expressed doubt that all of the outstanding issues could be solved in a couple of weeks. President Clinton and Prime Minster Barak, on the other hand, were both emphasizing the importance of coming to a final settlement at Camp David. The Israeli Prime Minister was especially emphatic about his "all or nothing" strategy. But one might have expected at least some of the journalists to raise questions about whether it was possible to solve age-old disputes over Jerusalem and the Palestinians' right of return in a fortnight. In the end, however, one can say that there was an almost perfect mesh between Barak's all or nothing strategy and the media's need for closure. It is worth noting in this regard that negotiations did resume after Camp David, and even continued after the outbreak of the Intifada. Reports suggest that considerable progress was made in this next set of negotiations. However, by that time Barak was heading for almost certain defeat in the elections.

Journalists covering such high-profile negotiations find themselves in an admittedly difficult position. Due to the high stakes involved, there is a tremendous thirst for information. Israeli reporters who have been sent to the United States to cover the summit are expected to continually produce news stories. Yet the flow of substantive information that actually emerges from such negotiations is both sporadic and limited. How many times can one report that Barak is offering to divide Jerusalem? Thus they must find alternative materials to fill the large news hole that has been prepared for their story. As might be expected, this leads to rather poor journalism.

One of the ways journalists cope with this problem is to look at the summit as a sort of sports event with winners and losers. Thus reporters analyze the tactics being used in order to gain advantages, talk about what each leader has to gain or lose from various developments, and continually try to assess whether the talks will end in success or failure. This tendency among journalists to use a "strategic focus" has received a great deal of attention with regard to election campaigns (Cappella and Jamieson, 1997; Patterson, 1993; Sabato, 2000; Valentino, Beckmann, and Buhr, 2001). In some ways the use of this focus is even more problematic with regard to a peace process. Elections are inherently competitive, while peace negotiations would be better seen as a cooperative effort to end conflict. It is true that each delegation is attempting to achieve the best possible agreement for their people. Nevertheless, by emphasizing the competitive aspect of this process, the media reinforce the assumption that one side's achievement is always the other side's loss. This zero-sum frame makes it difficult to promote the idea that a successful peace process can benefit both sides.

The frantic search for clues about how the summit will end can also lead to some ridiculous news stories. Starved for visual materials, analysts will attempt to interpret every picture they get. This phenomenon is reminiscent of the attempts by Kremlinologists to decipher changes in the Soviet leadership by dissecting pictures of leaders viewing the annual May Day parades. Probably the best-known example of this phenomenon at Camp David was the "wrestling by the door" segment, in which Barak and Arafat each insisted on letting the other enter the door first. The scene shows a playful, smile-filled struggle in which Barak eventually pushes Arafat through the entrance. It was an irresistible piece, susceptible to countless interpretations. Few pundits could resist the temptation of analyzing its inner meaning. At the very least, some said, it was an optimistic sign that the leaders were getting along with each other. The scene has since become an historical icon to be used whenever television news in Israel refers to Camp David. There is no reason to believe, however, that this incident meant anything at all.

The exaggerated importance attributed to this scene also demonstrates another important aspect of summit coverage: the emphasis on personalities. Not only was the summit often framed as a sports contest; it was a game of one-on-one. The news focused almost exclusively on Barak,

Arafat, and Clinton (as the referee). How was their mood? Did they look happy or concerned? What tactics was each using to place pressure on the other side? What were they wearing and eating? What did they have to gain or lose if the talks failed?

Consider an item from one of the television reporters for Channel 1 that appeared on the evening news after Barak had threatened to leave in negotiations. She began by quoting from a letter from the Prime Minister that had been written to Clinton and leaked to the Israeli press. Stressing the theme that would soon become familiar, Barak blamed Arafat for his unwillingness to conduct serious negotiations and warned that the Palestinian people would have to bear the tragic consequences. The reporter then provided her own interpretation of what was happening.

> This letter, more than it is directed at Bill Clinton, is directed at the Israeli public. Barak is starting his public relations [*hasbara*] campaign in the public relations war about how can it be that he returns, it seems, without an agreement. He will have to explain to many people, also among those that supported him, how it happened that after ten days they didn't come to agreement here. This letter is part of that public relations effort, which is why it was leaked so quickly after Clinton received it. (Karen Neubach, *Channel 1 Evening News*, July 19, 2000)

The most important element that gets lost in this type of reporting concerns the national goals and interests of the two peoples. Thus one might think that the more important question is what Israelis and Palestinians have to lose from the failure to achieve a settlement. The focus on the leaders themselves suggests that the summit is really more of a political contest than an historic opportunity to achieve genuine peace. Barak's chances of surviving politically if the summit should fail is far less important than what will happen if the enemies return to violence.

Many journalists would see these criticisms as unreasonable. Yes, they would argue, it would be very nice if we could provide serious analytical coverage of such events, but we are in the news business. The public has no interest at all in reading intellectual treatises that attempt to place the summit within a larger historical context. The more knowledgeable citizens will do that by themselves and the less informed refuse to look at that type of coverage. Our job, they would argue, is to provide interesting reports about current events. This argument makes a good deal of sense.

It is indeed unreasonable to demand of journalists more than the public will bear. Nevertheless, more could and should be done to raise the level of coverage. The task of critics is to point out the serious consequences of low-level journalism, and to hope that more journalists will strive to raise the bar.

ISRAELI GENEROSITY AND PALESTINIAN INTRANSIGENCE: UNMASKING ARAFAT

The overall story line that emerged in the aftermath of Camp David can be roughly summarized as follows: *Barak went to Camp David where he made Arafat an extremely generous offer that included 98 percent of the territories, half of Jerusalem, and even some land within Israel itself. Arafat stupidly rejected that offer and responded with a brutal terrorist wave in order to achieve through violence what he could not attain at the bargaining table.* It is also fair to conclude that this interpretation became the conventional wisdom within Israel, expressed in countless editorials and by a myriad of leaders from both left and right.

Whatever problems Barak and his team had in promoting peace, they faced few obstacles in driving the campaign against Arafat. There is also evidence that the "Palestinian Intransigence" frame was in place even before Camp David began. A number of reporters talked about the fact that Barak's advisors were already blaming the Palestinians from the start. The most convincing interview on this point comes from one of Barak's chief spokespersons, who talked about the public relations strategies that were prepared for the summit.

> We prepared public relations [*hasbara*] strategies for three scenarios. Scenario one: that there is an agreement that includes painful concessions on one hand but tremendous achievements on the other. The second scenario was that there is an agreement but it is a partial agreement and it will have an additional stage of negotiations that will come. The third scenario: that the summit does not give birth to an agreement. Naturally each of these scenarios was possible and we built a strategy to deal with each one. And in the end the result – because of our deployment during the summit – proved that while the summit failed politically, from a public relations perspective Israel's position was the dominant position in the international, American, and national media. (CD42; August 8, 2001)

The spokesperson goes on to talk about how important such a public relations strategy is in conducting a media campaign to convince world leaders. He was also pleased that – although some revisionist interpretations had since emerged – Israel's central argument about what happened at Camp David remained intact. The journalists who were interviewed also agreed on the success of the campaign to blame Arafat for the failure at Camp David. Aluf Ben (2001), who covered the summit for the newspaper *Ha'aretz*, wrote about the continued success of this message a full year after the Camp David summit had ended.

One also learns from the above quote that, despite all that was said publicly, Barak and his staff were prepared for a partial agreement. In any case what actually happened was somewhat different than any of the three scenarios that were anticipated. As noted, the summit ended in failure but the negotiations continued. They even persisted after the outbreak of the Second Intifada. One can only wonder if a more encouraging message concerning the peace process might have lowered the level of tension in the days that followed the summit.

In any case, the Israeli news media were more than willing to blame the Palestinians for the failure, even before the summit began. A telling illustration of this theme can be found in the coverage accompanying the opening day of the summit. A story in *Yediot Ahronot* (July 7, 2000, p. 7) provides a rather colorful description of the negotiating team representing the two sides. Each negotiator is given a nickname, designed to say something about the role they can be expected to play in the talks. The various members of the Israeli team are referred to as: the "creative one," the "intellectual," the "compromiser," the "insider," and the "joker." The members of the Palestinian delegation have rather different types of monikers: "the influential," "the sophisticated," "the obstinate," "the restrainer" [*hamechashek*], and the "rigid" [*hanukshe*]. Thus, already before the negotiations begin, the Israelis are generous and flexible while the Palestinians are obstinate.

One finds evidence of this spin in almost every news report about the summit. It is a story about Israel continually making extensive concessions and the Palestinians repeatedly refusing to compromise. Here are some examples:

Apart from a generally positive atmosphere, there is nothing positive to report. As it looks now, it is not at all clear that there will be an agreement, said the Israeli delegation . . . According to them there is no progress because Arafat brought with him the familiar merchandise from Gaza: return to the 67 borders, Palestinian sovereignty over East Jerusalem, and implementing the right to return. Unless there is a massive American intervention, accompanied by pressure on the Palestinians, there is no way to achieve an agreement. (*Yediot Ahronot*, July 16, 2000, p. 4)

In the meantime, there is a growing feeling of general pessimism . . . At this stage Arafat has rejected out of hand the compromise proposals of Ehud Barak concerning Jerusalem . . . The Israeli delegation has found Arafat to be a centralist leader who makes all the decisions himself and continually makes clear that he does not intend to compromise on less than the maximum. (*Ma'ariv*, July 18, 2000, p. 1)

[Large headline] Arafat Refuses Barak's Compromise Proposal for Jerusalem. (*Yediot Ahronot*, July 19, 2000, p. 1)

There were a number of reasons why this theme tended to dominate news of Camp David and its aftermath. One of the most important is that it resonated with so many different elements among the political elite. Once Barak had turned against the Palestinians, opposition from the right had no problem agreeing that Barak had been generous; their whole point was that he was being *too* generous. They were also in full agreement that the Palestinians should be blamed for any lack of progress in the peace process. The only political leaders that disagreed with the anti-Palestinian spin were the Arab Knesset members, whom the Hebrew news media regarded as extremists. The news media are incapable of expressing ideas that fall outside of what is considered mainstream consensus (Bennett, 1990).

It is also critical to understand something about just who was really telling the Israeli story about what is happening at Camp David. It was both natural and inevitable that the Israeli media depended on Barak's spokespeople for almost every piece of information they received. The normal reliance on official sources becomes even greater in a controlled environment such as Camp David. Israeli journalists tried to pump American and Palestinian sources for information, but the most useful information came from their own people. The construction of the news at Camp David was to a large extent a matter of Israeli journalists telling stories to their fellow Israelis based (mostly) on their Israeli sources. One of the reporters who was at Camp David talked about the situation.

Some of the media at the summit mostly used what the Prime Minister's spokesperson put out and one had to be careful not to be completely swept up. Some succeeded more and some less. The Israeli reporters had a problem, I think more than in any other summit. There was very little information from the Americans, and during all of the various stages there was almost nothing from the Palestinians . . . There was very little information in comparison to Wye [plantation talks] or to Shepherdstown. Even in Shepherdstown with the Syrians, they passed information through the Arab media, but they still passed on information. At Camp David there was very little information from the Palestinians. (CD43; July 9, 2001)

In addition few journalists had any reason to raise any doubts about the Palestinian Intransigence frame. Although there were some earlier hints about what the government was going to do, the reporters were just as amazed by what Barak was offering as everyone else in Israel. To the vast majority of Israelis this was indeed a generous offer and thus Arafat's refusal to agree was not only unfathomable, it was infuriating. This brings us back to the fundamental ethnocentrism of all media. The same journalist quoted above made this point rather well when asked why there was such an emphasis on Israel's generosity.

Because the Israeli reporters come from the Israeli way of life. Because by Israeli standards the concessions that Barak offered at Camp David, regardless for now what there exactly were, especially when it came to Jerusalem, were really above and beyond anything that anybody else had offered. The Israeli reporters, given that they were Israeli citizens, were amazed at the acuteness of the concessions. Less thought was given to the issue of the distance between those concessions and Arafat's bottom-line demands. (CD43; July 9, 2001)

An important turning point in the Camp David story took place on July 19. There was a major crisis in the talks and Barak had given the order for the Israeli delegation to "pack their suitcases." This was a well-known tactic used by Israelis and Palestinians in the past, and the talks did continue for a few more days. Far more important, however, was that Barak spoke publicly against Arafat and knowingly established the "Palestinian Intransigence" frame that would become so important in the coming months. Here is the quote as it appeared in *Yediot Ahronot*: "The Prime Minister Attacks: 'Arafat lost an historic opportunity to achieve peace because of his obstinacy. He is not a partner for peace'" (July 19, p. 4). The Prime Minister and his advisors continually stressed this theme throughout the remainder of the summit.

Three important details are worthy noting about this spin. The first is that the media's emphasis on Israeli concessions could now be turned to Barak's advantage: It proved that Israel had been generous. Second, this was probably the first time that the Prime Minister officially declared that Arafat was not a "partner for peace." This was an important development for, once such an idea became widely accepted in Israel, it signaled the end of the Oslo peace process. The notion that "there was no one to talk to" was an extremely pervasive belief in Israel in the past, especially before President Sadat of Egypt recognized Israel. Although Barak vacillated on this issue in the following weeks, he would return to it after the outbreak of the Second Intifada. The third point has to do with Arafat "losing an historic opportunity," which was also alluded to earlier. The rather condescending argument that the Palestinians were being "foolish" or that "they would be the ones to suffer the most" was another message that would be constantly repeated in the wake of Camp David.

The fact that Barak turned to the media at this juncture in the talks provides an important lesson about the role of the press in such negotiations. A great deal of emphasis is placed on the damage that the presence of the media can have on such talks. Much less understood is the fact that relationship between media involvement and the success of negotiations actually runs to both directions. When negotiations are going well, both sides have an interest in keeping the news media away. A high level of cooperation behind closed doors leads to cooperation with regards to the media outside of the doors. As mentioned earlier, however, when there is a crisis in the talks, each side is anxious to turn to the media in order to ensure that the blame will be placed on the other side. This, of course, is likely to make things even worse. Thus this dynamic provides yet another demonstration of the PMP cycle. A change in the political climate (crisis in the negotiations) leads to a change in media coverage (negative coverage of the other side) that leads to further changes in the political climate (more tensions between the antagonists).

Robert Malley (2001), a senior member of the Clinton's team at Camp David, provides an alternative perspective on what took place at Camp David. He published his argument in an editorial that was published in the *New York Times* a year after the summit was over.[6] He begins by admitting that he too was "frustrated almost to the point of despair by the Palestinians' passivity and inability to seize the moment." Malley argues, though, that "there is no purpose – and considerable harm – in adding to their real mistakes a list of fictional ones." He then talks about what he considers three of the "most dangerous myths about the Camp David Summit." The first myth is that Camp David was an ideal test of Mr. Arafat's intentions. Malley points out that Arafat had told the Americans on many occasions that he did not want to go to Camp David because the gaps between the two sides were too great. Arafat argued that any premature convening of the summit could lead to disaster. The second myth was that Israel's offer met most if not all of the Palestinians' legitimate aspirations. One piece of counter-evidence to this claim has to do with the "land exchange" offered by Israel in exchange for the territories it was planning to annex in the West Bank. The amount being offered, argued Malley, was one-ninth the size of what was being taken. The third myth was that the Palestinians made no concessions of their own. The author argues that the Palestinians did accept the annexation of West Bank territory for the settlement blocs and that significant limits would be placed on the number of Palestinian refugees that would be allowed into Israel. Malley concludes by placing a certain amount of blame on both sides for the failure at Camp David.

It is not being argued here that the Palestinian Intransigence frame was incorrect. It is only fair to point out that President Clinton also contributed to this interpretation by placing most of the blame for the failure at Camp David on Arafat. Perhaps Barak was right in placing all of the responsibility on the Palestinians. It is also unreasonable to demand that the Israeli news media bring a "balanced" form of coverage that would attribute equal credibility to the Palestinian version of what took place. There is certainly no evidence that the Palestinian coverage of the summit was any less subjective. The problem with how the news media operate at such junctures is that the dominant frame becomes taken as a given, as a fact. Because there were no "legitimate" sponsors of alternative frames, the Hebrew news media were incapable of even considering any other perspectives. The official spin quickly became the

---

[6] The article was also translated into Hebrew and published in *Ha'aretz* (July 10, 2001, p. B1). Other "revisionist" interpretations of what happened at Camp David soon joined it.

official history of the event. It was only a year later that careful observers could find a few cracks in this official wall.

Prime Minister Barak often claimed after Camp David that one of his greatest accomplishments had been the "unmasking of Arafat in order to show his real face." This metaphor also became widely used within Israel as a shortcut device for describing what happened at Camp David. Barak also warned that as a result of the failure, the Palestinians might turn to violence.[7] Barak wanted to make it clear, however, that if that happened: "we would be able to look at our children straight in their eyes and know that we had done everything, everything we could to prevent the conflict" (*Yediot*, July 26, 2000, p. 2). The violence between the two sides erupted only a short time later and with an intensity few could have imagined just a few months before.

THE ISRAELI NEWS MEDIA AND THE OUTBREAK OF THE SECOND INTIFADA

The rapid shift from Camp David to the outbreak of the Second Intifada provides a powerful demonstration of how differently the news media deal with conflict and peace. The ongoing difficulties in promoting the Oslo peace process to the media become more vivid when one compares the relative ease of mobilizing the Israeli media in the battle against the Palestinians. The same journalistic values that were considered obstacles in attempts to tell pro-peace stories became major assets in the war effort. Unlike a peace process, for example, it is relatively easy to divide a war into an ongoing series of dramatic events. In addition, while wars can be thought of in complex terms, they can also be translated into fairly simple news stories. Such news stories deal with concrete details such as where the various confrontations are taking place, what happened, and how many were wounded or killed. Perhaps the most important value for promoting wars has to do with the fundamental ethnocentrism of

---

[7] One interesting fact is often left out of this story. After the failure of Camp David, a number of Palestinians were expressing quite a bit of optimism that the two sides could still reach an agreement. Sa'eb Arikat, for example, claimed that he believed the agreement would be signed by September 13 (*Ma'ariv*, July 26, 2000, p. 6). In that same press conference it was reported that he made every effort not to place the blame for failure on the Israelis. This approach was consistent with their early claims that a final settlement would require a series of talks rather than one summit. It also suggests that the Palestinians were not necessarily preparing their people for war after the failure at Camp David.

the news media, which facilitates the demonization of the enemy. Given the long and bitter history of most conflicts, the media and the public have little problem accepting stories that are rooted in traditional views of the other side.

Once again the discussion begins by examining the political environment in Israel surrounding the Second Intifada. As discussed, Prime Minister Barak had been extremely successful in blaming the Palestinians for the failure at Camp David. It was difficult to find a Jewish leader who was willing to disagree with this position. Thus there was broad consensus against Arafat and a general pessimism about the chances for peace. Nevertheless, there were also some reasons for optimism concerning the subsequent negotiations. The most positive development took place on September 25th. Arafat came to Barak's home at Kochav Yair for the first time and both sides reported that serious progress was being made towards an agreement.

On September 28, 2000 Ariel Sharon – then head of the Israeli opposition – came to the Temple Mount in order to demonstrate his determination to maintain Jerusalem as the undivided capital of Israel. The Palestinians saw this as a provocative act and some form of violence was inevitable. In the coming weeks there was a great deal of local and international debate over whether Sharon's visit was the "real" reason for the outbreak of the Intifada. The Barak government defended Sharon, arguing that Arafat had only used the visit as a pretext for initiating a wave of violence against Israel. In keeping with his earlier warnings, Barak argued that Arafat's goal was to achieve further concessions from Israel. Israel had no intention, he said, of giving in to Palestinian aggression.[8] There was no choice, it was said, but to fight.

It was argued earlier that political waves often provide important advantages to particular frames. When such waves run in a particular

---

[8] One of the historical facts that is often left out of this debate concerns the sequence of events at the Temple Mount. While there was a good deal of violence associated with Sharon's visit on Thursday the 28th, no one from either side was killed. Far more important were the events of the following few days, in which scores of Palestinians were killed. Thus on Friday the 29th five Palestinians were killed during riots at the Temple Mount. The level of violence rose considerably after that and on Saturday eleven were killed including twelve-year-old Mohammed al-Dura, whose tragic death was broadcast around the world. Thus one could certainly argue that the failure to use non-lethal means of quelling the Friday riots was far more important than Sharon's visit. One might also ask whether the failure to deal with this aspect of the issue has to do with the relatively low level of prominence given to Palestinian deaths in Israeli news reports.

direction they provide compelling "evidence" that one frame is correct and the other wrong. The larger the wave is, the more significant and long-lasting its impact. Given this, the outbreak of the Second Intifada could only be described as a tidal wave. It was the ultimate proof that Oslo had failed and that any hopes for real peace with the Palestinians were illusionary. After the Rabin assassination, the press had demanded that the right wing "search their souls" about where they had gone wrong. Now it was the architects of Oslo that were being asked to do the same. The political pendulum took a dramatic swing to the right and every Israeli death pushed it further in that direction.

The fact that a Labor Prime Minister was leading the initial attack against the Palestinians ensured the ultimate success of the Anti-Palestinian frame. This is similar to what happened in the United States during the early years of the Vietnam War (Halin, 1986). In both cases the broad consensus among political elites led to the press adopting a relatively uncritical view of the war effort. The few who came out publicly against government actions were seen as extremists. If nothing else, many Israeli pundits claimed, at least the Intifada had brought the country together again. This new sense of unity became especially apparent after Sharon was elected Prime Minister and had formed a National Unity government, appointing Shimon Peres as his Foreign Minister. In addition, despite the change in government, there was little change in either frames or policy. Given the fact that Barak had unmasked the true Arafat, no alternatives were available.

As before, the news media not only reflected such changes in the political environment, they served as central agents for intensifying them and providing them with narrative structure. This process becomes manifest in times of war, especially when the war enjoys a broad level of public support. Political passions run high and most citizens expect the press to be patriotic. The news media lose a great deal of their independence during such crises and political and military leaders find it much easier to promote their messages to the public (Wolfsfeld, 1997a). Only if there is a serious breach in this elite consensus can the news media regain some semblance of independence and articulate a more critical voice.

The outbreak of the Second Intifada led the Israeli news media to adopt a war mode of reporting. While it is possible to develop a long list of norms and routines associated with such crises, the present discussion will zero in on three important professional devices. Each of these mechanisms facilitated the promotion of an anti-Palestinian frame to the Israeli media and public. The first was a major change in *news slots* whereby the topic of Palestinian violence dominated the media agenda. The second change was an increasing *level of cooperation with government and military officials*, with little criticism of their policies. Finally, and perhaps most importantly, was the *ethnocentric coverage of death*: the Israeli news media related to Israeli fatalities as major tragedies while Palestinian deaths were given little attention. None of these news routines are unusual; they are typical of what happens when a country goes to war. Nevertheless, understanding how each of these engines operates helps illuminate why it is so much easier to promote war than peace.

CHANGES IN NEWS SLOTS: PALESTINIAN VIOLENCE AT THE CORE

The most general mechanism has to do with the change in news slots. It was argued in previous chapters that one of the benefits of the Oslo and Jordanian peace processes was that they had provided journalists with new ways of covering the other side. The very fact that there were news stories about meetings and negotiations provided Israelis with a different perspective on the conflict. Even bad news about a peace process, it was argued, was better than scenes of war. The problem was that there was not enough peace news to fill up these slots. Even during times of relative calm, the most important stories often focused on the threat posed by the Palestinians. The case of Jordan was even more revealing, for this was a peace process that enjoyed a tremendous amount of public support. Nevertheless, once the hoopla over those peace ceremonies had died down, there was little of any interest to report about that country. The news slot for peace stories was available but nothing was considered interesting enough to fill it.

There is rarely any problem filling news slots created for wars.[9] There is an unlimited supply of valuable news stories about threats and destruction. While even a successful peace process provides a limited number of major events, wars provide multiple waves that continue for an extended period of time. While there is rarely any reason for journalists to put in overtime covering a peace process, during a war they are lucky

---

[9] There are, however, some interesting lulls in which the media carves out a major news hole for the conflict, but a lack of concrete events makes it difficult to fill. A good example can be found by viewing the US coverage of the "War Against Terror" that preceded the actual attack on the Taliban in Afghanistan.

to get home. The biggest challenge facing editors during war is to find an efficient method for shifting through the flood of information and images.

It is true that certain events become routine. Thus, while the first few times shots were fired on the Jerusalem neighborhood of Gilo (which the Palestinians consider a settlement) it was considered big news; such stories received much less prominence as time passed. Nevertheless, all such shootings continued to be reported on Israeli television and radio on a daily basis a full year after they began. Unlike the relatively narrow slot reserved for routine peace stories, the amount of time and space reserved for war is huge and expandable. Week after week, month after month, news of the Intifada dominated the public agenda, driving out almost any other concern.

Reverting back to previous news slots not only had an impact on what was being covered, but also on how it was being covered. The changing political environment associated with the outbreak of the Intifada meant that major framing question had again changed. The major question was no longer whether peace was possible, but what Israel could do to protect itself from Palestinian terrorism. In addition to the factual reports about the violence, virtually all of the news stories revolved around the three dimensions discussed in an earlier chapter: grief and mourning over the victims, anger at the Palestinians, and a frantic attempt to find solutions. The entire society felt threatened and thus it was not surprising that almost all news dealt with this aspect to the exclusion of all else. The competition between the Peace and Security frames was – at least for a time – over; concerns over personal and collective security were the only ones that mattered. Perhaps one of the most telling indicators of this change was that the term "peace process" simply vanished from public view.

The change in the news slots were also reflected in the way the press dealt with Palestinian sources. One of the intriguing anomalies of this period was the continued interest in interviewing Palestinian leaders on Israeli television and radio. This was a radical change from the first Intifada in which – due to the fact that all of the territories were under Israeli rule – such leaders remained hidden and nameless for fear of being arrested (Schiff and Ya'ari, 1990). This was one of the Oslo-related changes that remained in place even after the outbreak of violence. It would seem that the drama associated with interviewing the enemy was more important than any fears about offending members of the local audience.[10] This dynamic is also interesting from a Palestinian perspective. Despite the dramatic rise in the level of hostility towards Israel, there were still quite a few Palestinian leaders who were willing to be interviewed (in Hebrew) in order to convey their message to the Israeli public.

Nevertheless, the deterioration in relations was reflected in the tone of these interview sessions. From an Israeli perspective there was really only one question: what will the Palestinian do in order to end the violence against Israel. The Palestinian leader stood as the accused and the Israeli interviewers were the prosecutors. The Palestinians, on the other hand, strived to use such opportunities to promote their own claims against Israel. Every such interview was a political struggle in which each side attempted to drag the other into his/her own world. As an example, consider the following exchange between an Israeli anchorman and a Palestinian who was thought to be a leader of one of the local militias associated with the PLO. The interview was conducted in the wake of a meeting that had been held the day before between Foreign Minister Peres and President Mubarak of Egypt. The goal of that meeting had been to find a way to achieve a "ceasefire" between Israel and the Palestinians. The interview was conducted in Hebrew.[11]

> Israeli Interviewer: So, is there a ceasefire?
>
> Palestinian Leader: The word ceasefire is not the right word, it leads to a distortion. There aren't two armies that are fighting one another. There are the Palestinian people and against them there is the Israeli army, which has all of the means of combat, and they are the side that is carrying out the crime of violence. So if one side wants to call for a stop to the violence, it is the Israeli side.
>
> Israeli Interviewer: In other words, if I interpret your words, there is no ceasefire and the war goes on.
>
> Palestinian Leader: Look, I want tell you that cannot use the word ceasefire . . . There is an uprising against the occupation. We don't need an agreement for a ceasefire. We need an agreement for the end to the occupation.

---

[10] There were some objections raised about these interviews by the government and a number of right-wing groups. It is not clear whether these objections reduced the number of Palestinians who appeared.

[11] I have shown the tape of this interview to Israeli students. One can often hear laughter when the Palestinian makes mistakes in Hebrew. This illustrates another problem Palestinians have in passing their messages on to the Israeli public.

Israeli Interviewer: In other words, the war goes on.

Palestinian Leader: The atmosphere that the occupation generates is the atmosphere that brings violence. If the Israeli occupation of our land ends, I think the situation in the whole area will change.

Israeli Interviewer: Because again I interpret what you are saying, because the message is clear, but it seems like you are trying to avoid talking about it, I understand that in the field for now the violence, the armed struggle will continue.

(*Five O'clock with Gadi Sukenik*, Channel 2, April 30, 2001)

It is hard to find a better example of a dialogue of the deaf. The positions taken by the two sides are typical of what happens in many unequal conflicts. The more powerful antagonist promotes a "Law and Order" frame emphasizing the need to quell the violence, while the weaker side focuses on the injustices perpetrated by the more powerful side (Wolfsfeld, 1997a). The news media from each side adopt the appropriate frame. The struggle over the terms of reference is actually a struggle over meaning.

Thus, while the transition from conflict modes of reporting to those associated with peace tends to be slow and gradual, the move back to war is often sudden and devastating. Protecting oneself and one's people from violence is a primal instinct and this becomes the only issue.

THE SYNERGY BETWEEN JOURNALISTS, THE MILITARY, AND THE GOVERNMENT

There was a second mechanism that ensured a relatively easy transmission of the Anti-Palestinian frame to the Israeli news media. The outbreak of violence led to an unusual amount of collaboration on the part of Israeli journalists with government and military sources. The Israeli press normally prides itself on being critical and aggressive. As in other countries, however, reporting about war is a very different affair.

There are at least two major reasons for the increasing tendency of the media to echo the official line. One is more structural, the other more cultural. The structural reason is that during a military crisis journalists become much more dependent on official sources, especially those in the armed forces. These are the only sources that are in a position to give massive amounts of critical information in an extremely short amount of time. The most important news stories all center on the battle against the enemy and thus the most valuable information comes from the military and from those political sources, such as the Minister of Defense, who are involved. This also raises the prominence of military reporters whose major function is to provide the military's perspective. All of this inevitably increases the ability of such sources to take greater control over story lines (Wolfsfeld, 1997a).

The cultural reasons for such collaboration once again returns us to the wide level of consensus in support of official policy. Thus, despite a serious amount of international condemnation for Israel's actions, the amount of criticism within the country was relatively minor. There was never any serious internal debate concerning the charges that Israel was using excessive force against the Palestinians. As with the "unmasking of Arafat," there was little disagreement between the major political parties. Thus, when Prime Minister Barak was still in office he argued that the Israeli Defense Forces (IDF) were exercising the maximum amount of restraint possible. The right-wing opposition condemned the restraint and demanded that Barak "let the IDF win." Thus there was a high level of agreement that the IDF was using restraint; the only question was whether such moderation was justified. The international community had a very different view of Israel's actions, but there were no legitimate domestic sources to provide a competing frame.

The atmosphere in Israel turned even more hostile as terrorism became the major form of violence. The massive riots that had characterized the first weeks of the Intifada gave way to an increasing number of suicide bombers and there was a shocking rise in the number of civilian deaths. Anger and fear were rampant as the conflict turned from bad to worse. Given this climate, the government had little difficulty mobilizing the political elite, the news media, and the public for the war effort. What at one time would have been considered drastic actions against the Palestinians seemed reasonable given the growing number of Israelis killed and wounded. This process is almost identical to what happened in the United States after September 11, 2001.

The only leaders crying out against Israel's actions against the Palestinians were the Arab Knesset members, who were again discounted as extremists. The Arab minority became even further ostracized when violent riots broke out within those communities in the early weeks of the Intifada. Thirteen Arab citizens were shot and killed during these disturbances. Here, too, it was difficult to find Jewish voices condemning the police actions; most saw it as simply another part of the battle with the Palestinians. Only months later was a Committee of National Inquiry established to investigate what had happened. The final report of this committee was issued in the fall of 2003 and was extremely critical of the government and the police.

The increasingly high level of cooperation between Israeli journalists and the military is an especially important factor to understand, for this phenomenon provides a stark contrast to what happens in the course of a peace process. In war, the military elite represents a major asset in promoting government policies to the domestic news media. The military is often seen as "above politics" and thus assumes a stature few politicians can hope to achieve. Thus, when the Israeli Chief of Staff refers to the Palestinian Authority as a "terrorist entity," it is more likely to resonate within Israeli society. Given the fact that the military is forbidden to deal with political issues, such pronouncements are seen as a form of strategic analysis rather than political polemic. Political leaders attempting to promote peace, on the other hand, rarely have such powerful allies.[12]

One method for assessing the independence of a news media during wartime is to look at what might be called "the frustration gap." While the military is often irritated by the way the news media are covering the war effort, the level of frustration varies over time and circumstance. When generals are mostly pleased with media performance it suggests that they are finding little difficulty in getting their message across. In other words, the lower the level of frustration among the military, the lower the level of media independence. A good example was the media campaign conducted by the Allies during the Gulf War, in which expert informants from the American military were mostly pleased with the results of their public relations efforts (Wolfsfeld, 1997a).

One receives a similar sense of satisfaction when talking to those responsible for getting the IDF messages out to the public. There is a sharp and revealing contrast between the anger such officers expressed when talking about the foreign media and their opinions about the domestic press. While those in charge of the Israeli army spokesperson's office found themselves constantly on the defensive with regard to the international news media, they had few complaints about the Hebrew press. These information officers had an especially strong connection with the military correspondents, whose expertise was based on their

---

[12] One might point to an exception to this rule in Northern Ireland. The British and Irish governments do serve as important allies for the local proponents of the peace process.

connections with the army. It is worth remembering that all of these correspondents – like most other Israelis – had themselves served in the military. Many reporters continue to do reserve duty and thus often find themselves serving in the same army they are supposed to cover.[13] One of the senior officers in the army spokesperson's office talked about the close relationship with the military correspondents.

> So, in the end they cooperate with us. After all they are military correspondents so they are very connected to the army, they have a commitment. When it comes to the army they don't just come to attack us. They are not army spokespeople; they are not little army spokespeople. But they do have a commitment to the IDF and they want to explain what the IDF is doing. (CD51; March 19, 2001)

As he notes, the fact that these reporters cooperate with the IDF does not mean that they are mere sounding horns for the army spokesperson's office. These reporters will exploit a variety of sources. However, almost all of those sources come from within the defense establishment. Although there may be disagreements over the effectiveness of certain tactics and strategies, such informants are unlikely to question the overall righteousness of the cause. When asked about this issue, one of the military correspondents argued that his job was to provide the military vantage point. It was up to others, he said to provide other perspectives.

> Military correspondents are connected to the army and talk to the army and thus they pass on materials that come from the army. Reporters from the territories, or those who deal with the settlers, are supposed to bring their own materials in order to create "auto-balance." But you can't come to a particular beat and ask the reporters, Why do you deal with the army? We deal with the army because we cover the army. We don't cover the Palestinian side. (CD49; May 25, 2001)

A radio reporter talked about the difficulties military correspondents faced in their attempts to achieve a certain amount of independence.

> There are many military terms that all of us, all of us that work with the army on a day-to-day basis, fall into using. We start talking like officers, using the military terminology ... It is easy to fall into that. I don't think we deserve a grade of ten [out of ten] but we do our

---

[13] If one wanted to be nasty, one might speculate about the possible effects of having diplomatic reporters moonlighting in the Foreign Office.

work. We do commit many sins of mobilization, of ignoring the suffering of the other. The people we cover, I mean the army, often talk through our throats. I can't explain why it happens. (CD55, October 24, 2001).[14]

It is interesting to note that a number of Israeli reporters who were interviewed after September 11 felt somewhat vindicated. Certainly, they argued, the American press was no less one-sided in their coverage of their "War on Terror" than the Israeli media. While some might balk at this comparison, the political atmosphere surrounding the two campaigns was similar.

One might have thought that an alternative perspective might have come from those covering the Palestinian beat. The Israeli news media did place an increased emphasis on gathering information about the re-actions and intentions of the Palestinian leadership. A typical evening's newscast, for example, would include a report by the military corre-spondent, the political correspondent, an Israeli Arab reporting from the territories, and an arab affairs analyst (who was Jewish). However, the outbreak of violence led to a serious crisis between many Jewish jour-nalists and their Palestinians sources. One manifestation was discussed earlier in connection with the "dialogue of the deaf" characterizing tele-vision and radio interviews. As the death toll continued to rise it was inevitable that connections between the two sides would sour. One jour-nalist described the change in relations.

> Every journalist as a private person went through a crisis. Even those who worked with the Palestinians and tried to be balanced went through a crisis. The reaction led to a more extremist approach towards the Palestinians – for the worse: a complete lack of trust in what they say and tell and to a great extent towards their claims. It is impossible to look for objectivity, because this is a real armed conflict. (CD54, May 3, 2001)

The increased level of hostilities also led to additional structural dif-ficulties for those covering the occupied territories. Many Jewish jour-nalists were understandably scared to go into the areas and Palestinian groups threatened others. One of the journalists said that he had received seven death threats from Palestinians for what he had written. It also be-came illegal for Israeli journalists to go into the territories, supposedly

---

[14] This interview was carried out by my student Roni Sorek as part of a seminar paper on the topic. I appreciate her allowing me to use it.

for safety reasons. Thus most Israeli journalists had little choice but to depend on phones and faxes in order to keep up with events. This can hardly be considered the optimal method for finding out what is happening or for understanding the other side's perspective.

There were a few Israeli journalists who refused to accept the government frame with regard to the Intifada. They were extremely critical of the government and army from the beginning. Two names continually came up in such interviews and both were from the liberal, non-sensationalist paper *Ha'aretz*: Amira Hess and Gideon Levy. The role of such rebels was also discussed in chapter 4. It is extremely helpful to read such pieces because they – along with news produced outside of Israel – provide an alternative frame about the conflict. These articles, as well as some that appeared in a number of local newspapers, place a major emphasis on what is seen as Israeli aggression and Palestinian suffering. It is also revealing that a number of people from the army spokesperson's office referred to these two reporters and their paper as the ones who were least willing to cooperate with them. This helps illustrate why the "frustration gap" provides a useful indicator of the relative independence of each news medium.

Looking at those journalists who were more critical of the government and the army, one discovers yet another difference between the promotion of peace and war. It is much more difficult, and even dangerous, for a journalist to take a critical stance against war than against peace. At worst, those who oppose a popular peace process – say in Northern Ireland or with regard to Jordan – are likely to be considered die-hards or troublemakers. Those who oppose a war effort, on the other hand, are often considered traitors. While it is always difficult for journalists to swim upstream against a strong current, it is especially dangerous to be considered advocates for the enemy. Owners and editors who allow such reporting are also taking certain risks. Thus one of the editors at *Ha'aretz* reported that numerous readers of that newspaper canceled their subscription, because of what they said was a "pro-Palestinian" bias.[15] A rival newspaper, the *Jerusalem Post*, attempted to exploit the anger against *Ha'aretz* in its advertising strategy.[16] The *Post* published a full-page ad displaying a letter they had received from a new subscriber who had left *Ha'aretz* because of that paper's "unbalanced coverage" of the Intifada.

---

[15] Remarks made at the annual conference of the Israel Communication Association's annual meeting held at the University of Tel Aviv on December 24, 2000.

[16] The *Jerusalem Post* competes with the English version of *Ha'aretz*.

Ethnocentric view of death

The third mechanism that facilitated the success of the Anti-Palestinian frame was probably the most powerful. As in any conflict the Israeli news media covered their own dead and wounded very differently than they covered casualties on the other side (Liebes, 1997). Israeli deaths are always considered major tragedies and the news media were the central forum for collective mourning. Palestinians deaths were, for the most part, discounted. Apart from a few exceptions they were treated as relatively minor, unimportant incidents. This emphasis, although understandable, provides an extremely one-sided view of the conflict. There can be little doubt that continual exposure to such coverage serves to demonize the enemy and sanction the use of force as a means of self-defense.

It is once again important to stress that the coverage in the Palestinian press was probably even more one-sided. Television broadcasts included blood-filled scenes of the dead and wounded accompanied by stirring music and emotional appeals. Here, too, there was little coverage or sympathy for Israeli deaths. These stories conveyed the idea that the only true victims of this conflict were the Palestinians, the only aggressor Israel. The Palestinian media were important tools in mobilizing and maintaining public support for the war effort.

The values and routines for covering the two types of deaths all served to reflect and reinforce cultural beliefs concerning the conflict. While some of these points were alluded to in an earlier discussion about terrorism, it is important to think about these differences in a situation when people from both sides are being killed. The most obvious difference concerns the prominence given to different deaths. Israeli deaths are considered front-page, top of the line-up news stories in the Hebrew media. Such events are considered breaking news; television and radio stations interrupt their normal broadcasts with bulletins of such deaths. There is also a tremendous amount of time and space devoted to such coverage, especially in the case of multiple deaths.[17] Stories of Israeli casualties are also very detailed, often including maps,

---

[17] It is interesting to note, however, that the ongoing coverage of death became less intensive than in the early stages of Oslo (see chapter 2). There were very few "mourning marathons" and unless many people were killed at once, the entertainment media quickly returned to normal. Given the ongoing number of casualties, isolated shootings and the like became almost as routine as traffic accidents. It would seem that the weight editors attribute to novelty is sometimes more important than the weight given to drama.

eyewitnesses, interviews with police or soldiers, and chronologies of the events. In addition, as discussed before, such coverage is also relatively dramatic and emotional and this too raises the prominence of such stories.

Not surprisingly, Palestinian deaths are given much less attention, although here, too, the amount of prominence varies. When suspected terrorists are killed – which is considered a success for the IDF – such stories receive somewhat more time and space. When other Palestinians are killed such deaths are granted a relatively brief mention within more general reports about the day's events. It is rare for such reports to include details of what happened and even rarer to have eyewitnesses talk about what they saw. These reports are usually factual, analytical, and fairly easy to overlook.

There are also important differences in the level of personalization afforded to the types of victims. Israeli victims have names and faces. They have families and friends that mourn for them, that want to talk about them. The first few times the names of the victims are read on the air, the anchor always utters the Jewish prayer: "May their memories be blessed." The times and places of each funeral is announced on radio and television. It is also customary to include portions of the funerals themselves as part of the evening news. The Palestinian victims, on the other hand, are, for the most part, nameless and faceless. Here, too, suspected terrorists enjoy a somewhat higher level of media status in that some of these names are published in the press. The Israeli press will also cover the funeral marches associated with these higher-profile deaths. This coverage, however, is much more likely to center on Palestinian threats for revenge than on grief.

It is hard to conceive of another circumstance in which the media's ability to construct reality has such a powerful effect. Israelis and Palestinians are being told completely different stories about the conflict. Each population becomes emotionally linked to its own victims, who are killed by a vicious, inhuman enemy. We come to "know" our victims, we know nothing about "their" victims, and we do not really care. It is an ongoing and horrifying story of one side's righteousness and the other side's evil. Given the daily scenes of (our) horror, how can anybody accuse us of being aggressors? We observe each ceasefire and they continually violate it. They continue to kill us and we are only acting in self-defense.

Amira Hess talked about the impact of these differences in an editorial that appeared one year after the start of the uprising:

Let's assume that for one week the entire Israeli media – radio, television, and the daily papers – would decide to report on everything that that happened . . . to the Palestinians. On the same week the Israeli media would not only report on every mortar that fell on a Jewish settlement, but (also) on every Israeli shell that fell on a Palestinian home . . . They would tell about the Jews that were killed, but also about the Palestinians. The Palestinians would be given names, ages, and histories . . . The first goal of such an effort would be basic journalism: to try to report on what is happening and not only the Israeli perspective. But such a project would also have a secondary result . . . because without complete information one cannot direct rational policy. It would also force the Israeli public to place more serious questions before their leaders. (*Ha'aretz*, September 26, 2001, p. B1)

When Israeli journalists are asked about such differences in the way the two sides are covered, they almost always refer back to the audience. While a number pointed to the logistical difficulties in finding out what really happened when Palestinians are killed, most pointed to their audience. There is little point, they argued, in spending much time on such stories because very few Israelis have any interest in them. One of the military correspondents put it this way:

The number [of Palestinians] killed doesn't interest anybody. But that's already a social problem, not the media's problem . . . Why isn't anything published about Palestinians killed? Because there's no demand. It doesn't interest anybody. Except for Mochamad Dura [sic]. The faces are not interesting. [CD62, March 31, 2001]

As this quote implies there are deeper reasons for these media routines. It is not simply a question of public apathy. Many citizens become very angry when the news media display sympathy for victims on the other side. The amount of anger and hate directed at the more critical journalists demonstrates this point. Thus, attempting to change such routines carries with it a certain amount of professional risk. Some also believe that providing such sympathy plays into Palestinian hands. Consider, for example, the remarks made by one of the television correspondents responsible for covering the territories about the reasons why he probably covers things differently than a reporter from CNN.

Yes, the [Israeli] reporter might relate to a cordon around a Palestinian town less severely than a foreign journalist because the reporter says to himself, "My God, they started it and now they are crying to me. They want me to come and cover their suffering? . . . So don't [you Palestinians] shoot at people, there won't be a cordon. What you want me to run after you with a camera and show how miserable you are? After all, it is clear that you are miserable because war is cruel, and you started the war." (CD48, March 20, 2001)

Anger and hate permeate throughout the society during such conflict and affect journalists as much as everyone else. There is nothing surprising or discordant about this type of coverage. It is only natural to mourn over one's own victims and not the enemy's. This is what makes this routine such an efficient and powerful engine for converting cultural energy into political motion. It is a collaborative effort between leaders, journalists, and the public and few have the interest, the will, or the political strength to slow it down.

All of which returns us to the major point of this discussion. There is simply no comparative mechanism in the news media for the promotion of peace. The closest equivalent would be the peace ceremonies that provide an enormous amount of time and space for promoting such a frame. Such media events pale, however, when compared to an ongoing story of death and destruction. The euphoric news stories associated with such ceremonies are brief. Images of the pain and suffering associated with violent conflict not only last much longer, they also leave deep scars. Even worse, those who hope to build peace must do so only after so much damage has already been done. From a political and media perspective one never gets to begin a peace process from zero.

The anger and pessimism among Israelis and Palestinians was compellingly revealed in polls that were taken in July of 2001, nine months after the outbreak of the hostilities.[18] The proportion of Israelis who believe there is "no chance to reach a peace agreement in the immediate future" rose from 19 percent immediately after Camp David to 41 percent (which was the most frequent answer). The change among Palestinians was similar: it rose from 23 percent to 46 percent. There was a similar change in the proportion that believed that the relations between the two sides would be conflictual and violent for the next five to ten years. Among the Israelis the proportion rose in less than a year from 10 percent to 46 percent while among Palestinians it rose from 31

---

[18] The results of all these types of polls can be found at: http://truman.huji.ac.il, the website of the Harry S. Truman Institute for the Advancement of Peace.

percent to 59 percent. There was also a great deal of support among the two populations for the continued use of violence against the other side.

It was a tragic end to the Oslo story and it left plenty of blame to go around. The point of this book is to suggest that at least part of the responsibility should be attributed to the news media. It may not be appropriate to blame the messenger for bringing bad news. On the other hand when messengers tell only one side of a story they can be certainly be held accountable for the consequences.

Conclusion

The basic argument is this. All other things being equal, the news media generally play a negative role in attempts to bring peace. At the same time, the exact part the press will take in a given peace process varies in conjunction with the political and media environments in which journalists operate. The news media are most likely to play a constructive role when there is a high level of support in favor of a peace process, when the number and intensity of crises are low, when there is a relatively high level of shared news organs and when journalists feel less need or desire to construct sensationalist news stories. It was also claimed that the role the news media play in any political process is best seen in terms of a cycle: Any changes in the political environment leads to changes in media performance that can lead to further changes in the political environment.

The validity of these arguments was demonstrated by examining three different peace processes. The most telling evidence about changing environments came from comparing the role the news media played in the Oslo process with what happened in Northern Ireland. There is good evidence that in the case of Oslo the Hebrew media made a difficult situation worse, while in Northern Ireland the press probably enhanced the prospects for peace. It's not that the journalists in Israel have any less desire for peace than their counterparts in Belfast. It is rooted in the differences in what they were covering, how they chose to cover it, and the ethnic diversity of their intended audience.

The role of the press played in the Israel–Jordan peace process fell somewhere in the middle of these two extremes. In Israel, there was little evidence that the news media played any significant role at all with regard to Jordan, in part this was because Israelis have so little interest in that country. The Jordanian press, on the other hand, appears to have played the more traditional role of exacerbating the situation. The situation might have even been worse were it not for the attempts of the Jordanian government to exercise a certain amount of control over the news. This comparison proved rewarding because it provided insights into the ways in which the political and media environments can pull in such different directions. Whereas the cases of Oslo and Northern Ireland seemed more consistent in this regard, here the influences were more complex. In Jordan it was the political environment that was most problematic, while in Israel it was the media environment. In addition, the lack of many encouraging findings from this relatively successful peace process reinforces the belief that the case of Northern Ireland is rather unique.

Which brings us to the concept known as the politics-media-politics cycle. The cycle can be divided into two major parts. The first has to do with the influence of the political environment on media performance. This part of the cycle is relatively simple to demonstrate. It is clear, for example, that the level of political consensus surrounding a peace process has a major impact on how that process is covered. The same can be said about the number and intensity of political crises. It is the second part of that cycle that is more problematic. How does one demonstrate that such changes in media performance also have a supplementary impact on the political environment?

The research strategy taken in this study tried to collect evidence on this point through interviews with expert informants. These informants were in the best position to talk about the effects of varying media values, routines, and coverage on the ongoing interactions between political actors and journalists. Those actually involved in the peace processes also shed light on how they personally coped with variations in news coverage. While no single piece of evidence can be considered conclusive, the preponderance of data does lead to the conclusion that the news media can have a profound impact on the course of a peace process.

One can elucidate the evidence concerning this second part of the cycle by returning to the four types of influences that were discussed in chapter 1. The news media, it was said, can help define the political atmosphere surrounding the process, have an impact on the debate over the process, influence political actors' strategy and behavior, and raise and lower the public standing and legitimacy of the various antagonists.

In some ways the influence of the media on the political atmosphere surrounding a peace process is the most obvious to understand but the hardest to prove. On the one hand, there can be little doubt that the news media serve as the central reference point for elites, journalists, and the broad public to monitor a peace process. The important question is whether the news media merely reflect a particular political mood or also help define it. Do editorial choices about how to cover political events alter the impact such incidents have on the political environment?

One good piece of evidence on this point has to do with historical changes in media coverage of terrorism in Israel. Prime Minister Rabin's advisors complained about the fact that the Israeli news media's hysterical coverage of terrorism made it difficult for his government to deal with the issue in a thoughtful manner. The political advisors and the journalists who were interviewed were old enough to remember a previous time when the Israeli news media were less likely to spread fear and panic. It would be difficult to accept that such major differences in media presentation had no influence on the mood of the Israeli public.

There were also episodes in which editorial choices served to *improve* the political atmosphere in support of peace. The behavior of the Israeli news media during the initial weeks of Oslo known as the "Peace Festival" is a case in point. In hindsight most expert informants believed that the active search for optimistic stories during that brief period served to underplay the risks and dangers that lay ahead. But this too would be an example of a supplementary media effect. Some in Northern Ireland made a similar point with regard to role of the news media at the time of the Good Friday referendum. Given the fact that so many are tuning in, it is hard to avoid the conclusion that editorial choices about content and volume do have an effect on the overall political atmosphere.

There is also pretty good evidence that media routines had an impact on the nature of the various debates over peace. The influence on public discourse was found in two major areas. First, the emphasis on conflict and drama raised the *intensity* of the debate over peace. Second, the need for simple story lines and the media's inability to question conventional wisdom narrowed the *range* of frames that were made public.

With regards to the first problem, the comparison between the relatively sensationalist media environment in Israel with the more reserved milieu in Northern Ireland was especially telling. While Israeli political actors expressed universal dissatisfaction with this problem, there were few such complaints in Northern Ireland. Equally important, the journalists in each of these countries confirmed these differences in professional values. All of these informants had years of experience in this area and most were extremely aware of the impact sensationalist coverage can have on conflicts. The difference was that journalists in Northern Ireland felt an ethical obligation to avoid such effects, while their Israeli counterparts rarely expressed such qualms. The sensationalism of the Israel news media appears to have been particularly damaging in the period leading up to the assassination of Yitzhak Rabin; the prominence given to extremist rhetoric and actions appears to have exacerbated an already tense situation.

The ability for the news media to narrow the range of debate about peace was found in both Israel and Northern Ireland. In Israel, this became especially apparent during major political waves. The Israeli press seemed particularly eager to develop a unified interpretation for such events; the "lessons" always seemed obvious. Anyone following the news during these periods would find it hard to escape the conclusion that "incitement' was the major cause for the Rabin assassination, or that the Palestinians were completely to blame for the failure at Camp David and for the outbreak of the Second Intifada. There were dissenting voices to these story lines, but it was almost impossible to hear them over the roar of the crowd. In Northern Ireland those opposed to the Good Friday accords also felt that they were continually shortchanged in the media, and there is some reason to believe they were right.

Demonstrating the impact of the news media on actors' strategies and behaviors is more clear-cut. All of the political actors and advisors who were interviewed stressed the importance of the news media as tools for achieving their goals. This realization, in turn, meant that they were forced to invest time and resources courting the media. As anticipated, this adaptation was especially blatant with regard to the weaker political actors. The oppositions in both Israel and Northern Ireland were both frustrated about the need to use extraordinary tactics in order to be heard. Palestinian interviewees spoke in similar terms when talking about their attempts to get their message across to the Hebrew news media. The Palestinian leadership talked about how difficult it was to "compete" with their more violent and extremist opposition. Supporters of Hamas disclosed that exploiting the Israeli news media was part of their overall strategy for fighting Israel.

Governments attempting to promote peace also found themselves adapting and reacting to the news media. Every political offensive, be it for war or for peace, must include a media strategy. Modern leaders have little choice but to hire an increasingly large number of profession-als to deal with the press. Public relations experts are not only expected to translate government policy into news, they must also find ways of regulating the flow of information about the peace process, and to limit the damage caused by unwanted news stories. One of the best-known influences of the news media on a peace process takes place during nego-tiations. When leaks about possible concessions are published they have an impact on both the home front and the talks themselves. As discussed, the fact that initial talks in Oslo were kept secret was certainly one of the reasons they were so successful. Similar efforts to distance the press were made in all of the peace processes that were studied, with varying degrees of success. It was also found that the news media were especially likely to get involved in those negotiations that were already having problems, a fact that further demonstrates the validity of the PMP cycle.

Which brings us to the final influences of the news media on a peace process: the ability to raise and lower the public standing and legitimacy of the various antagonists and their frames. The role of the news media can play in raising the level of public standing proved to be especially pronounced with regard to the Palestinians. The historical content anal-ysis presented in chapter 4 showed a significant increase in the number of Israeli news stories that relate to the Palestinians as independent actors. Such an analysis does not prove that such changes in media attention had any impact on the Israeli political environment. Nevertheless, it would be surprising if such a focus on the part of the media did not reinforce public beliefs that the Palestinian "problem" is an important issue that needs to be addressed.

The role the media played in raising the standing of terrorist groups was more rapid. Of all the various antagonists, the ones that enjoyed the largest rise in public standing were the Palestinian opposition movements Hamas and Islamic Jihad. The enormous amount of media attention granted by the Israeli news media helped transform these groups into major players, much to the annoyance of the Palestinian Authority. If, as some suggested, these groups were attempting to send the message that they could not be ignored, they certainly succeeded. Although the change was less dramatic, one can make a similar claim with regards to the Real IRA in Northern Ireland.

As always, however, the actual influence of the news media on standing depended on the surrounding political environment. In other words, one can never ignore the first part of the PMP cycle. The asymmetrical relations between Jordan and Israel again provide an excellent example. While Israel is a major news story in Jordan, Jordan is a relatively minor news story in Israel. The formal inauguration of peace had no long-term impact on this situation, because there was no significant change in the relative weight each country attributed to the other. At the same time there can be little doubt that the news media in both countries remain important agents in reinforcing public beliefs about the other side's importance. Thus, Jordanian leaders and citizens are constantly being told to think (usually negatively) about Israel, while Israelis have little reason to even think about Jordan. To put it differently, while the Jordanians are constantly debating about their relations with Israel, the question of how to promote peace and reconciliation with Jordan is rarely even considered an issue in Israel.

The news media also appear to have played an independent role in raising and lowering the legitimacy of different groups and frames. It is important to distinguish between more short-term and long-term types of changes. Consider, for example, the fall and rise of the right-wing opposition in Israel. After the Rabin assassination the news media played an active role in accusing them of some level of responsibility for the murder. As discussed, this event also provided important opportunities for the Peres government to promote the Oslo peace process as part of "Rabin's legacy." Public support for the process rose to a new high. Only a few months later, however, it was the Peres government that stood as the accused, due to the large number of people killed in bus bombings. Netanyahu was then able to ride the terrorism issue to victory by successfully influencing the electoral agenda of the media. When Israeli interviewers start to ask whether you have "searched your soul" for guilt, you know you're in trouble.

There are two examples of the news media having similar types of effects on the legitimacy of peace and its sponsors in Northern Ireland. The first has to do with the referendum over the Good Friday agreement in May of 1998. The decision of the Unionist *Ulster Newsletter* to support the accords provided the agreement and its supporters with an important public boost at a critical time. The second example took place after the terrorist attack in Omagh. The news media in both the North and the South launched a vicious attack on the perpetuators. Similarly to what happened after the Rabin assassination, opposing the peace agreements became very politically incorrect. This illustrates that the news media – and no doubt the public – often find it difficult to distinguish between an idea and its sponsors.

As always, the long-range effects in this area are more difficult to es-tablish. Nevertheless the study did provide some suggestive data in this area, especially concerning changing media images of the enemy. The findings concerning the Israel–Jordan peace process proved intriguing. As a result of the peace process, Israel's media image in Jordan did im-prove for a time. There was an important rise in the number of favorable news stories and in the creation of news slots that had been unavailable in the past. Some Jordanian journalists were even planning joint ventures with their Israeli counterparts that might have raised the public legitimacy of Israel. Once previous tensions began to resurface, however, the Jordanian news media became important weapons to be used against Israel. As noted, King Hussein, whose personal reputation was linked to the peace treaty, made a conscious attempt to tone down these attacks. This internal struggle over how to portray Israel suggests, at the very least, that both the Jordanian government and the press believe that the nature of such stories can have an effect on Israel's public image in Jordan.

One can make a similar point concerning long-term images of the Palestinians in the Israeli press. Here, too, the establishment of a peace process led to certain improvements in how that group was covered. Israelis were suddenly introduced to Palestinian diplomats and negotiators and peace often seemed just around the corner. Nevertheless, whatever progress was made was completely destroyed with the outbreak of the Second Intifada. Arafat and the Palestinians had again become terrorists and the only important issue was how Israelis could best defend themselves. Indicative of this reversal were the increasing number of voices calling for Arafat's "removal."

Here, too, some might argue that the news media play an unimportant role in all this. Any hatred for the enemy, they would say, is rooted in the conflict itself, not in how it is covered. In order to accept such an idea, one has to minimize (among other things) the impact that the ethnocentric coverage of death can have on the public. Day in and day out Israelis and Palestinians are exposed to horrific scenes of death and destruction in which those on the other side are framed as murderers. Anyone who has had the misfortune to live through the experience of continually watching one's own people die will find it difficult to react with anything but hatred and rage. The news media not only intensify that anger through graphic presentations, they also play a role in channeling it towards the enemy. As in Plato's allegory of the cave, the prisoners have little choice but to accept the images on the wall as reality. The ultimate power of the media to influence the course of a conflict is rooted in the fact that antagonists are almost always kept in separate caves.

One can only speculate about whether it will become easier for Israeli journalists to rehabilitate the Palestinians the next time around. As always, the key variable will be the ability of the leaders on both sides to take control over the political environment. There are two necessary conditions for the Israeli news media to become optimistic about a peace process with the Palestinians. First, there would have to be a relatively broad consensus within the Israeli political elite in support of the process. This could conceivably happen if it was a right-wing leader who was promoting it – such as what happened when Prime Minister Begin signed the Camp David accords with Egyptian Prime Minister Anwar Sadat. Second, it would have to be a process with little or no violence. This condition is rooted in the second component of the political environment – the amount and severity of crises associated with the process. If both these conditions were met then the Israeli news media could conceivably serve as important tools for promoting peace. The ongoing relations between Palestinian sources and Israeli journalists could smooth this process, especially if some of these contacts assumed new positions of power. Even if all this were to occur however, it is hard to believe that the Israeli press would express the level of enthusiasm they had during the first days of Oslo.

When taken as a whole all of this makes a pretty good case for the underlying validity of the politics-media-politics cycle. It is true that there is no "smoking gun" and given what we know about media effects research, there never will be. Nevertheless, the fact that the testimonies come from so many different sources performing under such a variety of circumstances adds weight to the argument. Changes in the political environment surrounding a peace process inevitably lead to changes in how the media perform, which in turn often has its own impact on the political environment. The news media not only reflect the level of elite consensus, they augment it. Journalists do not merely report on political crisis, they help define it. The press makes some ideas appear more obvious and clear-cut than they really are. The model is far too primitive to make specific predictions about the exact nature of these effects or about the amount of importance one should attribute to each link in the chain. Hopefully, however, this study does provide a useful basis for exploring these issues.

IMPLICATIONS FOR JOURNALISTS AND POLICY MAKERS

I argued in the introduction to this work that journalists have an ethical obligation to encourage reconciliation among hostile populations. While there is no reason to expect journalists to support any particular peace initiative, they are obliged to do what they can to lower the risk of violence and war. At the very least, it was argued, journalists should do no harm:

They should refrain from carrying out any practices that could exacerbate a conflict.

There is no reason why social scientists should be exempt from this rule. We too have an obligation to do what we can to encourage peace. Studies in conflict resolution should not be considered any more controversial than research that deals with racism, murder, or – for that matter – cancer. As in those cases, researchers (and their critics) have to be especially careful that the desire to find solutions does not overly influence the collection and interpretation of data. This problem, however, is not unique to peace studies: researchers always have a vested interest in certain kinds of results. The difference is that in this field claims based on research often appear to be more politically charged.

Given this obligation, the final section will be devoted to discussing some of the implications of this study for both policy makers and journalists. The underlying assumption is that the vast majority of people want to prevent violence and war. Political differences over a peace process usually center on either the "price" that has to be paid or whether the other side can be trusted to keep agreements. These are perfectly legitimate debates. None of the suggestions raised below should be seen as an attempt to limit such disputes. Rather, they should be seen as an attempt to prevent the news media from being significant obstacles to peace.

The results of this study contain good news and bad news for those who are interested in the promotion of peace. The bad news is that leaders cannot depend on the news media to help them when they are in trouble. Political leaders often buy into the myth that if only they can hire the right publicity people or produce the proper spin, they could create a positive image for their policies. The construction of news about peace, however, is directly related to the state of the political environment. Leaders who are unable to mobilize a broad political consensus for their policies will have little success in promoting those policies to the media.

This dynamic has a number of unfortunate implications for those interested in the promotion of peace. First, it means that the news media are least likely to help in those cases where they can do the most good. When elites and the public are fairly divided over a peace process, the media have the potential of tilting the balance in one direction or the other. Given the way news is constructed, they are most likely to tilt the scales against peace. Some might argue that this is for the best; a peace process lacking a broad range of internal support is in any case doomed to failure. On the other hand, almost every peace process eventually runs into trouble. It is at just these junctures, when leaders are trying to keep public attention focused on long-term goals, when the impact of the media can be so critical.

There is another negative consequence more particularly linked with the news media's obsessive search for drama. It is often said that it is much easier to destroy than to build, and this is certainly true in the area of media and peace. Hamas was extremely successful at using terrorism to derail the Oslo peace process, and the hysteria of the Israeli news media was an important element in this dynamic. A peace process is mostly composed of long, complicated negotiations, where the need for secrecy far outweighs the need for publicity. Opponents can easily exploit this situation by providing the media with the drama they desire.

It is important for policy makers to understand this situation and find better ways to deal with it. It is critical to develop a long-range political strategy that also takes into account the needs of the media. The Rabin government, for example, was extremely meticulous in planning the peace ceremonies that followed every success. There was little preparation, on the other hand, for dealing with disasters. The better leaders understand how and why the role of the news media can change, the better prepared they will be to exploit their opportunities, and to limit the damage associated with failures.

The adoption of such a strategy could include two major components. First, it would involve continually promoting a long-range perspective to journalists and the public. Leaders and spokespeople would have to fight their natural political tendencies of exaggerating successes and presenting optimistic visions of the future. It is important that they also provide warnings about future crises down the road, lower expectations concerning when to expect a breakthrough, and constantly attempt to place current events within a longer historical context. The (George W.) Bush administration appeared to adopt just this type of strategy in their updates concerning the "War on Terror." While such an approach conflicts with journalists' preference to focus on the immediate, such efforts can make a difference. At the very least leaders would be in a better position to react to disasters by pointing to their previous warnings.

A second component of such a policy would be to set up a crisis team responsible for dealing with such situations. In quiet times the team would be responsible for developing crisis scenarios and policy recommendations for dealing with news media during such situations. When a crisis does break out, this team could form the equivalent of a "war room" that would be responsible for implementing the policies in as rapid and efficient a manner as possible. It is important for political leaders to look at the struggle for peace as part of a permanent campaign.

There are also implications from this study that have to do with how journalists operate. The idea of a shared media is an important one. Although it is not realistic to attempt to create a shared media where they do not already exist, it is possible to increase the level of interaction among journalists working in different news media. Organizing joint meetings of editors and reporters from the rival communities could lead to greater cooperation between them. The organization "Search for Common Ground," which is based in Washington, DC, carries out such seminars in a number of conflict areas, including the Middle East. Efforts might also be made to persuade certain news media to hire journalists from the opposite camp in an effort to provide their audience with an alternative perspective. At the very least journalists could be better educated about ways they might make a contribution towards easing tensions between antagonists (Davison, 1974; Weimann, 1994).

It is also worth considering more significant changes within the news media. The differences in the journalistic cultures of Israel and Northern Ireland demonstrate that professional values and routines do vary over time and circumstance. The notion of ethics should not be limited to the single value of "objectivity." Journalists working in conflict-ridden areas could adopt values that would minimize the risk of escalating conflict and maximize the potential for reconciliation. Robert Manoff (1996, 1997, 1998) is one of a number of scholars who have put forth a model of "peace journalism" which includes a series of practical suggestions for changing editorial policies along these lines. Examples include counteracting misperceptions about the conflict and the other side, using analytical frameworks that have been developed in the field of conflict resolution, and reporting on areas of cooperation between the antagonists.

It must be emphasized, however, that a more conducive form of journalism depends on making structural changes in the news production process. Such a change would involve creating special sections in newspapers and the broadcast media dedicated to peace issues. Such sections would force reporters to search for materials that would be consistent with the values of peace journalism. The stories could include essays written by people living on the other side, stories about the other side's culture and society, stories that deal with various peace proposals, and stories about individuals and groups that are working for peace and reconciliation.

Many news people would object to such changes, arguing that they violate important journalistic values. Nevertheless, the goal of such sections is not to replace conflict journalism but merely to add some elements of peace in order to provide a minimal amount of balance. Given the fact that almost all news is dedicated to conflict, it hardly seems unreasonable that a small section be devoted to peace. Galtung (1998) has suggested a provocative parallel in this regard. How, he asks, would the "Health" section of the newspaper look if it were only devoted to the study of diseases? There would never be any news devoted to preventive medicine, to research being carried out about possible cures, or about the advances medicine has made in understanding and curing disease. Instead such news would focus almost exclusively on the most frightening diseases, on any illness or epidemics on the horizon, and on sad stories about the sick and the dying. This is exactly how conflict journalism looks today.

Another idea would be to wage war against sensationalism. Such a battle is never easy because owners and editors are understandably reluctant to risk losing audience share. However the notion that "sensationalism can cost lives" can be a powerful message in war-torn societies. Peace groups and other organizations could attempt to place this issue on the national agenda, and editors might adopt more responsible policies. The success enjoyed in recent years by women's groups and minorities in changing media routines demonstrates that such efforts can produce results.

At the very least there is a need to begin a dialogue about these issues among policy makers, journalists, researchers, and peace activists. As noted in the introduction, there is very little research on this topic, even among those who study conflict resolution. This is in stark contrast to the enormous amount of research and public discussion about the role of the news media in terrorism and war. It is to be hoped that the growing awareness about the central role the media play in other political processes will also lead to more attention to the significant role they can play in peace.

Methodological appendix

This appendix includes a list of the interview schedules and coding sheets that were used in the course of this research. All interviews were carried out using a semi-structured type of format. While a core set of questions was used to guide every interview, new questions and ideas emerged within the course of each session. It was also sometimes necessary to skip some questions because of a lack of time. Interviews usually lasted between an hour and an hour and a half and all were taped and then transcribed. All interviewees were promised anonymity.

The appendix is organized in the order of the chapters in which each method was first utilized.

CHAPTER 2: THE INITIAL STAGES OF OSLO

The research on the role of the news media in the Middle East peace process began in the summer of 1994, about nine months after the first major breakthrough at Oslo. A central source of data for this research comes from forty-one in-depth interviews that were carried out from that summer until December 1995, about a month after Prime Minister Rabin was assassinated. Interviews were carried out with representatives from the Rabin/Peres governments (seven interviews), the Israeli opposition parties (eight interviews), the Palestinian authority (six interviews), and the Palestinian opposition (seven interviews) and journalists (thirteen interviews). The major criterion for political actors being interviewed was that the individual had an ongoing relationship with the Israeli press concerning the Oslo peace process. The journalists were selected based on the importance of their news organ and their area of responsibility. Most interviews lasted for about an hour. All were taped and then transcribed.

The research schedules included a set of core questions that were asked of all interviewees as well as questions that were designed more specifically towards journalists, politicians, and Palestinians.

Core questions for all interviewees.

1. Can you tell me something about your professional background and your current responsibilities?
2. Would you say that the Israeli news media played a mostly positive, negative, or neutral role in the Oslo peace process?
3. To what extent do you believe the Israeli government was able to promote its messages about Oslo to the Israeli press?
4. Many argue that the political bias of the media affects its coverage. What do you think?
5. How would you describe the way the media dealt with those groups and political parties who opposed the Oslo peace process?
6. Would you say the press provided a positive forum for debate over the Oslo peace process?
7. How would you describe the coverage of the Palestinians in the Israeli press?
   a. Do you think the media image of the Palestinians changed because of the Oslo peace process?
   b. What differences do you see in how Israeli news media covered the Palestinian authority and how they covered the opposition (e.g. Hamas)?
8. What kinds of influences would you say the news media had on the government, the opposition, the public, or others in the debate over the peace process?
9. Many people have talked about the negative effects the news media can have on negotiations while others have said there could also be positive effects. What do you think?
   a. Can you give any examples of either negative or positive influences the media had on the negotiations?
10. A number of people complain that the Israeli news media are too sensationalist? What do you think?
11. How would you describe the role the Israeli news media played in covering terrorism?

12. What differences do you see in the ways the various news media dealt with the Oslo process?
    a. Can you point to differences between specific journalists in the way they related to the Oslo process?

Additional questions for journalists (not all questions were relevant to all journalists).

1. How would you describe your relationship with the government over the course of the Oslo peace process?
    a. Would you say that relationship changed during different periods of the process?
    b. Did you often get criticism from people in the government about things you reported?
2. How would you describe your relationship with the various parties and movements who were opposed to the Oslo process?
    a. Would you say that relationship changed during different periods of the process?
    b. Would you say that the opposition suffers from certain ongoing disadvantages in their relations with the news media?
    c. Did you often get criticism from the opposition about things you reported?
3. How would you describe your relationship with the Palestinian leadership and the various Palestinian organizations that opposed the peace process?
4. Did you feel any pressure from your management concerning coverage of the Oslo peace process?

Additional questions for policy makers and members of the opposition (not all questions were relevant to all political actors).

1. How would you describe your relationship with the press over the course of the Oslo peace process?
    a. Would you say that relationship changed during different periods of the process?
    b. What differences can you think about concerning your relationship with different journalists or media?
2. Which parts of your message about Oslo did you think you were the most successful at promoting to the Israeli news media? Which parts were you the least successful at promoting?

3. How difficult was it to provide the news media with information and events that helped you promote your message about Oslo?

4. To what extent would you say you took the news media into account when deciding what to do? Can you give some examples?

5. Would you say the way the media reported about terrorism had much of an effect on your decisions, strategies, or tactics? Can you give some examples?

Additional questions for Palestinians (results discussed in chapter 4).

1. To what extent would you say that the Palestinian leadership has a strategy for dealing with the Israeli news media? What about the opposition?

2. To what extent do you feel that ideological considerations influence media strategy and your relationship with Israeli journalists?

3. To what extent does the topic of the news media come up during political discussions?

4. To what extent would you argue that the Palestinians have devoted serious resources for dealing with the news media?

5. How would you describe your relationship with the Israeli news media?

   a. Are there certain reporters who are more willing to cooperate with you?

6. There are those that say that the Israeli press has an influence on the competition between various Palestinian leaders. What do you think?

7. Do you think that the Palestinian leadership/opposition has been successful in getting their message conveyed by the Israeli news media?

8. How would you describe the role of the Palestinian press in the peace process?

CONTENT ANALYSIS OF THE FIRST 250 DAYS OF OSLO

The analysis was based on fifty days of news articles that appeared between August 27, 1993 and May 5, 1994. This period starts with the initial news of the breakthrough in Oslo and ends with the signing of agreement in Cairo which came to be known as "Oslo A" or "Oslo 1." The fifty days were selected at random and the analysis looked at all news articles about the peace process that appeared in the first three pages of two newspapers: *Yediot Ahronot* and *Ha'aretz.* A total of 577 articles were included in the analysis. Editorials and personal columns were excluded.

The news stories were divided into a total of seventeen subject categories based on headlines. Two separate coders were trained and given a sample of seventy-five articles to test the reliability of the coding sheet. There was an 87 percent rate of agreement between the two coders.

The subject categories were then classified into those considered "positive" news about the peace process, "negative" news, and "mixed news." The positive news categories included stories about progress in the peace process, negotiations, peace ceremonies (including preparations and the aftermath), economic benefits related to agreement, non-economic benefits related to agreement, international support for agreement, new relations with Gulf states or other Muslim countries, and general optimistic statements in favor of the peace process. The negative news categories were: dangers associated with agreement, terrorism (including aftermath), standstill or difficulties in negotiations, parliamentary opposition to agreement, and extra-parliamentary opposition to agreement. The following categories were considered mixed news: mixed reports on the negotiations, reports about the negotiations with Syria, reports about the negotiations with Jordan, reports on the discussions in the Knesset, and the Baruch Goldstein massacre.

CHAPTER 3: THE ISRAELI MEDIA AND THE DEBATE
OVER OSLO

CONTENT ANALYSIS OF ISRAELI EDITORIALS

A content analysis was conducted of Israeli editorials that were written about the peace process in the wake of seven major events that took place between the start of Oslo in September of 1993 and the major terrorist attacks at the end of February 1995. The seven events were: the opening week of the peace process (September, 1993); the Baruch Goldstein massacre (February, 1994); the terrorist attacks in Afula and Hadera (April, 1994); the Cairo Agreement (May, 1994); the terrorist attack in Dizengoff (October, 1994); the attack on Beit Lid (January, 1995); and the terrorist attack in Tel Aviv and Jerusalem (February–March, 1995).

A total of 229 editorials were taken from the newspapers *Ha'aretz*, *Ma'ariv* and *Yediot Ahronot*. The editorials were coded as either supportive of the peace process, opposed to the peace process, or ambivalent. Two separate coders were given a sample of forty editorials and the agreement rate was 92 percent.

CONTENT ANALYSIS OF THE RABIN ASSASSINATION

A content analysis was conducted of all of the news articles and editorials dealing with the Rabin assassination that appeared in two newspapers (*Yediot Ahronot* and *Ha'aretz*). A total of 761 articles were analyzed including 183 editorials.

The articles were broken down into four major categories: those having to do with the funeral and memorial events, those concerned with the implications for the peace process after Rabin's death, those concerned with the crime itself (e.g. how Yigal Amir got through the security ring), and questions having to do with responsibility. This last category of articles dealt with the reasons why Rabin was murdered.

The most important questions looked at three major issues: the reason given for the assassination, which actors were blamed for the murder, and who was the major source for the news item. The final categories that were developed were based on initial readings of the articles and the initial testings of the coding sheet.

The reasons given for the murder were initially divided into nine categories: incitement by the right; actions of the extreme right; religious education; Bar Ilan (the university attended by Yigal Amir); fundamentalism (extremist religion); madness; desperation (of those opposed to the government); a blunder by the security forces; and other. The list was then compressed by including the third, fourth, and fifth reasons under the category of religious reasons.

The categories for blame included: the right; the parliamentary opposition; the Likud; Benyamin Natanyahu; Bar Ilan; the Rabbis; fundamentalists; settlers (in the West Bank and Gaza); the security forces; extremists; right-wing groups; everyone; the left; and Yigal Amir. This list was made shorter by combining the right with parliamentary opposition ("the right"), Likud with Natanyahu ("Likud"), and Bar Ilan with the Rabbis and fundamentalists ("the religious").

The source categories included: government and leftists sources; Likud sources; right-wing parliamentary sources; extra-parliamentary sources from the right; police sources; religious sources; expert sources; foreign sources; and others. The coding of sources was only carried out in reference to news items. The sources were identified in 44 percent of the articles.

The coders were allowed to list three possible answers to each of these questions. The agreement rate was over 85 percent for all three of the items.

Content analysis of 1996 elections

The analyses were based on two major sources of data. The first was the election news appearing on television during the sixty days (April–May 1996 before the election. The news programs were taped and then analyzed by coders. Any news item in which the word "election" was mentioned was included in the analysis. A total of 627 news stories were coded.

The news items were then classified according to whether they were "substantive issues" (related to Israeli security, economy, welfare, relationships with the Palestinians, peace talks, etc.) or "campaign issues" (related to campaign strategies, surveys and polls, "sleaze campaigns," "deals," predictions of outcome, etc.). Those items that referred to substantive issues were then divided into the eleven categories: terrorism; relations/negotiations with the Palestinians; Jerusalem; Golan Heights and Syria; settlers/settlements; economy/finances; religion and state; education; Israeli Arabs; immigration/absorption; and other. If more than one issue was raised coders were instructed to code according to the first topic mentioned.

The second source of data came from a content analysis of the election ads that appeared every evening. The allocation of airtime was proportional to the size of the party in the Israeli parliament (ten minutes for every campaigning party plus three additional minutes for every member in the outgoing Knesset). Thus, in both elections the Labor, as the leading party, was given more airtime, followed by Likud. All commercials aired by the two leading parties were content-analyzed by a group of coders trained together and using a simple and standard codebook containing the variables ISSUE (the same categories from the codebook used to analyze the news coverage), DATE, and PARTY.

Inter-coder reliability for both sets of data was tested by comparing the codes given by two additional coders with those of the original coders. Only those items for which the calculated reliability measures exceeded 85 percent were included in each database.

CHAPTER 4: THE PALESTINIANS AND
THE ISRAELI MEDIA

INTERVIEWS

For interview schedule for Palestinians see comments to chapter 2, above.

CONTENT ANALYSIS OF THE PALESTINIAN IMAGE IN ISRAELI
NEWS MEDIA

The analysis looked at fifty days of newspaper coverage about the Palestinians that appeared during four different years: 1965, 1985, 1995, and 1997. The year 1965 represents a period before the PLO was created and the year 1985 represents a full two years before the outbreak of the Intifada. As Oslo was initiated in September of 1993, the data from 1995 provides some evidence about the Palestinian image after the early euphoria had worn off. In 1997, the Labor government was replaced by a more right-wing administration led by Prime Minister Netanyahu. Given the change in atmosphere, the period chosen allows for sufficient distance to examine some more enduring changes in the Palestinian image.

There were two major coding categories that were used in the analysis. The first related to the topic of the article and the second asked about the first source that was identified in the piece. Although the coders were allowed to list more than one topic, they were asked to list the most important topic first. These are the topics that are used in the analysis. The topics presented in the coding sheet were first divided into six major topic areas: disorder/violence; security; economics; peace process; relations between Palestinians and the Palestinian Authority; and miscellaneous. Within each general topic area, coders were asked to identify more specific topics. The economic heading, for example, included economic cooperation, the economic effects of closures, poverty/poor living conditions among Palestinians, work permits for Palestinians, and international aid for the Palestinians. There were a total of forty-seven categories in all. The level of inter-coder agreement for the broad categories was 87 percent, and the level of agreement for the small categories was 73 percent. The subcategories were than collapsed in order to create the final five categories: general Arab; security; peace process; internal society; victims.

There were a total of sixteen possible sources identified in the coding sheet (e.g. Israeli security source, Israeli expert). The level of coding agreement on type of source was 91 percent. These categories were then collapsed into the three categories that were used in the analysis: Israeli; Palestinian; and other.

CHAPTER 5: THE MEDIA AND THE ISRAEL–JORDAN PEACE PROCESS

INTERVIEWS WITH JORDANIAN AND ISRAELI JOURNALISTS

Nine Jordanian journalists and twelve Israeli journalists were interviewed during 1997. The expert informants came from newspapers, radio, and television and all had been responsible for covering the other country. The relatively small number of interviewees reflects the meager number of people who are directly responsible for reporting in this area. This number constitutes the vast majority of journalists who were responsible for constructing news stories about the two countries.

Questions for Jordanian/Israel journalists

1. Please describe your professional background and the nature of your current responsibilities.
2. How important would you say stories about Jordan/Israel are in the media?
3. Where do you get most of the information about Jordan/Israel? Who are your major sources?
4. What are the major types of news stories relating to Jordan/Israel?
5. Do you think that fact that Jordan and Israel have signed a peace treaty has had much of an effect on news coverage of the other country?
6. In what ways does the story about Jordan/Israel vary over time and circumstance?
7. Would you say that the Jordanian/Israeli news media are biased towards Israel/Jordan? In what ways?
8. Do you believe that your own attitudes towards Jordan/Israel influence the way you relate to that country in the news?
9. To what extent do you believe that government policies effect how you cover Jordan/Israel?
10. Do you feel any pressure from outsiders concerning coverage of Jordan/Israel? Can you give some examples?
11. Do you speak Hebrew/Arabic?
12. How much time have you spent in Jordan/Israel? Does anyone from your organization go there on a regular basis?

CONTENT ANALYSIS OF ISRAELI/JORDANIAN NEWS ABOUT THE OTHER

The content analysis was based on a sample of newspaper articles that were published in each country during three different years. Two newspapers were selected from each country. The newspapers selected from Jordan were *Al-Ra'i* and *Addustour*, respectively with majority and minority government shareholdings. The two newspapers used in Israel were *Yediot Ahronot* and *Ha'aretz*.

A coding sheet was developed that looked at two major variables: the general topic area of the news story and the overall valence (evaluative direction) of the story. Based on an extensive pretest, it was found that the stories could be divided into six topic categories that were applicable in both countries: Stories having to do with the peace process and/or normalization between the two countries; political and economic meetings/relations; multilateral relations (Jordan/Israel and others); the foreign policy of Jordan/Israel; security issues related to Jordan/Israel; and the internal affairs of the other. The level of agreement for topic area was 83 percent in Jordan and 88 percent in Israel.

The stories were also divided into three evaluative categories in order to gauge the overall valence of the story: positive, neutral, and negative. The level of inter-coder agreement for valence was 82 percent in Jordan and 85 percent in Israel.

CHAPTER 6: THE MEDIA AND THE STRUGGLE FOR PEACE IN NORTHERN IRELAND

INTERVIEWS WITH NORTHERN IRELAND JOURNALISTS AND POLITICAL LEADERS

Interviews were carried out in Belfast in April of 1999. A total of twenty semi-structured interviews were conducted with leaders from a variety of political parties, their spokespeople, and a range of reporters responsible for covering the peace process for the local press.

Core questions for all interviewees

1. Please describe your professional background and your current responsibilities.
2. Would you say the press in Northern Ireland played a mostly positive, negative, or neutral role in the peace process?
3. To what extent do you believe the various parties were able to promote their messages about the peace process to the media?

4. Many argue that the political bias of the media affects its coverage. What do you think?
5. How would you describe the way the media dealt with those groups and political parties who opposed the peace process?
6. Would you say the press provided a positive forum for debate over the peace process?
7. What kinds of influences would you say the news media had on the government, the opposition, the public, or others in the debate over the peace process?
8. Many people have talked about the negative effects the news media can have on negotiations while others have said there could also be positive effects. What do you think?
   a. Can you give any examples of either negative or positive influences the media had on the negotiations?
9. Would you describe the press in Northern Ireland as sensationalist?
10. How would you describe the role the Northern Ireland news media played in covering political violence?
11. What differences do you see in the ways the various news media dealt with the Northern Ireland process?
12. Can you point to differences between specific journalists in the way they relate to the peace process?

Additional questions for journalists (not all questions were relevant to all journalists).

1. How would you describe your relationship with the government over the course of the peace process?
   a. Would you say that relationship changed during different periods of the process?
   b. Did you often get criticism from the various parties about things you reported?
2. How would you describe your relationship with those who were opposed to the peace process?
   a. Would you say that your relationship changed during different periods of the process?
   b. Would you say that the opposition suffers from certain ongoing disadvantages in their relations with the news media?
3. Did you feel any pressure from your management concerning coverage of the peace process?

Additional questions for policy makers and members of the opposition (not all questions were relevant to all political actors).

1. How would you describe your relationship with the press over the course of the peace process?
   a. Would you say that relationship changed during different periods of the process?
   b. What differences can you think about concerning your relationship with different journalists or media?
2. Which parts of your message about the process did you think you were the most successful at promoting to the news media? Which parts were you the least successful at promoting?
3. How difficult was it to provide the news media with information and events that helped you promote your message about the peace process?
4. To what extent would you say your party took the news media into account when deciding what to do? Can you give some examples?
5. Would you say the way the media reported about the process had much of an effect on your decisions, strategies, or tactics? Can you give some examples?

CONTENT ANALYSIS OF EDITORIALS IN THE NORTHERN IRELAND PRESS

This analysis was carried out in parallel with the content analysis of Israeli editorials about Oslo (see description given in the comments to chapter 3, above). The editorials came from the *Irish News* and the *Belfast Telegraph*. The coding had three categories: support for the peace process, opposition to the peace process, and ambivalence. A total of 147 editorials were analyzed.

Twenty-two events were selected that cover a period extending both before and after the signing of the Good Friday agreement. The events include the violence associated with an Orange March (July, 1997); announcement of an IRA ceasefire (July, 1997); Sein Fein joins the talks (September, 1997); Sein Fein leaders meet with Prime Minister Blair (October, 1997); Sein Fein leaders first visit Downing street (December, 1997); LVF leader shot in Maze prison (December, 1997); Loyalist and Catholic killed (January, 1998); UDA member killed (February, 1998); IRA terrorism, Sein Fein expelled from talks (February, 1998); attack on Armagh police station (March, 1998); Sinn Fein back in talks (March 1998); Good Friday agreement (April, 1998); referendum (May, 1998);

Drumcree stand-off (July, 1998); Omagh bombing (August, 1998); Meeting between Adams and Trimble, first Assembly Meeting (September, 1998); Hume and Trimble nominated for Nobel Peace Prize (October, 1998); Loyalists murder Catholic (November 1998); Violence following Protestant march (December, 1998); Loyalist violence (January, 1999); human rights activist murdered (March, 1999); Hillsborough Declaration (April, 1999).

CHAPTER 7: THE COLLAPSE OF OSLO AND THE RETURN TO VIOLENCE

A total of thirty semi-structured interviews were conducted concerning the role of the news media in the Camp David summit and the initial months of the Second Intifada. Ten of these interviews focused on Camp David and were conducted between July and October of 2001. Twenty interviews focused on the role of the media in the Second Intifada and were carried out between March and November of 2001. The Camp David interviews included both representatives from the government and journalists who covered the event. The interviews concerning the Second Intifada were conducted with members of the Israeli army's spokesperson's office and journalists who were responsible for constructing news about the ongoing events. Interviews lasted for approximately an hour.

Questions about the Israeli media and the Camp David summit (exact question format depended on role of interviewee).

1. Please describe your professional background and your current responsibilities.
2. How would you generally describe the role of the news media at Camp David?
3. To what extent was the US government able to close off Camp David from the press?
   a. How did reporters gather information about what was happening?
   b. What effects did the closed environment at Camp David have on the news coverage that appeared? Would you say it sometimes led to "trivial" coverage?
4. What were the major news stories that emerged at the summit?

5. How would you describe the relationships between the various delegations and the various news media (including those from other countries)?
6. To what extent would you say news stories had an influence on the negotiations?
7. How would you describe the Israeli strategy with regard to the news media?
   a. How did this change during the course of the negotiations?
8. Would you say the Israelis were successful at using the news media to get their message out?
9. Would you say there was a good deal of attention in the Israeli press on Israeli concessions?
10. How would you describe the Palestinian strategy with regard to the news media?
    a. How did this change in the course of the negotiations?
11. Would you say that there was a good deal of attention in the Israeli press about Palestinian concessions?
12. Would you say the Palestinians were successful at using the news media to get their message out?
13. Could you say something about any changes that took place in your relationship with the delegations during different stages of the summit?

Questions about the Israeli media and the outbreak of the Second Intifada (exact question format depended on role of interviewee).

1. Please describe your professional background and your current responsibilities.
2. How would you describe the role of the Israeli news media in the Second Intifada?
3. How would you describe the nature of the relationship between the Israeli news media and the government/military?
   a. Did you notice any changes during different periods?
4. Can you tell me something about how the IDF/news media were organized for dealing with the Second Intifada? Did this involve any major reorganization?
5. Some critics have claimed that the Israeli news media have basically been "mobilized" by the government to support the official version of events. What is your opinion?
6. To what extent would you say that the Israeli news media depend on the IDF for getting information about what is happening?

7. How much do media considerations influence military planning and strategy?
8. How successful would you say the Israeli government/military has been in getting their message across to the Israeli news media?
   a. What about the foreign news media?
9. Would you say that there were certain stories in which the IDF was particularly successful in getting its message across?
10. Would you say that there were certain stories over which the Israeli military simply lost control?
11. Can you give any examples of Israeli news coverage that has been especially critical of actions taken by the government or the IDF?
12. What differences do you find in the way various journalists or news media cover the Intifada?
    a. Would you say that the military reporters find it more difficult to achieve independence than others?
13. How much would you say the initiative for stories about the Intifada comes from the IDF and how much from the journalists themselves?
14. In what ways did the IDF attempt to restrict the flow of information to journalists? Would you say they were successful?
15. What is your opinion about the ways in which the Israeli news media have covered acts of terrorism?
16. Would you say that the way the Israeli news media have covered the Intifada has had any effect on policy?
    a. What about the way the foreign news media have covered the Intifada?
17. In what ways has the relationship between the Israeli journalists and Palestinian sources changed since the outbreak of the Second Intifada?
18. Are many Israeli reporters scared to go into the territories today? How has this affected the coverage?
19. Would you say that the Israeli news media have an obligation to present the Palestinian perspective on what is happening?
    a. How would you describe the way the Israeli news media relate to Palestinian victims as opposed to Israeli victims?

References

Abu-Odeh, A. (1999). *Jordanians, Palestinians, and the Hashemite Kingdom in the Middle East peace process.* Washington DC: United States Institute of Peace.

Adam, G. F. and Thamotheram, R. (1996). *The media's role in conflict: Report reviewing international experience in the use of mass-media for promoting conflict prevention, peace and reconciliation.* Geneva: Media Action International.

Adoni, H. and Mane, S. (1984). Media and the social construction of reality: Toward an integration of theory and research. *Communication Research* 11, 323–340.

Arian, A. (1995). *Security threatened: Surveying Israeli opinion on peace and war.* New York: Cambridge University Press.

Arian A., Weimann, G., and Wolfsfeld, G. (1999). Balance in election coverage. In A. Arian and M. Shamir (eds.), *The elections in Israel, 1996.* Albany: State University of New York Press.

Arterton, C. F. (1993). Campaign '92: Strategies and tactics of the candidates. In G. M. Pomper (ed.), *The election of 1992.* Chatham, NJ: Chatham House.

Avraham, E., Wolfsfeld, G. and Aburaiya, I. (2000). Dynamics in the news coverage of minorities: The case of the Arab citizens of Israel. *Journal of Communication Inquiry* 24, 117–133.

Ayres, R. W. (1997). Mediating international conflicts: Is image change necessary? *Journal of Peace Research* 34, 431–447.

Bar-Tal, D. and Teichman, Y. (in press). *Stereotypes and prejudice in conflict: The case of the perception of Arabs in Israeli society.* Cambridge: Cambridge University Press.

Barzilai, G. (1996). *Wars, internal conflicts and political order: A Jewish democracy in the Middle East.* Albany, NY: State University of New York Press.

Baumgartner, F. R. and Jones, B. D. (1993). *Agendas and instability in American politics.* Chicago: University of Chicago Press.

Becker, J. A. (1996). A disappearing enemy: The image of the United States in Soviet political cartoons. *Journalism and Mass Communication Quarterly* 73, 609–619.

Ben, A. (2001). Now everyone knows: They're guilty. *Ha'aretz*, July 21, p. b3 [Hebrew].

Bennett, W. L. (1990). Toward a theory of press-state relations in the United States. *Journal of Communication* 40, 103–125.

Bennett, W. L. and Entman, R. M. (2001). Mediated politics: An introduction. In W. L. Bennett and R. M. Entman (eds.), *Mediated politics: communication in the future of democracy.* New York: Cambridge University Press.

Bennett, W. L. and D. L. Paletz (eds.) (1994). *Taken by storm: The media, pubic opinion, and U.S. foreign policy in the Gulf War.* Chicago: University of Chicago Press.

Blumler, J. G. and Kavanagh, D. (1999). The third age of political communication: Influences and features. *Political Communication* 16, 209–230.

Bowles, S. (1999). Fewer violent fatalities in schools. *USA Today*, April 28, p. 4A.

Brants, K. (1998). Who's afraid of infotainment? *European Journal of Communication* 13, 315–338.

Brants, K. and Neijens, P. (1997). The infotainment of politics. *Political Communication* 15, 149–164.

Brosius, H. and Eps, P. (1995). Prototyping through key events: News selection in the case of violence against aliens and asylum seekers in Germany. *European Journal of Communication* 10 (3), 391–412.

Bruck, P. A. (ed.) (1988). *A proxy for knowledge: The news media as agents in arms control and verification.* Ottawa: Carleton International Proceedings.

Bruck, P. A. (1989). Strategies for peace, strategies for news research. *Journal of Communication* 39, 108–129.

Bruck, P. A. and Roach, C. (1993). Dealing with reality: The news media and the promotion of peace. In C. Roach (ed.), Communication and culture in war and peace. Newbury Park: Sage.

Cappella, J. N. and Jamieson, K. H. (1997). *Spiral of cyncism: The press and the public good,* New York: Oxford University Press.

Caspi, D. and Limor, Y. (1999). *The in/outsiders: Mass media in Israel.* Cresskill, NJ: Hampton Press.

Cobb, R. and Elder, C. (1983). *Participation in American politics: The dynamics of agenda-building.* Baltimore, MD: Johns Hopkins University Press.

Cohen, A. and Wolfsfeld, G. (eds.) (1993). *Framing the Intifada: People and media.* Norwood, NJ: Ablex.

Cohen, R. (1987). *Theatre of power: The art of diplomatic signalling.* London: Longman, 1987.

Cohen, Y. (1986). *Media diplomacy: The foreign office in the mass communications age.* London: Frank Cass.

Cooke, T. (2003). Paramilitaries and the press in Northern Ireland. In P. Norris and M. Kern (eds.), *Framing Terrorism.* New York: Routledge.

Cottle, S. (1997). Reporting the troubles in Northern Ireland: Paradigms and media propaganda. *Critical Studies in Mass Communication* 14, 282–296.

Davison, P. W. (1974). *Mass communication and conflict resolution.* New York: Praeger.

Dearing, J. W. and Rogers, E. M. (1996). *Agenda-setting.* Thousand Oaks, CA: Sage.

Delli Carpini, M. and B. Williams. (2001). Let us entertain you: Politics in the new media environment. In W. L. Bennett and R. M. Entman (eds.), *Mediated politics: Communication in the future of democracy.* New York: Cambridge University Press.

Dorman, W. and Livingston, S. (1994). News and historical content: The establishment phase of the Persian Gulf policy debate. In W. L. Bennett and D. L. Paletz (eds.), *Taken by storm: The media, public opinion, and U.S. foreign policy in the Gulf War.* Chicago: University of Chicago Press.

Dorman, W., Manoff, R. K., and Weeks, J. (1988). *American press coverage of U.S.-Soviet relations, the Soviet Union, nuclear weapons, arms control, and national security: A bibliography.* New York: Center for War Peace and the News Media.

Eckhardt, W. (1991). Making and breaking enemy images. *Bulletin of Peace Proposals* 22, 87–95.

Edelman, M. (1988). *Constructing the political spectacle.* Chicago: University of Chicago Press.

Entman, R. (2004). *Projections of power: Framing news, public opinion, and U.S. foreign policy.* Chicago: University of Chicago Press.

Entman, R. and Herbst, S. (2001). Reframing public opinion as we have known it. In W. L. Bennett and R. M. Entman (eds.), *Mediated politics: communication in the future of democracy.*

Fawcett, L. (2002). Who's setting the postdevolution agenda in Northern Ireland? *The Harvard International Journal of Press/Politics* 7, 14–33.

First, A. (1998). Who is the enemy? The portrayal of the Arabs in the Israeli TV News at the beginning of the Intifada. *Gazette* 60, 239–254.

First, A. (2000). Are they still the enemy? The Represenation of Arabs in the Israeli News. In P. Tudor (ed.), *Mediating the other: Jews, Christians and the Media.* London: The Centre of Near and Middle Eastern Studies.

Fromm, J., Gart, M., Hughes, T. L., Rodman, P., and Tanzer, L. (1992). The media impact on foreign policy. In H. Smith (ed.), *The media and the Gulf War.* Washington, DC: Seven Locks Press.

Galtung, J. (1998). High road, low road: Charting the course for peace journalism. *Track Two* 7, 7–10.

Gamson, W. A. (1992). *Talking politics.* New York: Cambridge University Press.

Gamson, W. A., Croteau, D., Hoynes, W., and Sasson, T. (1992). Media images and the social construction of reality. *Annual Review of Sociology* 18, 373–393.

Gamson, W. A. and Modigliani, A. (1987). The changing culture of affirmative action. In R. G. Braungart and M. M. Braungard (eds.), *Frontiers in social movement theory.* New Haven, CT: Yale University Press.

Gamson, W. A. and Modigliani, A. (1989). Media discourse and public opinion on nuclear power: A constructionist approach. *American Journal of Sociology* 95, 1–37.

Gamson, W. A. and Stuart, D. (1992). Media discourse as a symbolic contest: The bomb in political cartoons. *Sociological Forum* 7, 55–86.

Gamson, W. and Wolfsfeld, G. (1993). Movements and media as interacting systems. *The Annals of the American Academy of Political and Social Science* 528, 114–125.

Gannett Foundation (1991). The media at war: The press and the Persian Gulf conflict. New York: Gannett Foundation Media Center, Columbia University.

Gilboa, E. (1998). Media diplomacy: Conceptual divergence and applications. *Harvard International Journal of Press/Politics* 3, 56–75.

Gitlin, T. (1980). *The whole world is watching.* Berkeley: University of California Press.

Glasgow University Media Group (1985). *War and peace news.* Philadelphia: Open University Press.

Gowing, N. (1996). Media coverage: Help or hindrance in conflict prevention? Unpublished paper. New York: Carnegie Commission on Preventing Deadly Conflicts.

Graber, D. (1994). The infotainment quotient in routine television-news – A director's perspective. *Discourse and Society* 1994, 483–508.

Griffen, E. (1996). *A first look at communication theory.* New York: McGraw Hill.

Hackett, R. (1991). *News and dissent: The press and politics of peace in Canada,* Norwood, NJ: Ablex Publishing Co.

Hallin, D. C. (1994). *We keep America on top of the world.* London: Routledge.

Hallin, D. (1986). *The uncensored war.* New York: Oxford University Press.

Hass, A. (2001). Once again Israel is operating according to a concept. *Ha'aretz,* July 29, p. B1.

Henderson, G. (ed.) (1973). *Public diplomacy and political change: Four case studies, Okinawa, Peru, Czechoslovakia, Guinea.* New York: Praeger.

Himmelfarb, S. (1998). Impact is the mantra: The 'common ground' approach to the media. *Track Two* 7, 38–40.

Horowitz, D. and Lissak, M. (1990). *Trouble in utopia: The overburdened polity of Israel.* Albany: State University of New York Press.

Hroub, K. (2000). *Hamas: Political thought and practice.* Beirut: Institute for Palestinian Studies.

Ito, Y. (1990). Mass communication theories from a Japanese perspective. *Media, Culture and Society* 12, 423–464.

Ito, Y. (2002). Climate of opinion, *kuuki,* and democracy, In W. Gudykunst (ed.), *Communication yearbook.* Mahwah, NJ: Lawrence Erlbaum.

Just, M. J., Crigler, A. N., Alger, D. E., Cook, T. E., Kern, M., and West, J. (1996). *Crosstalk: Citizens, candidates, and the media in a presidential campaign,* Chicago: University of Chicago Press.

Kellner, D. (1991). *The Persian Gulf TV war.* Boulder, CO: Westview Press.

Kepplinger, H. M. and Habermeir, J. (1995). The impact of key events on the presentation of reality. *European Journal of Communication* 10 (3), 371–390.

Kershner, I. (1999). The rise and rise of Colonel Dahalan. *Jerusalem Report,* February 1, pp. 22–24.

Kimmerling, B. (1993). Militarism in Israeli society. *Theory and Criticism* 4, 123–140 [Hebrew].

Kingdon, J. (1995). *Agendas, alternatives, and public policies.* 2nd edn. New York: Longman.

Lawrence, R. G. (2000). *The politics of force: Media and the construction of police brutality.* Berkeley: University of California Press.

Lawrence, R. G. and Bennett, W. L. (2000). Civic engagement in the era of big stories. *Political Communication* 17, 377–382.

Liebes, T. (1997). *Reporting the Arab Israeli conflict: How hegemony works.* London: Routledge.

Liebes, T. (1998). Television disaster marathons: A danger for the democratic process. In T. Leibes and J. Curran (eds.), *Media, Culture, and Identity.* London: Routledge.

Liebes, T. and Curran, J. (eds.) (1998). *Media, ritual, and identity.* London: Routledge.

Livingston, S. (1997). Clarifying the CNN effect: An examination of media effects according to the type of military intervention. Research Paper R-18. Cambridge, MA: The Joan Shorenstein Center on the Press, Politics, and Public Policy, Kennedy School of Government, Harvard University.

Livingston, S. and Eachus, S. (1995). Humanitarian crises and US foreign-policy – Somalia and the CNN effect reconsidered. *Political Communication* 12, 413–429.

Lynch, J. (1998). Findings of the Conflict and Peace Journalism Forum. Unpublished manuscript. Tablow Court, Talow, Buckinghamshire, England.

Manheim, J. B. (1991). All of the people, all the time: Strategic communication and American politics. Armonk, NY: M. E. Sharpe.

Manheim, J. B. (1994a). Strategic public diplomacy and American foreign policy: The evolution of influences. New York: Oxford University Press.

Manheim, J. B. (1994b). Managing Kuwait's image during the Gulf conflict. In W. L. Bennett and D. L. Paletz (eds.), Taken by storm: The media, public opinion, and U.S. foreign policy in the Gulf War. Chicago: University of Chicago Press.

Manheim, J. B. (1998). The news shapers: Strategic communication as a third force in news making. In D. Graber, D. McQuail, and P. Norris (eds.), *The politics of news, the news of politics*. Washington, DC: CQ Press.

Manoff, R. (1996). The mass media and social violence: Is there a role for the media in preventing and moderating ethnic, national, and religious conflict? Unpublished paper. New York: Center for War, Peace, and the News Media, New York University.

Manoff, R. (1997). The media's role in preventing and moderating conflict. *Crossroads Global Report* (March/April), 24–27.

Manoff, R. (1998). Role plays: potential media roles in conflict prevention and management. *Track Two* 7, 11–16.

McQuail, Denis and S. Windahl (1993). Communication models for the study of mass communication. London: Longman.

Makovsky, D. (2001). A voice from the heavens: Al-Jazeera's satellite news broadcasts inflame emotions across the Arab world. usnews.com, May 14.

Mermin, J. (1999). *Debating war and peace*. Princeton, NJ: Princeton University Press.

Mishal, S. and Sela, A. (2000). *The Palestinian. Hamas: Vision, violence and coexistence*. New York: Columbia University Press.

Mitchell, G. J. (1999). *Making peace*. New York: Alfred A. Knopf.

Mowlana, H., Gerbner, G., and Schiller, H. I. (1992). *Triumph of the image: The media's war in the Persian Gulf – A global perspective*. Boulder, CO: Westview Press.

Mutz, D. and Reeves, B. (2001). Exposure to mediated political conflict: Effects of civility of interaction on public opinion. Paper presented at the Annual Meeting of the American Political Science Association, San Francisco, California.

Naveh, C. (2001). The role of the media in shaping Israeli public opinion in the peace process (1992–1996). In S. Sofer (ed.), *Peacemaking in a divided society*. London: Frank Cass.

Newton, K. (1999). Mass media effects: Mobilization or media malaise? *British Journal of Political Science* 29, 577–599.

O'Heffernan, P. (1993). Mass media and U.S. foreign policy: A mutual exploitation model of media influence in U.S. foreign policy. In R. J. Spitzer (ed.), *Media and public policy*. Westport, CT: Praeger.

Ottosen, R. (1995). *Enemy images and the journalistic process*. Journal of Peace Research 32, 97–112.

Owen, D. (2000). Popular politics and the Clinton/Lewinsky affair: The implications for leadership. *Political Psychology* 21, 161–177.

Patterson, T. (1993). *Out of order*. New York: Alfred A. Knopf.

Peri, Y. (1983). *Between battles and ballots: Israeli military in politics*. Cambridge: Cambridge University Press.

Peri, Y. (2000). Introduction: The writing was on the wall. In Y. Peri (ed.), *The assassination of Yitzhak Rabin.* Stanford, CA: Stanford University Press.

Peri, Y. (2004). *Telepopulism: Media and politics in Israel,* Stanford, CA: Stanford University Press.

Pundak, R. (2001). From Oslo to Taba: What went wrong? Unpublished Paper.

Rabin, Y. (1996). The promise and problems of the Israeli press. *The Harvard International Journal of Press/Politics* 1, 106–112.

Reese, S. D. and Gandy, O. (eds.) (2001). *Framing in the new media landscape.* Mahwah, NJ: Lawrence Erlbaum Associates.

Reese, S., Grant, A., and Danielian, L. (1994). The structure of news sources on television: A network analysis of "CBS News," "Nightline," "MacNeil/Lehrer," and "This Week with David Brinkley." *Jounal of Communication* 44, 84–107.

Roach, C. (1993). Information and culture in war and peace: Overview. In Roach (ed.) *Communication and culture in war and peace.* Newbury Park: Sage.

Robinson, P. (2002). *The CNN effect: The myth of news, foreign policy and intervention.* London: Routledge.

Rolston, B. and Miller, D. (eds.) (1996). *War and words: The Northern Ireland media reader.* Belfast: Beyond the Pale Publications.

Roy S. (2001). *The Gaza Strip: The political economy of de-development.* 2nd edn. Washington, DC: Institute for Palestine Studies.

Rubinstein, D. (2001). Who needs politics when there is *Al-Jazeera? Ha'aretz,* October 30, p. B3.

Ryan, C. (1991). *Prime time activism: Media strategies for grassroots organizing.* Boston, MA: South End Press.

Sabato, L. J. (2000). *Feeding frenzy: Attack journalism and American politics.* Baltimore, MD: Lanahan.

Scheufele, D. A. (1999). Framing as a theory of media effects. *Journal of Communication* 49, 103–122.

Schiff, Z. and Ya'ari, E. (1990). *Intifada: The Palestinian uprising – Israel's third front.* New York: Simon and Schuster.

Schudson, M. (1996). *The Power of News.* Cambridge, MA: Harvard University Press.

Serfaty, S. (ed.) (1991). *The mass media and foreign Policy.* New York: St. Martin's Press.

Shamir, J. and Shamir, M. (2000). *The anatomy of public opinion.* Ann Arbor, MI: University of Michigan Press.

Shinar, D. (2000). Media diplomacy and 'peace talk': The Middle East and Northern Ireland. *Gazette* 62, 83–97.

Shoemaker, P. (1996). Hardwired for news: Using biological and cultural evolution to explain the surveillance function. *Journal of Communication* 47, 32–47.

Shoemaker, P. and Eicholz, M. (2000). Good news vs. bad news: News valence as a theoretical construct. Paper presented at the Annual Conference of the International Association for Mass Communication Research in Singapore.

Simon, A. and Xenos, M. (2000). Media framing and effective public deliberation. *Political Communication* 17, 363–376.

Small, M. (1987). Influencing the decision-makers: The Vietnam experience. *Journal of Peace Research* 24, 185–198.

Sparks, C. (1992). Popular journalism: Theories and practice. In P. Dahlgren and C. Sparks (eds.), *Journalism and popular culture*. London: Sage.

Sprinzak, E. (2000). Israel's radical right and the countdown to the Rabin assassination. In Y. Peri (ed.), *The assassination of Yitzak Rabin*. Stanford, CA: Stanford University Press.

Strobel, W. P. (1997). Late breaking foreign policy: The news media's influence on peace operations. Washington, DC: The United States Institute of Peace.

Swanson, D. L. (in press). Political news in the changing environment of political journalism. In P. Maarek and G. Wolfsfeld (eds.), *Political communication in a new era: A cross-national perspective*. London: Routledge.

Tami Steinmetz Center for Peace Research (1996). *The Peace Index Project: Findings from June, 1994 to May, 1996*. Tel Aviv: University of Tel Aviv [Hebrew].

Underwood, D. (2001). Reporting and the push for market-oriented journalism: Media organizations as businesses. In L. Bennett and R. Entman (eds.), *Mediated politics: Communication in the future of democracy*. New York: Cambridge University Press.

Valentino, N. A., Beckmann, M. W., and Buhr, T. A. (2001). A spiral of cynicism for some: The contingent effects of campaign news frames on participation and confidence in government. *Political Communication* 18, 347–367.

Van Dijk, T. A. (1996). Power and the news media. In D. Paletz (ed.) *Political communication in action*. Cresskill, NJ: Hampton Press, Inc.

Vedel, T. (2003). Public policies for digital democracy in the European Union and the US. In P. Maarek and G. Wolfsfeld (eds.), *Political communication in a new era*. London: Routledge.

Weimann, G. (1994). Can the media mediate? Mass mediated diplomacy in the Middle East. In G. Ben Dor and D. Dewitt (eds.), *Confidence building measures in the Middle East*. New York: Westview.

Weimann, G. (2000). *Modern media and the reconstruction of reality*. Thousand Oaks, CA: Sage.

Weimann, G. and Wolfsfeld, G. (2002). The struggle over the media agenda in the 1996 and 1999 elections. In A. Arian and M. Shamir (eds.), *Election in Israel 1999*. Albany, NY: State University of New York Press.

Weymouth, L. (2001). Barak: Die or separate. *Newsweek*, July 23, pp. 28–29.

Wolfsfeld, G. (1997a). *Media and political conflict: News from the Middle East*. Cambridge: Cambridge University Press.

Wolfsfeld, G. (1997b). Fair weather friends: The varying role of the news media in the Arab–Israeli peace process. *Political Communication* 14, 29–48.

Wolfsfeld, G. (1997c). Promoting peace through the news media: Some initial lessons from the peace process. *Harvard International Journal of Press/Politics* 2, 52–70.

Wolfsfeld, G. (2000). Political waves and democratic discourse: Terrorism waves during the Oslo peace process. In W. L. Bennett and R. Entman (eds.), *Mediated politics: Communication in the future of democracy*. New York: Cambridge University Press.

Wolfsfeld, G. (2001a). *The news media and peace: From the Middle East to Northern Ireland*. Peace Works, No. 37. Washington DC: United States Institute of Peace.

Wolfsfeld, G. (2001b). The news media and the Second Intifada: Some initial lessons. *Harvard Journal of Press/Politics* 6, 113–118.

Wolfsfeld, G. (2003). The role of the news media in peace negotiations: Variations over time and circumstance. In J. Darby and R. MacGinty (eds.), *Contemporary peace making: Conflict, violence and peace processes*, New York: Palgrave-Macmillan.

Wolfsfeld, G., Avraham, E., and Aburaiya, I. (2000). When prophesy always fails: Israeli press coverage of the Arab minority's land day protests. *Political Communication* 17, 115–131.

Wolfsfeld, G. and Rabihiya, Y. (1988). Communication and control in times of crisis: Israeli censorship in the occupied territories. *Canadian Journal of Communication*, special Issue, December, 96–101.

Index